D0606395

Iron Will

Memories of vintage tractors
from the readers of
Farm & Ranch Living magazine.

If it weren't for farmers and their tractors,
this world would be a much hungrier place.
Here in their own words, farmers and
ranchers tell how they bought, restored
or learned to drive on the tractors
that help feed humanity.

Country Books

Iron Will

Memories of vintage tractors from the readers of *Farm & Ranch Living* magazine.

Publisher: Roy Reiman
Editor: Nick Pabst
Art Director: Thomas L. Hunt
Associate Editors: Deb Mulvey, Cliff Muehlenberg, Kristine Krueger, Rick Van Etten
Production Assistants: Ellen Lloyd, Claudia Wardius
Photo Coordinator: Trudi Bellin
Technical Adviser: Ed Bezanson "The Yankee"

© 1997 Reiman Publications, L.P.
5400 S. 60th St., Greendale WI 53129

Country Books
International Standard Book Number:
0-89821-193-X
Library of Congress Catalog
Card Number: 96-71402
All rights reserved. Printed in USA.

For additional copies of this book or information about other Reiman Publications books, magazines or calendars, write: Country Books, P.O. Box 990, Greendale WI 53129.

Credit card orders, call toll-free 1-800/558-1013

Cover Photo: Scott Anderson

Photos on page 4, chapter title pages and pages 158-163 were taken by Scott Anderson at the 33rd Annual Badger Steam & Gas Engine Show in Baraboo, Wisconsin in August 1996.

Page 157: Michael Shedlock

Back Cover: Richard Thomas of Davie, Florida hugs his tractor (see story on page 13).

Behind Every Great Tractor Story Is a Real Live Person

The editors of *Farm & Ranch Living* invite you to meet some of these "tractor folks"…and we've created this book from the "Tractor Talk" section of our magazine just so you can. Hope you enjoy making their acquaintance!

THERE ARE plenty of books about old tractors...but how many are there about the folks who own, drive, restore and love all those old tractors? Well, now there's at least one, and you're holding it.

With more than 200 stories and photos by the folks these "tractor experiences" actually happened to, this book is a bit unusual. It's also a "twofer"—you get entertaining and inspiring tales about people *and* informative stories about tractors.

Iron Will is being published by *Farm & Ranch Living* magazine, which regularly fills its pages with stories and photos from readers—ordinary folks just like you. We're an agricultural magazine, all right...but not one about crops, production, farm politics or the economy.

Instead, we're about *people*—the farm and ranch families who live and work on the land and who think agriculture is

not just a business, but a way of life. And we believe the people most qualified to tell a story are the ones who actually experienced it.

Each month, we receive about as many letters and photos from readers as there are nuts and bolts on an old "Johnny Popper". Not all the letters are about tractors, of course. But in every issue of *F&RL*, we devote at least 6 pages to Old Iron.

The rest of the magazine is chock-full of beautiful color photographs of farm and ranch scenes plus stories about life on the land. Joy...pride...humor ...nostalgia—these are the things you'll find in each issue of *F&RL*.

Although we fill as many pages as we do with Old Iron stories, we often don't have room for all the great letters and photos we receive. So when readers began suggesting that we use some of those stories to create either an annual Old Iron calendar or a book, we jumped at *both* ideas.

Farm & Ranch Living's first *Old Iron Calendar* came out in 1996. Each edition contains tractor photos and stories from *F&RL* readers, as well as listings of tractor shows throughout the U.S. and Canada.

And now this book is off the press!

We decided to call it *Iron Will* because that's what it takes to get the crops in—both the will to overcome often difficult conditions, and the iron tractors required to pull, plow and tote. No matter how hot or cold the weather...or how good or bad that year's crop...farmers and their iron machines stay in the field till the job is finished.

If the book looks at all familiar to you, it's because we have tried to make it an expanded version of "Tractor Talk", one of the regular features that appears in each issue of *Farm & Ranch Living*.

Like the rest of the magazine—and as in this book—all the stories in "Tractor Talk" are from our readers. All we do is sand off some of the corners and occasionally dab on a little linseed oil.

Mighty Good Reading

Besides making room for some of the great tractor stories that we haven't been able to fit into "Tractor Talk", this book has another purpose—folks who restore Old Iron deserve a special "thanks". Many of them played a role in the historic switch from horses to tractors, and their stories and restoration work are helping preserve a bit of the past.

Maybe the best reason for producing this book, however, is the fact that the "tractor talk" within these pages makes very *interesting and entertaining reading*! Some of the tales are dramatic...others heartwarming. You'll get a good laugh from many...and a few will likely bring a tear or two to your eye.

Send Us Your Stories. We hope you will read and enjoy them...and send your tractor story to "Tractor Talk", *Farm & Ranch Living*, 5925 Country Lane, Greendale WI 53129. You may see your story or photo in a future calendar, book or issue of *F&RL*!

Again, we hope you enjoy this book. As you can see from the photos on these pages, these stories aren't just about tractors—they're about the people who own, restore or learned to drive on 'em. ⚏

MEET THE PEOPLE. Pictured clockwise from left are some of the folks you're about to meet: Otto Haman pulling his brother Elmer on a binder (page 10)... ...Aubrey Dodson working on a vintage Fordson (page 100)... Tom Bickel and his family's Minneapolis-Moline (page 90) 3-year-old Crawford Ifland (page 155)...and Carl Lynes on his Farmall A (page 67).

Chapter One

Learnin' to Drive

What better place to practice driving than on a tractor? And once you got the hang of it, you could help Pa farm.

Tractor Love Started Early

By George Taylor, Carthage, Texas

MY DADDY and my uncle, farming and ranching partners, bought the Taylor family's first John Deere equipment in June 1949. They paid $1,200 for a 1950 MT tractor and a No. 5 mower.

The new equipment joined a 1939 Farmall H used for cultivating cotton fields. During the 1950's, however, these tractors were used less and less for cultivating cotton and more and more for mowing pasture as farmland was converted to ranchland.

I was born in 1952, and my love affair with tractors began soon thereafter. By the age of 2, I rode in my uncle's lap as he mowed. By the time I was 6, Daddy and my uncle (to my mother's dismay) allowed me to mow alone on the MT for short periods of time.

When I was 10, my uncle's two sons

ALL IN THE FAMILY. George Taylor, above at age 3 on John Deere MT and below with son Clint, daughter Kelli, wife Emily and JD 420, says his love of "green machines" began with his dad and uncle on Texas ranch.

and I mowed pastures daily during the summer with the Farmall, the MT and a newer acquisition—a 1960 John Deere 435. Along with our dads, we three cousins mowed, repaired tractors, fixed fence and fed cows all throughout our teenage years.

When the three of us moved away to attend college, however, significantly decreasing the labor supply for the Taylor ranching enterprise, my dad and uncle bought a large tractor—a John Deere 4030 and a 15-foot batwing mower.

When my dad died in 1990, I inherited his share of the Taylor ranchland, becoming partners with my uncle. During our first year of operation, we decided to sell the old MT. It was inoperable with a cracked block, and we felt we really didn't need it anyway.

What a mistake! Three years later, I embarked on a desperate search for the MT. I had developed an intense interest in antique tractors, and I desperately wanted to find the MT from my youth.

I called the man to whom we had sold the MT. Three owners later, I finally located the MT—with all its mechanical problems corrected! I was extremely happy to pay $1,800 for the tractor I had junked 3 years earlier for $100.

My tractor restoration partner and I cosmetically renovated the MT so that it now looks like it did that day in 1949 when it arrived to become a new member of the Taylor family. In addition,

---

Massey-Harris Pulled Out Neighbors' Stuck Combines

By John Vitt
Bartlesville, Oklahoma

THE MASSEY-HARRIS four-wheel-drive tractor was the first I learned to drive on our Kansas farm. Dad used it on an Allis-Chalmers 60-inch grain combine and for plowing, but he broke me in on easier jobs like disking.

Dad used the Massey-Harris to help many a neighbor get "unstuck" as they combined grain. Most of our neighbors' combines were powered by a PTO or pulled by a tractor, even if the combine itself had a motor. One neighbor pulled his motor-driven combine with horses.

But we never had to worry about our tractor getting stuck—with its lugged steel wheels, that was virtually impossible.

When I was 12, the tractor seemed big, loud and clumsy to me. I can't believe how much it shrank over the years!

---

we have restored a John Deere 70, a JD R and a JD 420. We are currently working on a 320 and have the original 435 and another MT waiting in the wings.

That 435, by the way, is still being used. Although it's no longer needed for primary tasks at the ranch, I still use it for small mowing jobs around the neighborhood and loan it to close friends.

One neighbor mows his pasture with it and another friend uses the 435 to cultivate his garden. The pastor of our church mows a shopping center lot with it, so the tractor is affectionately known as "the ministry tractor".

Besides ranching, I'm now a mixed-practice veterinarian. I'm also a member of the very active East Texas Antique Tractor and Equipment Association, and my family participates in shows and parades.

During the 1995 Christmas season, we took part in four parades, including one in which my wife, Emily, drove the 435, daughter Kelli drove the 420, son Clint drove the MT and I drove the R. My love affair with tractors has now come full circle: from my father and uncle to me, and from me to my son and daughter.

AN UNUSUALLY LONG exhaust stack was used on the 1930 Farmall Regular being driven by a young Larry Haman (left) to pull a grain binder. The long stack reduced the chances of starting a fire if the tractor was in a tall stand of grain. Above, Larry is driving a 14-tooth hay sweep with his little brother standing on the back, and below, Larry's dad, Otto, is pulling Uncle Elmer on a binder with the same Regular.

Farm Sale Was Sad Event... But Tractor Got New Home

By Larry Haman, San Francisco, California

THE TRACTOR I learned to drive on—a 1930 Farmall Regular—was used on the same farm for 64 years...and today, it's still being used on a neighbor's farm!

As a youngster, I worked on a farm near Meadow Grove, Nebraska. The farm was run by my uncle, Elmer Mueller, because my grandfather, Jacob Mueller, was going blind. Jacob purchased the Farmall Regular in 1930...later, Uncle Elmer taught me how to drive it.

When the tractor arrived in Meadow Grove by train, it had lugs on the rear wheels and disk wheels on the front. Uncle Elmer drove the tractor home because in those days, the streets and roads were still gravel, and there wasn't any pavement to tear up.

As a teenager, I windrowed the alfalfa with a horse-drawn rake, then used the Regular with a 14-tooth sweep on the front to push the hay into the stacker. The stacker was horse-drawn, too, and hoisted the hay up to Elmer on top of the stack.

The Regular had a hand crank and no battery or starter. I learned early that if I ever had to crank the Regular, I needed to place my fingers and thumbs on the back of the crank handle. Otherwise a backfire would have broken some fingers or a thumb.

At the end of the day, I always switched the Regular's main fuel tank off before shutting down the engine. The tractor had two tanks—a big one for kerosene and a small one for gasoline. Because kerosene was cheaper, that's what we ran the tractor on. But starting the tractor with kerosene was difficult—if not impossible—and you needed to make sure all the kerosene in the fuel lines and combustion chambers was used up before turning the engine off. Thus, I always switched off the kerosene and let the Regular run on gasoline for a short time, making it easier to start in the morning.

Although the lugs and disk wheels gave the Regular a rough ride, they provided good traction and a more positive turning capability. Especially at slow speeds, the Regular was hard to turn with disk wheels...but once you got those front wheels turned, the tractor didn't skid or slide along as it sometimes later did on rubber.

In those days, there were lots of mishaps on tractors. Fortunately, the worst thing that ever happened to me on the Regular was that a few sweep teeth got broken. I guess I was lucky...and I had a good teacher in Uncle Elmer.

He always said that if it hadn't been for that Regular, he never would have been able to keep the farm going through the Great Depression and World War II. (It was during World War II that we managed to put rubber on all four wheels.)

Elmer died recently and the farm was sold. Although the occasion was a sad one, I was pleased to see that a neighbor bought the old Regular. Now the tractor I learned to drive on is at work in its new home only a few miles away from the old one.

CASE ROW CROP STILL CRANKS UP WITH EASE

By Raymond Muessman
Charleston, Illinois

IT WAS a 1936 Case CC Row Crop and ran on steel wheels. It had to be cranked to start, but the hand clutch made it fairly easy to drive. "It" was the tractor I learned to drive on.

I waited a long time to drive it, though. Dad bought it in 1939, and I rode on it with him whenever he'd let me. I was always begging to drive, but he'd say, "You need to be bigger and more grown-up to handle a tractor on your own." As time went by, he started letting me steer, but only in open spaces.

After World War II, Dad converted the tractor to rubber tires and added a battery, generator and lights. The last time the Case was overhauled, Dad put in 4-inch sleeves and aluminum pistons, a gasoline manifold, and a high-compression head so the tractor could burn gasoline, not low-grade fuel.

Dad used the Case for every job on his 120-acre farm until 1959, when he bought a new Allis-Chalmers D-17. He kept the Case for mowing and odd jobs and still owned it when he died in 1979. After inheriting the tractor, I made some minor repairs and took it to several antique tractor pulls, always placing in my weight class. The Case won several trophies at antique tractor shows, too.

Today, I still drive the Case at least twice a year. It still starts with just a couple of cranks—not bad for a tractor 60 years old. 🚜

HAND CRANK. Raymond Muessman shows off his 1936 Case CC Row Crop at an antique tractor pull. The Case, which features a tricycle front, still starts easily with its hand crank.

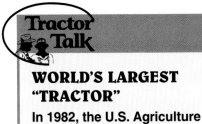

Tractor Talk

WORLD'S LARGEST "TRACTOR"

In 1982, the U.S. Agriculture Department built a vehicle it called a "tractor". This unusual vehicle measured 33 feet between wheels, weighed 24.5 tons and cost $459,000.

Fast Turn in Wheat Field Had Him Going in Circles

By Elmer Strahm, Sabetha, Kansas

IN THE SPRING of 1939, Dad bought a used John Deere General Purpose on steel wheels. He paid $300 for it, but I'm not sure what he intended to use it for. We had a barn full of workhorses at the time.

That summer was hot and dry. Wheat harvest was at hand, and we were cutting a beautiful field that was ripening fast. It was a beastly hot afternoon—not a breeze blowing—and the horses were getting hot.

Finally Dad said, "This is enough." He went home and got the tractor, a handsaw, a brace and bit, and a couple of strap irons he'd made. He sawed the binder tongue in half and bolted on the strap irons. We hitched on the JD and away we went, with Dad on the binder and my older brother on the tractor. Round after round, everything was going great.

It was getting late, and we had quite a few cows to milk. Dad said, "Walter, you go home and do the milking and let Elmer drive the tractor—we're going to get this field of wheat cut."

So I rode the tractor a few rounds to get the hang of it, and soon I was on my own. Piece of cake. When we came to the first corner, I forget to slow down. I made a sharp left turn but wasn't able to straighten out the tractor again. Around the corner and into the wheat we went, with Dad yelling, "Whoa! Whoa!" I didn't think to pull the clutch!

About the second time through the corner, I let go of the steering wheel and pulled on the clutch with both hands. I was small for an 11-year-old, and it took all I had to stop that beast.

We did manage to finish cutting that field, although I never heard the last of my tractor-driving "skills". But even Dad had to laugh about it when it was all over. 🚜

'Growing up with a Tractor Enriched My Life...'

By Rick Campbell, Sherwood, Oregon

FARM TRACTORS...garden tractors...wheel tractors...cleat tractors—the type doesn't matter. As my wife will tell you, any tractor turns my head.

My earliest memories are of riding a mid-1940's John Deere B with my dad. It was the only tractor on our 80-acre central-Oregon farm. Watching the plow turn the earth, the cultivator uproot weeds and the rake windrow the alfalfa was a great way to spend a childhood. The sounds and feel of a working tractor still give me a thrill.

When I was 4, my parents gave me a John Deere pedal tractor for Christmas. I rode it all the time. When I came down with chicken pox, Mom even let me bring it into the house and ride it.

A few years later, I made a wooden "dozer blade" for it and had the time of my life pushing dirt and gravel around. It was my favorite toy, and I rode it until I was so big that my knees hit the steering wheel when I tried to pedal.

As I got older, I could stand in front of Dad and drive the big tractor, using the hand clutch. Controlling that powerful machine made me feel like a man. I don't remember the first time I drove it alone, but from then until we sold the farm, "Johnny" and I were close friends.

After I began working with the tractor, I learned to operate a two-way single-bottom plow, a rubber-tired cultivator and a wheel rake. It was a special treat to drive along slowly while Dad and my older brother loaded hay bales onto the trailer.

My favorite job was raking alfalfa. I had to get up very early, when the dew was still on the leaves and there was just enough light to see. It was just me and Johnny, converting a blank field of mowed hay into windrows just the right size and with just the right spacing for the baler.

Raking became my specialty. When I was 12, a neighbor stopped me as I rode my bicycle to the mailbox and asked if I'd rake hay for him. He had a big farm and five or six tractors. It was the first time I received money to work off our farm. Driving a tractor and being paid for it—I thought I was in heaven.

Our John Deere was bought for work, but Mom and Dad made it a source of family fun, too. In winter, we'd hitch a toboggan behind it with a long rope and pull each other through the snow. This inspired me to build a heavy sled out of old fence posts and 2-by-12's. It had multiple uses, and we pulled it year-round.

Growing up with a tractor gave me a practical education. Learning to drive a car was a piece of cake, and I learned the basics of repairing engines and equipment by watching and helping Dad. I also learned to get along with less. There were several periods when Dad hand-cranked Johnny because we couldn't afford a new battery.

But the most important lesson was that working is fun. I've had six different types of jobs as an adult, and I've enjoyed each of them. My parents, not the John Deere, deserve the credit for instilling this attitude. But growing up with a tractor enriched my life and left me with fond childhood memories. ⚷

NO LEAKS. Walter Wright of Pleasant Garden, North Carolina learned how to drive this 1928 Fordson at age 10. "My father and grandfather bought it in 1930, and it's still in running condition today," he says. "It has the original radiator—and it doesn't leak." Walter re-bored the block and installed new rings and pistons in the late 1940's.

Tractor Talk

MAIL-ORDER TRACTORS

In 1931, Sears & Roebuck offered the Graham-Bradley two-plow tractor for sale. It was manufactured by the Paige Motor Car Co. of Detroit, which also produced some fast and sporty roadsters. The car business influenced the tractor in design and performance—the tractor's top speed was 22 mph.

From Pulling Wagons to Pulling Floats

By Richard Thomas
Davie, Florida

DAD BOUGHT the tractor that I learned to drive on from a dealer in 1940 for $800. It was a 1940 Farmall H on steel wheels.

We lived on a farm in Ohio then, and when I was about 5, I got my first driving lesson on the H. By then, Dad had changed from steel to rubber, making the H a much smoother ride.

By the time I left the farm when I was 18, I'd put in thousands of hours on that tractor and gotten to know it better than a friend.

When Dad brought the H home to our farm, it was the first Farmall in our part of the county. That didn't last for long—when our neighbors saw how good the little tractor was, many soon had one, too!

Today, the H is retired and lives with me in Florida. The only work it does is pull floats in parades...and draw admiring glances!

A BIG HUG. Richard Thomas expresses some of the affection he feels for the 1940 Farmall H that his dad bought and that he later learned to drive on. Still later, Richard put in a lot of hours restoring the tractor.

Tough Wallis Tractor Was 'Hard to Beat'

By Gordon Gottschalk, McAllen, Texas

PLOWING CONTEST. Gordon Gottschalk, his father and their Wallis tractor were photographed after a plowing contest in 1940. Competing against much newer, modern tractors, Gordon placed third in the junior division and his dad took first place in the senior division.

MY FATHER was an expert at tractor work. From 1919 to 1933, that was his main job for the farm corporation of Everson & Ferry in Lake Mills, Wisconsin.

Dad spent much of his time on a Wallis that was manufactured in 1919 or '20. For years, I had to be content to just ride along on it. There was a great place for that, too—a large oblong iron toolbox just in front of the operator, between the high steel fenders.

When the company dissolved in 1933, we started farming on our own, and Dad was able to buy the Wallis. He'd always said, "If I'm going to farm on my own, that tractor has to come with me."

I was 11 then and got to drive the Wallis when Dad put a stub pole on the grain binder. He sat on the binder and adjusted the reel and sickle bar, and slid the knotter back and forth to tie the bundles.

I had a lot of room to turn around on the field, and it didn't take me long to become pretty good at cutting a full swath and making some good corners. After that, I did a lot of plowing, disking and dragging while Dad did the planting with the horses.

With its long spade lugs and deep-cutting iron rings on the front wheels, that old Wallis was hard to beat. It was one of those tractors that followed the furrow. In cold weather, the operator could step off and jog along it for a while.

We traded the Wallis for an Allis-Chalmers WD in 1954. Rubber tires were the way to go then, but the memories of that tough old Wallis live on.

Rejuvenated W-30 Again Runs Thresher And Baler

By Joe Catron, Salem, Virginia

DAD BOUGHT a McCormick-Deering W-30 in June 1936 at the local hardware store, which was also the IH dealer in those days.

He used it to thrash, bale straw and hay and fill silos all over the county. When I was old enough to drive, I followed Dad and the tractor as they traveled from one farm to another.

When Dad retired the W-30 around 1960, it was almost forgotten. It sat under an oak tree until 1986, and by then, the motor was stuck.

My cousin Jimmy Huddle and I got it running on Thanksgiving Day 1988 and played with it all winter. That spring, I used it to help Jimmy disk 10 acres of corn ground.

Now the tractor is all painted, and I take it to a lot of shows. I still pull the thrashing machine and baler at the Rural Retreat tractor pull and show.

The W-30 was the first tractor I ever drove, and I still enjoy driving it, working with it and showing it. 🚜

HE NO LONGER THOUGHT OF TRACTORS AS 'PUTT-PUTTING'

By Carmen Brandt, McFarland, Wisconsin

IN THE EARLY DAYS of World War II, farm tractors were hard to come by. We had the good fortune to buy a Co-op tractor assembled and sold by the Farmers Union, with mostly Mopar parts. It had rubber tires, a starter, lights, PTO and a wide front. That wide front was important, as the tractor had a road speed of 40 mph.

Dad and my uncle drove the tractor from St. Paul, Minnesota to my uncle's farm in Deerfield, Wisconsin. The trip took the better part of a day.

As a 12-year-old farm kid, I spent the first part of that summer anxiously awaiting the moment when I would climb onto the Co-op. But I had to wait my turn—behind Dad, Mom, two uncles, an aunt and an older sister. By the end of the following summer, I felt like a veteran tractor driver.

When our parents went to town, my brother and I would jump on the Co-op for a thrill ride up and down the farmstead's long driveway, rounding the bend at full throttle as the tractor skidded in the loose gravel. We also discovered that if we attached a wire to the governor linkage, the Co-op would go well over 40 mph!

We discovered other uses for the Co-op, too. After early spring planting, we'd turn the team out to pasture—but they were never eager to return to the barn a few weeks later, at cultivating time. After a few trips around the pasture with the tractor at their heels, they were more than glad to head home!

In the late 1940's, a buddy and I ventured into the custom hay-baling business. For several years, we used the old Co-op to pull the gigantic New Holland 76 baler from farm to farm.

One afternoon, we were heading down the highway to a baling job, following an elderly man traveling about 35 mph. The poor fellow was so startled at being passed by a farm tractor pulling a hay baler that he ran completely off the road.

We stopped, of course—the fellow wasn't hurt. I'm sure that from then on, however, he didn't think of tractors as "putt-putting" through a field! 🚜

BELT LIGHTNING. Joe Catron, at the controls on his father's McCormick-Deering W-30, tightens the belt connected to a thrashing machine. Joe and a cousin started restoring the tractor in 1988, after it had sat outside for 26 years.

Tractor Talk

WATERLOO BOY

In 1893, the Waterloo Gasoline Traction Engine Co. was founded in Waterloo, Iowa. One of the first companies formed to produce gas-powered tractors, it later became the Waterloo Gas Engine Co. Chief engineer Louis Witry designed the highly successful and lightweight "Waterloo Boy" tractor in 1914. The design so impressed Deere & Co. that it purchased Waterloo in 1918 for $2.1 million!

Thundering Emerson Made Vivid Impression

By Lowell Stirratt, Hermosa Beach, California

I STILL REMEMBER the day Dad brought home our first tractor. It was the fall of 1917, and I was only 5 years old. The huge tractor thundered toward me as Dad drove it into the yard. I don't recall being frightened—only awed.

The tractor was an Emerson-Brantingham, built in Rockford, Illinois. To my knowledge, there were no others anywhere in our neighborhood. Apparently it wasn't a best-seller.

We used the Emerson primarily for plowing, as it had the capacity to pull a three-bottom plow. It also pulled a spring-toothed harrow, and a belt pulley was attached to run a feed grinder, silo filler, threshing machine, wood saw and other equipment.

The four-cylinder engine had to be cranked to start. On cold days when Dad needed to grind feed, he'd build a fire under the crank-case to warm the oil.

Sometimes he'd open the petcocks on the cylinders and squirt in a little ether—potent starting fuel, that was.

I don't remember the first time I drove the Emerson, but I do recall walking alongside it while plowing. It would follow the furrow, allowing the operator to dismount and walk to keep warm on cold days. One time when I was walking next to it, it must have hit a stone, because it climbed out of the furrow and started making a diagonal path. It took me some time to climb back on and get it back on track.

Stopped with a Bang

The tractor served us well until the late 1920's. We were threshing grain at a neighbor's farm when it suddenly stopped with a bang. A connecting rod had broken, and part of it came out the side of the engine, breaking the engine in half. We borrowed a neighbor's tractor for our own threshing and towed the Emerson home.

Then Dad bought a Huber—I don't remember any of those in our area, either. Its rear-drive wheels and gears weren't in good shape, but the Emerson's were close to the same size, so we transferred them to the Huber. Later on, I used the Emerson frame to make a hay wagon.

In 1934, Dad and I bought an Allis-Chalmers WC, the first rubber-tired tractor in Pierce County, Wisconsin. Farmers came from miles around to see a demonstration at our farm. Many shook their heads, saying those tires would wear out quickly and be a constant source of trouble.

Dependable Machine

They were wrong. The tires lasted for years, and they made the tractor a lot more versatile and comfortable to work with.

The "Allis" was my pride and joy—new and shiny, fast and versatile. I even used it to court my wife. When the car wasn't available, I'd crank up the Allis and head for town. It would do about 15 mph in high gear, so the 4-mile trip didn't take long.

That little tractor was still doing its job when I left the farm in 1947. Dad kept it until his retirement, when he sold it at auction. I don't know who bought it, but I hope they treated it with a lot of TLC.

It truly was a dependable little tractor.

NEXT BEST THING. Lowell Stirratt may not have photos of either the Emerson-Brantingham that was his dad's first tractor, or the 1934 Allis-Chalmers WC he and his dad bought together…but he does have the next best thing—scaled-down versions of the two tractors that he made himself (top right and below). A friend of Lowell's, David Lowrie, is driving the Emerson. Lowell has also built other smaller scale versions of his and his dad's farm equipment, including a bundle wagon, Case thresher and grain barge.

Chapter Two

Our First Tractor

Buying a first tractor could be emotional—it often meant putting a faithful team of horses out to pasture.

No Other Tractor Could Measure up to Ol' Red

By Peggy Norwood, Creedmoor, North Carolina

WHEN I WAS a child, we worked our tobacco field with mules and a horse. It was hard work, and we longed for a better way. When Daddy bought his first tractor, a shiny modern Farmall, we were all excited. Soon "Ol' Red" was doing the plowing and pulling the tobacco planter.

"Before tractors, we earned our living by the sweat of our brow," Mama told me. "All the hard work seemed much easier with Ol' Red."

Years later, when I asked Daddy about Ol' Red, his eyes lit up. He left the room and returned with the original operator's manual, still well-kept after all these years.

"I always fixed it myself when it wouldn't run," he recalled, thumbing through the pages with the wonder of a child looking at a Christmas catalog. "Red only had to go to the shop one time, to get the motor overhauled. I checked the oil and gas each day, and Red was greased every 2 weeks. The dirt was washed off once a week, and I never tied any bale wire on my tractor to fix it. Red looked good."

At 81, Daddy remembered everything about Red. "He had a good personality, you know. Red could pull trailers loaded with heavy green tobacco real easy and could hold back a weighty load coming down a hill. Often, Red stayed in the furrow while I got off and walked along beside him."

When Daddy retired, he used Red to plow Mama's garden. He kept Red spotless and shiny and painted him four times. After 36 years, though, there just wasn't enough work to keep Red busy. It was time to let him go.

The man who bought Red said he looked as good as new. Daddy thought he was ready to sell, but he soon regretted it.

"Your mama and I went to see him, and I wanted to bring Red home," he said slowly. "The man said we could visit Red whenever we wanted to, but it wasn't the same."

A year later, Daddy was at the International Harvester Co. and saw an old Farmall that had been brought in for repairs. Daddy recognized it immediately.

"I knew the sound of my tractor when the man cranked it," he said. "The exhaust pipe was broken, and the bumper and hood were bent. 'Ol' Red, you look bad,' I said.

"He needed new tires, and the brakes needed to be lined. The man should have put another paint job on him."

Daddy fell silent, a faraway look in his eyes. "I had other tractors, you know—a Ferguson and a Farmall 140—but they never got close to me. I never thought much of any other tractor except Ol' Red."

AND THEN HE SAID...

"When I was a young child, my brothers, sisters and I would go out to the dirt road in front of our house after Mr. Hood went by on his tractor and put our toes in the slits in the road made by the iron wheel lugs."

—*Max Brewer*
Paola, Kansas

'I Remember Thinking It Was the Prettiest Thing I'd Ever Seen'

By John Wilson, Rapid City, South Dakota

I GREW UP with the old steel-wheeled tractors and have always liked them. Looking back, one has to admire the engineering from those days. There was so much simplicity built into those old machines.

Our first tractor was a 1925 Fordson. One day when I came home from school, it was sitting in the yard with a new plow. I remember thinking it was the prettiest thing I'd ever seen. And, of course, I wondered how long it would be before Dad let me drive it.

Dad let me sit on his lap and "steer" when he was plowing, but there wasn't really any steering to do. The tractor would go from one end of the field to the other almost by itself.

But the day did come when Dad let me pull the grain binder. I was 12. I couldn't dump the bundles in a straight row and Dad didn't like that, so he tried me on the tractor. My, it was great to feel all that power.

We also farmed with horses, but cutting grain was much faster and easier with a tractor—no hitching up, watering or feeding, and no stopping at the end of the field to let the animals rest.

In the mid-'30's, my wife and I tried our hand at farming for a few years. Like everyone else at the time, we had no money for new equipment, so I bought two used Fordsons from an equipment dealer for $10. Believe it or not, I made one good tractor out of the two.

We used the tractor for 2 years, until we were able to buy a new one. And you know, I sold that Fordson for $100!

EXCELLENT ENGINE. John Wilson grew up with Fordson tractors, so this 1923 model was a natural choice for his first restoration project. "It had been used as a power unit on an irrigation pump in Wyoming, so the exterior was very rusty, but the engine was in excellent condition," John recalls. He has since helped a friend restore a 1926 Fordson.

Excitement Mingled with Fear On First Tractor Outings

By Harold Queck, Bridgewater, Iowa

IN 1925, when I was 12 years old, Dad bought his first tractor, a chain-driven International 8/16. I still remember the first time we plowed with it.

I sat on one of the large rear fenders as we drove down a dirt road to the field. It was a rough ride when the big wheel lugs hit a rut, but I wasn't going to miss this experience.

Along the way, Dad switched from the gasoline tank to kerosene and shifted into third gear, which had a speed of about 4-1/2 mph. At the field, he stopped and shifted into second, which had a speed of about 2 mph. He pulled a rope to drop the plow into the ground, the tractor belched smoke and we proceeded down the furrow. I think Dad was as excited and thrilled as I was.

Everything went fine until we reached the other end of the field. Dad pulled the rope to lift the plow out of the ground, but he didn't realize what a wide radius the tractor needed to turn and didn't throttle it down. Too late, he realized he was going to hit the fence.

So Dad did just what he had done for years. He pulled on the steering wheel, pushed with his feet and shouted "Whoa!" Of course, we hit the fence.

Dad finally stopped by pushing on the foot brake. We backed up, turned and continued on our way.

I think Dad was embarrassed to admit to others how his new tractor got those scratches, and why the fence needed repair. The power of the tractor was a little frightening.

As plowing season continued, Dad worked with the tractor and I drove five horses on the gang plow. When we had 7 acres left, Dad suggested I finish plowing with the tractor.

I tried to remain calm as I filled the fuel tanks and checked the fluid levels. When everything was ready, I retarded the spark and pulled up on the crank. I had to plant my feet firmly on the shed's dirt floor, grab the radiator frame, and pull hard and fast. When the tractor started, I hurried onto the seat, pulled the spark down, backed into the yard and hooked up the plow. I was so excited!

About a half mile from home, the tractor stopped. I knew immediately that I'd forgotten to switch from gasoline to kerosene. I had used up all the gas, so I couldn't restart the tractor. I walked home to fill a gas can, walked back and

cranked it again. This time I remembered to switch the tanks.

What a relief when I was actually in the field plowing! It was fun to drive down the furrow as black smoke rolled from the 2-foot exhaust pipe. When I was facing the wind, the fumes were blown into my face, but I never complained.

Toward the end of the afternoon, I noticed storm clouds in the west, but I had to finish the field that day, so I kept plowing. As I started for home, it began to rain. I put on my jacket and pulled up the collar, but that didn't provide much protection from the hail that came next. I had no choice but to keep going.

The steel seat filled with water, and the rain and hail beat the engine cover with a loud clanking noise. Suddenly there was a flash of lightning and I felt a burning sensation on the tractor seat. I stood up to drive the rest of the way.

As I turned into the yard, the tractor began to misfire—the spark plugs were wet. By the time I got to the shed, I was soaked, but I knew I had to take care of the tractor, just as we took care of the horses.

I kept the motor running until it was dry and firing correctly, then closed the kerosene valve and let all the fuel burn out of the carburetor. I was finally finished with a very exciting day. 🚜

TRIP TO ENGINE SHOW PUT HIM BACK IN DRIVER'S SEAT

By Ed Jensen, Battle Creek, Iowa

BACK IN 1947, when I was 17, I bought a 1934 John Deere A on steel in the hills near Oto, Iowa. That was the spring I started farming on my own, working 80 acres I'd bought the fall before at $100 each.

I paid $820 for the tractor, a cultivator, a spring-tooth harrow and a Deere wagon on steel. My uncle cut down the tractor's wheels, welded on rims and mounted rubber tires on it.

I farmed with the Deere until 1964, then used it to pull a 1905 15-horsepower portable gas engine. In 1988, I sold it to a collector from Iowa for $1,000.

In 1995, I was admiring the tractors at a gas engine show in Butterfield, Minnesota when I noticed a 1934 A just like the one I used to have. I checked the serial number to see how close it was to mine—and it was mine. The owner allowed me the honor of driving it in the show's parade. 🚜

Tractor Talk

THE COMFORTRACTOR

Minneapolis-Moline introduced the UDLX Comfortractor in 1938. It had a fully enclosed two-seater with insulated cab, heater, defrosters, windshield wipers, fenders on all four wheels and a radio! Unfortunately, while it offered more comfort, it cost about twice as much as the competition—$2,155.

Post-Depression farmers weren't ready for features that were 30 years ahead of their time. Only 125 to 150 were produced. This unique tractor may be the most recognizable tractor ever made.

A GOOD OFFER. Steve Carter leads a hayride on the 120-acre grounds of Friends of Israel Gospel Ministry in southern New Jersey, where he works. Steve accepted a job offer from the ministry on the condition that he be allowed to bring his Farmall H along with him.

When New Job Beckoned, His Tractor Moved, Too

By Steve Carter
Westville, New Jersey

AS A high school senior in 1978, I was in the market for a tractor. After graduation, my father and I were going to cut about 4,000 board feet of black cherry logs from a swamp forest, and we'd need a tractor to pull them out.

I first saw the 1941 Farmall H at a nearby farm in central New York State, buried in snow almost halfway up its exhaust stack. I agreed to buy it for $750 the following spring—providing it would run. Next time I saw it, it was purring away. It was the beginning of a long and satisfying relationship.

Dad didn't think we needed the tractor at first. However, after the H pulled out his four-wheel-drive International pickup a few times, he changed his mind!

After I married in 1981, my wife and I used the Farmall to clear land for our home in the woods. Seven years later, I was offered a job with Friends of Israel Gospel Ministry in southern New Jersey. I accepted—on the condition that I could bring the Farmall along and put it to use on their 120 acres.

Our first few years here, the H was doing quite a bit of work, pulling trucks and boats from boat ramps, loading mulch, pulling hayrides and doing other jobs. Sometimes it was the most dependable piece of equipment on the property.

My Farmall is a little different from any others I've seen. It has a Schwartz wide front end and a front-end loader, and its rear tires are larger than most. The most unique feature may be the M&W over-center hand clutch. This allows the rear wheels to be disengaged separately from the foot clutch, so the PTO and hydraulic pump can continue to turn—a big help for chopping or baling hay or using the loader.

As I've learned more about this tractor, I've developed great respect for the people who designed and built it, and for the owners who added some "extras". It may have run on steel originally, and the starter, battery and generator most likely were added later, along with the lights.

I've owned my Farmall H for almost half my life. Although the newer, smaller, fancier tractors have their appeal, I'm thankful to have this one. As we grow older together, I have more respect for the people who built it, and for what America stood for in 1941.

Fordson's Vibrations Put Their Feet to Sleep

DAD'S first tractor was a Fordson that whined so loudly it could be heard for a mile. It vibrated so much that it would put our feet to sleep as we rode, barefoot, with Dad while he plowed.

—John Vitt
Bartlesville, Oklahoma

PRIMITIVE DAYS. Power equipment replaced workhorses only gradually, as this 1927 photo shows. "Those were primitive days," recalls Ralph Bergerson of Vernonia, Oregon. "This McCormick-Deering 10/20 was heavy and durable but hard to steer—especially if the front wheels hit something or dropped into a dead furrow. That's my dad, Elmer, in the photo with a friend, William Anderson."

NEW HOME. Farmall A gets a good going-over after arriving (with chains) in sunny southern California from the snowy Midwest. In 1939, the A became the first tractor on a farm that eventually was swallowed up by a Chicago suburb. With the A in the photo is Scott, a great-grandson of the farmer who bought the tractor new.

Farmer's First Tractor Retires From Snowdrifts to Sun and Sand

By Elaine Schmidt Ponton, Holtville, California

C-R-A-N-K! With a roar, the brand-new, bright red 1939 Farmall A that my grandfather had just bought came to life.

It was the spring of 1939. I was 10 and living on my grandparents' farm. For months, Uncle Eddie had been trying to talk Grandpa Clark into trading his beloved team of matched horses for a tractor.

Finally, Grandpa agreed to at least go look at tractors. The whole family had piled into our 1933 Ford sedan and headed off to a dealership in Des Plaines, Illinois. The salesman told Grandpa that one little tractor could easily do what many horses had, and after much looking and dickering, a deal for the A was struck.

The little Farmall served my grandfather well. In spring, summer and fall, it was a workhorse on the farm. In winter, fitted with chains, it served as a snowplow, always starting with just one crank.

Many times, the A pulled cars out of snowdrifts along the road in front of our farmhouse. When Uncle Eddie was called to serve his country during World War II, I drove the A to help Grandpa plow, rake hay and do other work on the farm.

When the A was not in use, Grandpa always put it in the shed under a tarp so that its finish was kept spotless.

In the late '40's, when I was away at college, the farm was subdivided. Like many other farms in that area, my grandparents' place became part of a Chicago suburb. With no more farm work, the little Farmall A went into semi-retirement.

Continued Loving Care

It still plowed a lot of snow, but that was about it. Then when Grandpa Clark passed away in 1969, Uncle Eddie became the proud owner of the A. He took loving care of it just as Grandpa had, using it for snowplowing and frequently cleaning and polishing it.

Uncle Eddie even kept all the original manuals. When he passed away in December 1994, it appeared that the A and our family would part company—no relative in the Chicago area had any room for the tractor, and it would soon have to leave the garage to which it had been brought more than a half century earlier.

Then my two sons, Scott and Mark (both living in southern California), heard about the tractor's plight. They knew how much their great-grandfather and great-uncle had loved the little tractor.

Hauled 2,000 Miles

Neither Scott nor Mark was a farmer, but together they bought the A. After a lot of searching, they found a mover willing to haul it 2,000 miles in the back of an enclosed truck.

When it arrived in southern California, the first question the boys had was whether the A would start. It hadn't been used in several years…and the sand and sun of southern California were a lot different than the rich black dirt and deep snowdrifts of the Midwest.

C-R-A-N-K! With a roar, the 56-year-old 1939 Farmall A my sons had just bought came to life!

Suddenly Scott and Mark had a mission: Give the little tractor the same loving care it had gotten from Uncle Eddie and Grandpa Clark.

About the only difference between then and now is that instead of plowing snow, Grandpa Clark's first tractor sometimes plows sand!

Father and Son Overhauled Fordson Twice in Three Weeks!

By George Fichter, Crownsville, Maryland

DURING the first 2 or 3 years after my father bought a small farm in Luzerne County, Pennsylvania in 1926, he borrowed a neighbor's horses to till the fields. That had drawbacks, however, and he eventually found a rusty old Fordson instead.

When the tractor was delivered, Dad looked it over and decided to overhaul it completely before using it. I was about 9 or 10 at the time, and I helped Dad restore and repaint it. It took about 2 weeks, but when we were through, the old tractor looked like a showpiece.

The next day, before Dad had a chance to try the tractor out, the man who'd sold it to him came by. He'd leased some land in the Sugarloaf Valley and wanted to borrow or lease the tractor for a day to plow and sow grain.

Dad hesitated, but the man was persistent. Finally Dad gave in. The man promised to have the tractor back by nightfall. He and a helper loaded the tractor on a truck and left.

At his new acreage, the man plowed for about an hour and ran out of gas. As the sound of the engine faded, he heard thunder in the distance. He had only a few more rounds to go, and the storm was approaching fast. He'd have to hurry to finish the field before it began raining.

The man ran across the field, grabbed a 5-gallon gas can from his truck and hurried back to the tractor, nervous and out of breath. As he poured the gas in, some of it spilled out and hit the manifold, causing an explosion.

The ball of fire engulfed the man in flames from the waist up. His helper pushed him to the ground and covered him with a jacket, putting out the flames, then drove him to the nearest doctor for treatment.

When the two brought the tractor back to the farm that evening, my father couldn't believe his eyes. His newly overhauled tractor was nothing more than a burned-out hulk.

Dad was thankful the man hadn't been killed, but he was heartsick at the condition of the Fordson. The magneto and all the wiring was burned to a crisp, and most of the tractor needed to be sanded and repainted.

It was another week or so before we finished overhauling the tractor for the second time...and then Dad got to drive it for the first time. 🔧

ONE OF THE FIRST. Roger Abernathy drives his first tractor, a secondhand Fordson purchased in 1933, while his father works the binder at left. "Dad was one of the first in our area to farm with tractors," says Connie Greene of Blackstone, Virginia. "In 1937, he bought a Farmall F-12 and used it to cultivate tobacco. His neighbors had said it couldn't be done."

Tractor Talk

DOWNSIZING

By 1913, massive farm tractors had diminished in popularity. Farmers wanted smaller tractors for everyday chores. The demand was so great that even poorly designed tractors sold well, and by 1920, there were several hundred companies producing them. Many small companies faded almost as quickly as they appeared.

Original Owner Rescued, Restored Farmall F-12

By Earl Rockwell, Francesville, Indiana

I BOUGHT my first tractor, a 1935 Farmall F-12, in 1936. I paid $550 for it and hauled it 25 miles to our farm on a hayrack pulled by a Buick.

At a speed of 3-3/4 mph, a good day's plowing was 40 acres in 10 hours.

I used this tractor until 1942, when I traded it for a new H. I thought I'd never see the F-12 again. The dealer sold it to another farmer, who used it for many years, then drove it into the woods. That's where my friend George Miller found it 17 years later.

I was retired but still loved to work on tractors. So, at age 86, I bought it back—for $40. The tires and wheels were rusted and rotten, the motor was stuck and almost everything on the tractor needed to be replaced.

George and I went around looking for parts on other "junkyard" F-12's. It took us a year to restore it to running condition. 🔧

$800 Tractor Purchase Drove Mother To Tears

By Lucille Jensen
Independence, Kansas

IN THE 1930's, my parents were saving to buy some land—not an easy thing to do in those days. They managed to save $800, but it took a long, long time.

One day in 1938 or '39, Dad went to a farm sale and came home with a 1935 Allis-Chalmers WC, plus a plow, cultivator and mowing machine. The $800 was gone. My mother cried and cried. After years of doing without, they'd have to start saving all over again.

But Mom said the money seemed to come in easier and quicker once they had the tractor. Things were certainly easier on Dad and his team of mules. When Dad worked with the mules, though, he'd stop every round or two at the fencerow to "rest the team" and visit with his neighbor, who was "resting" his team. Of course, there was no excuse for that!

A couple of years after Dad bought

A WISE PURCHASE. Lucille Jensen's father bought this 1935 Allis-Chalmers WC in the late 1930's, using savings he and his wife had earmarked for land. It turned out to be a wise purchase. "Mom said the money seemed to come in easier and quicker once they had the tractor," Lucille remembers.

the tractor, he got a threshing machine to run with it. The thresher was always stopping up or having a belt slip, and Dad decided he needed someone along who could stop the tractor immediately when necessary. I started going out with the threshing crew to "run the tractor".

I sat on the tractor and started and stopped it many times a day. Boy, was that heaven! Until then, I'd been helping Mom with the cooking, making tea in a washtub and serving the guys. Now I got to eat with the crew—and I didn't have to wash dishes afterward.

Dad obtained other tractors through the years but could never seem to part with his "original", even when he retired. When Dad moved to town, he finally gave the tractor to us.

My husband used it for small jobs like mowing and plowing the garden. He kept it even when he retired, which pleased my dad.

Since then, Bill has painted the WC and worked on it a bit. While we still use it for small jobs, we also take it to exhibitions, antique tractor pulls and parades. Last December, I drove it in a parade as "Allis, the Christmas angel".

The AC still has the original rubber tires, though one of them is held together with a steel band. It gives the tractor character. Our kids and grandkids plan to keep my dad's beloved first tractor and see that it stays in the family. ⌘

Dad Laid Down the Law: Work Came Before Play

By Gertrude Nolan
Aurora, New York

FUEL STOP. Gertrude Nolan's father stands alongside his first tractor, a McCormick-Deering, in 1937.

MY FATHER'S first tractor was a McCormick-Deering. I was 10 when he bought it and learned to drive it 4 years later. There were 10 children in the family, and we all helped on the farm. One of my regular jobs was cutting wheat.

One Saturday evening, I wanted to go roller-skating. I left the wheat field, shut off the tractor and went to the house to take a bath.

My father came in and told me to get back on the tractor and get the wheat cut —there was rain predicted for Sunday. I was upset, but back then, we always did what our parents told us to do. ⌘

Greenhorn Farmers Bested Uncle in Plowing Contest

By John Arnold, Leesburg, Florida

IN 1941, with Dad unable to work, we moved from Bay City, Michigan to a farm my mother had inherited. The rent from the farm barely paid the property taxes, and Mother had inherited the farm's debts along with its acreage.

I was 13, and my 22-year-old brother was working in a factory. We could work the farm for Mother, but we had no equipment of any kind, and Mother was in no position to borrow money.

My brother borrowed enough to get us started, and we bought a 1941 Ford Ferguson with a hydraulic lift for a mere $650. For a lightweight youngster like me, that lift was a real lifesaver. The tractor also came with a three-section spike-toothed drag, a two-bottom plow, a two-row cultivator, a quack grass rooter and a used three-section spring-toothed drag.

My first project was to plow a field so we could plant winter wheat. The day my brother and I decided to investigate the mysteries of running a tractor, our uncle spotted us from his farm next door and came over with his John Deere and a two-bottom trailer plow.

He was going to demonstrate what a good tractor could do compared to our "toy". He was not the least bit impressed with our little Ford Ferguson.

He suggested we start plowing the field at opposite ends and work toward the middle. My crafty brother suggested we turn it into a contest, with a modest wager on the outcome. We took a 1-yard measuring stick, stepped off the length of the field and divided it in half.

My brother decided we should plow across the narrow width of the field. Our uncle didn't catch the significance of this. His John Deere had more power and would travel faster on the straightaway. But we could plow right up to the fence, stomp on one of the independent brake pedals and pivot 180 degrees, leaving only a tractor-length to plow later.

Our uncle couldn't duplicate this tight maneuver. Our plow was nestled between the fenders, but his was trailered—and his tractor was twice as long. He had to travel along the fence line a bit before turning, and ended up with two to three times as much headland to plow.

Of course, we made it to the middle of the field and plowed our headlands well before our uncle finished. So we got half our field plowed for free, finished the work in half the time and won our bet besides. What a deal! ☙

Daughter's Arrival Sent Him Tractor-Shopping

By Ada Wellman
York, Nebraska

WE WERE married in 1932 and started farming in central Nebraska with horses. Our first daughter was born in 1936, and in 1939, we were expecting again.

My husband said he'd farm another 5 years with horses if it was a boy, but that if it was a girl, he'd buy a tractor.

We had a girl, so he started looking at what we could afford. The local John Deere dealer came out and sold us a new 1940 B with steel wheels on the rear and rubber tires in front for $650.

The first time my husband took it out to plant corn, he gave the command "Ho!" and went straight through the line fence.

IOWA-MADE WETMORE SERVED FAMILY WELL

By Ralph Benton, Clarksville, Indiana

ALL OUR HORSES except the old mare got a disease called distemper back in May 1920. Normally, May was when we started planting corn, but because of the horses' sickness, we weren't even able to plow our furrows.

I was 14 at the time and Dad's right-hand man on our Nebraska farm. One day, I took the mare and two of the recovering horses, hitched them to a 16-inch walking plow and began plowing a field. The horses were "soft", and I didn't get much done.

Dad came out about 4 o'clock to see how it was going. He stood there for a few minutes, then said, "For 2¢, I'd go out and buy a tractor."

The next day, he did just that. Dad went to Sioux City, Iowa, about 25 miles away, and bought a Wetmore tractor. Made by a small company in Sioux City, it had a four-cylinder engine, was rated at 12/25 horsepower and could pull a two-bottom 16-inch plow.

Dad would get up at daylight and start plowing while I did the chores. Then he'd take over plowing at noon while I took a break. Working this way, we got the soil ready for planting in just 5 days.

I rigged up a hitch to pull the horse-drawn disk and harrow, and Dad started planting. By switching teams at noon, we managed to finish planting only a little later than usual. We used the Wetmore to pull the grain binder, with me driving the tractor and Dad riding the binder. We had a hitch that scissored so we could cut square corners.

That summer, Dad bought a 22-inch Case grain separator, and we used that on the Wetmore, too. It also powered a corn sheller, a feed grinder and a 30-inch buzz saw.

The Wetmore served us well for 5 years, and then Dad traded it for a Case tractor with a cross-mounted motor. It was good on the belt, but not as good as the Wetmore for fieldwork. ☙

He Needed Real Horsepower To Free Tractor from Muck

By Wilbur Paulson
Rosalia, Washington

I WAS ONLY 2 when Dad bought an International Harvester T-20 track tractor in 1929…but I believe I can remember when it was delivered. Dad's was only the second T-20 sold out of Spokane, Washington.

As soon as Dad took delivery, he used the T-20 to do some fall work and to seed winter wheat. The neighbor kids taunted my sister and me that it would never pull our 12-foot Rumely combine come spring.

Sure enough, when harvest came around, the tractor didn't work. It would pull the combine, but the rollers would heat up, the steering clutches would get hot and then it couldn't be steered. The first tractor harvest was a bust. Dad and Granddad used horses to cut 700 acres of wheat.

Dad and the tractor company discussed things, and the company sent out a man with a truck full of parts. He overhauled the track rollers, steering clutches and brakes.

Soon our new tractor was overhauled and ready to work, but there wasn't much to plant in May, so right away Dad got started plowing the summer fallow. He had the T-20 out with a three-bottom plow when he hit a wet boggy spring fairly well up a hillside. Dad wasn't too experienced in driving a tractor on soft ground and let the tracks spin a few times. Then he was really stuck, with water and mud high on the tracks.

Dad tied a truck on the front, and he and Mother tried to pull the tractor out. The truck got stuck, too. They shoved fence posts under the tractor, which only got it stuck deeper. By the time they finally got the truck out, it was nighttime.

The struggle continued for the next day or so, with Dad and Mother shoveling mud and sticking more posts under the track. Now the tractor was really mired down.

A neighbor came by with his team of four matched bays, and Dad waved him down to discuss the problem. Could Al's horses pull the tractor out? (If you're wondering why they didn't pull it out with another tractor, well, there wasn't one for many a mile.)

Al said, "These are the best four horses I've got. I think if you start the tractor and engage the clutch as I put them into the load, we can probably pull that tractor out."

Mother put me well out of the way of flying cables and horses' feet, but close enough that I could watch. The tractor got started, Dad got on, and the horses were hooked on with a strong cable, doubletrees and chains.

Al eased the horses in, and they swung back and forth as they tested the load. His horses trusted him, and they knew he wouldn't give them more than they could pull.

The chains and cable tightened, with Al talking to the horses all the while. They buckled down until their bellies touched the ground but kept pulling until the tractor moved. Then they really laid in, and the tractor surged up out of the mud hole and bounced down onto solid ground.

It was an unforgettable sight, still etched in my memory 65 years later. If only we'd had videotape to record it!

As for Dad and his T-20, the experience taught him just what to do whenever he got stuck and the tracks started spinning. He'd stop immediately, unhook his equipment, drive the tractor out to solid ground and use a cable to pull out the equipment. ⌫

Tractor Was Their First Modern 'Appliance'

By I.P. Grill, Santa Rosa, California

DAD MIGHT have wanted a bigger tractor than the first one he ever bought—a McCormick-Deering 10/20—but, in those days, we didn't have a nickel to spare. I'd just turned 10 when, in mid-November, the tractor was delivered and unloaded on a bank beside the road.

There was snow and ice on the ground, and the tractor had steel wheels without any lugs. Needless to say, our new tractor had no traction…almost before it was unloaded, it was stuck! We looked for the lugs, but for some reason they weren't delivered with the tractor.

However, the nuts and bolts used to secure the lugs to the wheels were included. My brother Frank screwed some of the bolts through the holes in the wheels, giving the tractor the traction it needed to at least reach the shed.

As soon as the lugs came, we put them on and Frank let me "drive" the tractor down the road so all the neighbor boys could see me. (Actually, if the truth were told, I was only steering—Frank was driving.)

When we got the tractor, Father predicted it would never replace our two teams of horses, but it eventually did. We loved our horses…but we soon loved that tractor, too!

Our farm was in Bloomer, Wisconsin, and the tractor arrived before electricity or indoor plumbing. In those days, we still used kerosene lamps and pumped all our water by hand.

The McCormick-Deering was a big step toward the modern era—and our first modern "appliance"! ⌫

FARMER AND HIS 'WC' REUNITED AFTER 28 YEARS

By Harvey Bolton, Henderson, Iowa

KEPT TRACK. This 1934 Allis-Chalmers WC came into Harvey Bolton's life when he was 5 years old. The family sold it in 1949, but Harvey kept track of every subsequent owner. In 1977, he worked out a trade that returned it to the family farm.

I WAS 5 years old when my dad bought a brand-new 1934 Allis-Chalmers WC. Rubber tires were available then, but Dad insisted on steel wheels. That cut the price tag to $675, and besides, he figured steel wouldn't get stuck in the mud as easily.

About 8 years later, Dad had to stop driving the tractor because of health problems, and I took over. My younger brother, Gene, could drive those horses —I wanted responsibility for the WC! For nearly 10 years, it was the only tractor we used on our 300 acres.

Around 1944, we bought a 1939 WC to provide some extra mechanical help. I was fascinated by its starter and lights. We put lights and a generator on the old WC so we could drive it at night, too.

Traded for "WD"

With both Gene and me on tractors, we could really get some work done. I remember plowing 12 acres in 6-1/2 hours. That doesn't sound like much now, but we felt we'd really accomplished something.

In 1949, we finally traded off the '34 for a new WD. I wasn't even sad to see it go, even though I'd spent years picking and shucking corn, combining and doing custom work with it. I was 21, and my mind was on other things.

Over the next 28 years, the tractor had four different owners. The last was a man named Burt McCollister, who'd given the WC the best cleaning it'd had in years. He'd even driven it in a couple of parades.

In September 1977, I called Burt to ask how much he'd take for the WC. He said there wasn't a person on earth he'd sell to, but when he learned my dad was the original owner, he agreed to trade if I could find him a similar tractor. After searching at auctions, I found two 1937 AC's that, put together, made one tractor that worked.

Burt liked the offer, and in December 1977, the WC finally returned to our farm. After 28 years, we were finally reunited. ᕦ

John Deere A Has Seen Embarrassing Moments

By Pauline Mercer, Middleburgh, New York

MY HUSBAND bought his first tractor in 1952, when he was 18—a new John Deere A that cost $2,500. It's proven to be a fine tractor…but it's also been involved in a few embarrassing moments.

We still have the A, and it's in good working condition. We use it daily on our 120-acre dairy farm, where our "Deere family" now includes a 2510, a 3020 and a 4020.

The baby of the family is a 1969 110 lawn and garden tractor.

The A has a hand clutch, and that led to one embarrassing moment. I had been driving the A in the hay field all day while my husband picked up bales. Although I grew up on a farm, I didn't have much tractor-driving experience.

When I took the A back to the barn at the end of the day, I forgot that the clutch was a lever and not a foot pedal. When I entered the barn and tried to stop, I couldn't find the clutch.

I applied the brake and the tractor turned sideways, damaging the barn slightly before it came to a stop. I wasn't hurt, at least not physically …and after that, I've been very careful around the A.

Another embarrassing moment occurred when I sent one of our sons out to the field on the A to tell my husband that supper was ready. My husband was mowing hay with the 2510 and a haybine. My son caught up to him and jumped off the A with his message.

While the two of them were talking, they suddenly saw the A coming toward them. Our farm is hilly, and although our son parked across the hill, he'd left the engine running and hadn't set the brake.

My husband jumped off his tractor and both of them chased after the A, which turned downhill. It finally bounced over a stone boundary fence, where it high-centered and came to rest, still "putt-putting".

Once again, there wasn't much damage done, and no one was hurt. But my son learned a valuable lesson about the need to use your head and do everything right around farm equipment!

For all it's been through—embarrassing incidents and lots of hard work—our old A still has lots of spunk. At our local fair, it recently did itself—and us—proud by taking second place in a pulling contest.

The A has indeed been quite a "first tractor"! ᕦ

Ford 8N Got a Workout Plowing Area Gardens

By Louise Price
Grand Rapids, Michigan

AFTER OUR two children were born, my husband was working as a mechanic for the county, and things were looking up for us. We talked it over and decided we could afford to buy a tractor—something he'd always wanted. He bought a 1949 Ford 8N.

Victory Gardens had been a huge success in World War II, and gardening was still all the rage. Soon Bernard began getting calls to plow and prepare gardens. He bought a truck for hauling the tractor and equipment.

The plowing really boosted our income. Bernard would go out to plow a garden in the suburbs, and before he could leave, everyone in the area wanted a garden plowed.

A few years back, he decided to overhaul the tractor. He completely dismantled and repainted it. Now it looks like new…and it still runs like a charm.

GARDEN TRACTOR. This 1949 Ford 8N plowed many gardens around Grand Rapids, Michigan in the 1950's. Bernard Price overhauled it a few years ago, and then restored an International 450 diesel.

'Little Red' Was the Best

By Louis Mullins
Waterford, Michigan

I WAS ALREADY a grandpa when I got my first tractor. And I'll admit it: I was also a city boy, a farmer "wanna be".

My first tractor was a Farmall Cub. I named it "Little Red" and used it to mow the lawn all summer. Then in the winter, I plowed snow all over the neighborhood with its push blade.

I would spend hours outdoors on Little Red. I worked the afternoon shift, so I had the whole morning to play on Little Red, just like a kid with a new toy.

I also adapted a 10-inch dirt plow to use with the tractor. I bolted it to the drawbar and took out a bolt on either side of the drawbar so it could move up and down. With a pulley and a cable hooked to one end of the drawbar and then to the hydraulic lift, this system worked like a charm!

Then the ultimate occurred. A friend gave me a reclining bucket seat from an old car. I removed Little Red's old steel seat and mounted this nice comfy bucket seat in its place. Now I was really traveling in style, and I was soon the talk of the neighborhood.

We used that tractor for everything. My son hauled his boat down to the lake with it. My favorite pastime was giving rides to my grandchildren in a special seat, complete with safety harness, that I built and bolted to one of the fenders.

Then one day, Little Red's magneto broke. I searched all over for a replacement but had no luck. Little Red was "down" for almost 3 years.

Finally, while on a visit to Tennessee, I found a dealer who had two magnetos. I bought both of them, and I soon had Little Red running again.

While Little Red was "ill", I had bought myself a nice big blue Ford 2000 and all of the toys to go with it. Now I was faced with a tough decision. I had to admit that two tractors were really too many for a wanna-be farmer.

Reluctantly, I decided to sell Little Red. When the tractor's new owner drove it out of the yard, I almost cried.

The big blue Ford was there to help ease the loss of Little Red, however. Yes, I'm still a wanna-be farmer, plowing gardens, pushing snow and, of course, giving rides to the grandkids.

Tractor Talk

ALLIS-CHALMERS INNOVATION

Allis-Chalmers was the first to offer rubber tires as standard equipment (on its 1934 WC), and the first to include power steering (on its 1956 diesel-powered WD-45).

Rugged Case VAC Still Chugging After 50 Years

By Tony Dias, Clovis, California

OUR CASE VAC was purchased new in 1944, the year I was born. It had taken my mother weeks to convince Dad to buy a tractor instead of using a team of horses.

Dad knew how to farm with horses. He'd done it all his life. A tractor was very scary to him. But Mom prevailed, convincing him a team would cost almost as much as a tractor, without being as efficient.

We had great times driving that little VAC. It didn't have some of the tool-control sophistication of a Ford 8N or 9N, but it was the most rugged tractor I ever saw. My father, brother and I always taxed it to the maximum. Whether we were disking, plowing or making a ditch, we always made it "grunt". With only 18 horsepower on the drawbar, it could pull a 2-by-14 plow.

I remember making irrigation ditches with the VAC and a heavy steel drag ditcher. On the first round, the tractor had little trouble keeping the wheels in line and pulling the ditcher. But on subsequent passes, the narrow front end would slip down to the bottom of the ditch, along with a rear tire. As a result, it would pull the ditcher almost sideways for a quarter mile. The stress on the rear differential, front end and drive train was tremendous.

Only once in 20 years did that VAC break down. I was pulling a drag float to pack the soil. Since I was in a hurry to finish and play baseball, I was going as fast as I could in third gear (the highest farm gear). At each turnaround, I'd slip it into fourth (road transport gear). It lugged down for a few seconds, then eventually gained some rpm's.

I did this repeatedly until I heard a big bang from the engine. I limped back to the garage with the VAC firing on only three cylinders. The next day, Dad called his mechanic. He put in a new wet sleeve and piston, and we were back on our way.

The tractor is still running today. My brother-in-law uses it occasionally when his Massey-Ferguson doesn't cooperate. I think it will run until someone melts it down!

Sibling Rivalry Cured Her Fear of Hart-Parr

By Marge Hering
Great Falls, Montana

DAD USED horses on our farm until 1928, when he bought a Hart-Parr tractor. I was 4 years old, and it scared me to death.

Dad built a "kid-proof" fence around the house, and when he came in from the field at noon, I'd be waiting for him in the yard. He'd drive the tractor right up to the fence, and I'd run into the house, screaming. Then Dad would come in, pick me up and cuddle with me. Maybe that's why I continued to meet that tractor every day.

After dinner, I'd help Dad grease up the tractor and refuel it. But he could never convince me to get on it!

Five years later, when my little brother was 4, he started taking rides on the tractor. I wasn't about to let him get anything over on me, so I held my breath and climbed aboard. Riding the Hart-Parr turned out to be one of my favorite pastimes.

WAKING UP 'CRANKY'

By Gordon Heggenes, Seattle, Washington

MY BROTHER had just been born in 1939 when Dad bought a used Farmall F-12 to farm our 90 acres on Whidbey Island in Puget Sound. The tractor was red with an extremely loud exhaust and steel wheels with lugs that punched big holes in the ground. Soon after buying the tractor, Dad sold our horses, all seven of them.

The F-12 was the kind that had two fuel tanks, one for gasoline and one for stove oil. You had to start it on gas, then when it was warmed up, you could switch it over to stove oil. During World War II, gas was rationed and even farmers had a hard time getting it, so we almost always used stove oil to operate the tractor.

If you shut down the engine, it was hard to restart on stove oil unless you did it while the engine was still hot. If you forgot to switch back to the gas tank or just let it cool off too much, you had a real job to get it restarted.

This involved shutting off the stove oil and cranking the engine by hand—there was no electric start on that beast!—until the stove oil was cleared out of the fuel system. Then you switched on the gas and cranked the engine until it started. If you set the magneto timing lever too far advanced, it would sometimes kick back and hurt you.

We didn't pin the crank on the shaft like some people did. We just slipped it on and cranked the engine over and hoped it caught. If it decided to be contrary, you cranked it over and over and over.

I recall one day when I was about 16, I was mowing hay and shut off the tractor to check the fuel. When I cranked it to restart the engine, the crank slipped off the shaft and caught me over the left ear, knocking me out cold.

I don't know how long I was passed out, but I came to looking up at the sky, with the engine roaring and a knot like a goose egg on the side of my head.

Despite this mishap, I have mighty fond recollections of that old tractor. In fact, some of my most treasured memories are of the times I rode with Dad on the Farmall, long before I was old enough to drive it.

Chapter Three

Wrecks and Mishaps

In the early days of tractors, there were many mishaps. Some were serious, others funny. All provided lessons.

Worst Bruises from Accident Were to Granddad's Ego

By Marcia Webb, Chetopa, Kansas

WHEN MY grandfather, Barnet Hale, retired, Uncle Jim and his boys took over the farming operation. Granddad would remain on hand to advise and help whenever he was needed—and in his mind and heart, that was every day.

Several years after he "retired", Granddad went out to drill a wheat field. The 1974 International 574 diesel waiting for him had a bad starter switch, but that wasn't a problem. He started it by jumping it across the solenoid with a screwdriver.

But the tractor had been left in gear, and when the engine started, it lunged forward. Granddad jumped back, and the large rear wheel knocked him to the ground—in the direct path of the drill. He lay in the dirt, breathless, as the drill wheel ran over his legs with a thud.

Granddad slowly surveyed his legs. There were no broken bones or cuts. He eased himself up onto his knees and saw that the old International was still purring along, its rows straight and true.

As the tractor neared the end of the field, Granddad didn't know what to expect. To his surprise, it turned at the edge of the terrace and headed back in his direction!

As the tractor approached, Granddad stood on his bruised legs. He carefully climbed aboard the drill from the rear, and then onto the tractor, to finish his day's work. He told no one what had happened. He was 75—what if everyone thought he was too old to continue farming?

But by the next morning, it was clear to Uncle Jim that something was wrong with Granddad. After much prodding, Granddad told him everything. Uncle Jim took one look at Granddad's legs and firmly announced that he was taking him to the doctor.

The doctor shook his head disapprovingly. "You know, Barnet," he said, "I wouldn't believe this story if I'd heard it from anyone but you!"

Granddad was grounded for a while, but his legs soon were as good as new. The most severe bruising wasn't to his legs, but his ego!

Though Granddad has since passed on, I well remember him telling me about the horse teams he owned in the early days. He often said they were so well trained they could practically work a field on their own. I thought about the International making that turn by itself and wondered if Granddad had trained his tractors, too. 🚜

Dad's Quick Thinking Averted Tragic Plunge

By Virginia Jensen
Millington, Michigan

OUR first tractor, a used International 10/20 with steel wheels, didn't have one-wheel brakes. We weren't too concerned about that because it moved slowly, and with steel wheel lugs, it didn't take much to stop it.

We had just finished building a new barn, and the upper level didn't have back doors yet—just a vast opening that looked out over the barnyard below. It was haying time, so Dad decided to use the 10/20 rather than the horses to pull the wagon up the steep bridge into the barn.

When the tractor reached the back of the barn, inches from that huge doorless hole in the wall, Dad pulled back on the brake pedal—and it broke off in his hand! With split-second timing, he pulled down the throttle lever and the spark lever beside it. The engine immediately stalled, and the tractor stopped.

We had some close calls on the farm, but this was the closest we ever came to real tragedy. I still get chills when I think about it. I'm sure God was looking after us that day. 🚜

TWO VIEWS of the new barn where tragedy almost occured on an IH 10/20.

Lugs Cause Near-Accident

By Art Hoven
Springfield, Illinois

MY WIFE and I once had a scary moment involving a tractor. It was harvesttime…she was driving the tractor and I was on the binder, controlling the bundle carrier.

The tractor, an IH Farmall F-30, was purchased by my grandpa around 1928.

With a tricycle gear, it was the first row crop in our area and was still on steel wheels.

When my wife turned a corner in the grain field a little too tight, the lugs on the inside wheel got caught on the binder's stub tongue. The outside wheel kept turning, causing the tractor to jump around and the wheel to dig a hole into the ground.

CLOSE CALL. "Grandpa's old tractor sits outside on the farmstead he and Grandma built," explains Art Hoven. The IH F-30 is the same one Art's wife was driving when one steel wheel got caught on the binder tongue.

Because the tractor was jumping so much, my wife couldn't get her foot on the clutch. I bailed off the binder and ran around and shut off the engine. For weeks after that, my wife wouldn't get back on a tractor.

We have an old photo (below left) showing the tractor sitting outside on the farm started by my great-grandparents. They built a house, then when they retired, my grandparents moved in and built a second house onto the first.

The second house is freestanding, with its own entrance, fireplaces and basement.

Brothers Learned Dangers of Cleaning With Gasoline

By Paul Bliss, Atlanta, Michigan

I WAS RAISED on a 1954 Ford tractor and remember very well the day it was delivered, new, by flatbed truck. My brother and I took great pride in driving and caring for it.

One day while Larry and I were washing the engine with gasoline and a paintbrush, the brush's metal band sparked on the starter bolt, igniting a fire. Larry calmly started the tractor and backed it out of the toolshed. The fire quickly died without leaving so much as a smudge mark.

Failure to Heed Instructions Was a Tough 'Brake' for Mom

By John Arnold, Leesburg, Florida

MY BROTHER was drafted when I was 14, leaving me alone to work an 80-acre farm for my mother. I had a patch of sugar beets next to the house and asked Mother to drive the tractor for me while I handled my uncle's one-row beet lifter.

We'd only bought the tractor—our first—the year before, so before we started out, I tried to explain to Mother how the independent brake pedals worked. As we neared the house, she would have to apply just one brake to make the tractor pivot. Otherwise, the tractor would run headlong into the house. Mother indignantly informed me that she'd been driving a car since before I was born.

Well! When Mother got close to the house, she pushed the wrong pedal. Instead of pivoting away from the house, the tractor smacked right into it, destroying the Ford Ferguson's radiator and fan. Mother was so rattled that she sat frozen in place, yelling for me to turn the tractor off!

Tractor Talk

PARR FOR THE COURSE

The Hart-Parr Tractor Co. was formed in 1901 by Charles Hart and Charles Parr in Charles City, Iowa (naturally!). Hart-Parr was the first company begun for the sole purpose of building tractors.

The company was also the first to begin using the term "tractor" instead of "gasoline traction engine", and is regarded as having given birth to the industry.

Jump from Runaway Tractor
May Have Saved Teen's Life

By David Poulos, Falls Church, Virginia

ALMOST 20 years ago, when I was 14, I went to visit my uncle in southern Ohio. The only access to his cabin was a half-mile gravel driveway that ran straight up the side of a hill. At the bottom of the hill was a small gravel parking area for customers of his rustic-furniture shop.

Being a practical man, my uncle saw me not only as a houseguest, but a source of free labor. He assigned me to drive his 1940's-era Case tricycle up the gravel driveway, turn around at the top, load a half ton of firewood in the trailer and drive back down the hill to empty it.

I didn't have much driving experience and had never driven a tractor. Nonetheless, I performed my task successfully about three times, going up and down the hill without incident.

On my next trip down the hill, I saw a strange car parked in the gravel lot at the bottom—probably a customer at my uncle's shop. There wasn't enough room to turn the tractor around, so I coasted to a stop on a plateau to wait for the customer to leave. The engine promptly died.

The Case had a starter button on the dashboard with a very strong spring. As I leaned forward to push it, I must have nudged the gearshift lever into neutral. The tractor started to roll down the hill.

The engine hadn't caught yet, so I tried the brakes—to no avail. The right rear tire held 300 gallons of salt water for extra traction when plowing, so even if the brakes had worked, the results would've been unpredictable at best.

The tractor was now rolling freely down the steep incline toward the highway. This was a coal-mining area, and overloaded coal trucks were known to travel down Route 93 at great speed. I figured I had two options—jump off, or ride it out and hope no trucks were coming.

I was a high jumper in school, so I took what I thought was the safest route. I jumped. But the rear wheels were a little higher than I thought. A cleat on the left tire caught my heel as I dove over the side, slamming me to the gravel driveway and running over the whole right side of my body.

Dazed, I looked up just in time to see the tractor cross the highway, plow through the drainage ditch and smash into the neighbor's post-and-board fence. A few boards were broken, but the tractor wasn't even scratched.

All I can figure is that the tractor must have hit a bump just before it rolled over me, reducing the weight and downward

ONLY SCRAPES. A rear tire of this Case tractor ran over David Poulos when he was 14, but he escaped with only scrapes and cuts. David jumped off the tractor after its brakes failed on a hill leading to a busy highway.

force enough so that it didn't crush me. I escaped with a few scrapes and some stitches in my chin.

If I'd chosen to ride it out, there's no telling what might have happened. And if I'd jumped off the other side, that wheel full of salt water might have crushed me. So I guess I made the right decision, although it sure didn't feel like it at the time.

The next day, I was up and driving the tractor again, doing the very same job. And the tractor is still in use today—although it still doesn't have any brakes!

Swinging Bucket Toppled
City Slicker's Tractor

By Jerry King, Washington, Iowa

I BUILT a home in the country in 1979, then decided to add a sandy beach to my 5-acre pond.

I bought an old Ford 9N with a bucket on the front, filled the bucket with sand and drove downhill toward the pond.

As a transplanted city slicker, I knew nothing about how to safely run a tractor. I couldn't see too well in front of me, so I raised the bucket as high as it would go. Of course, the bucket started to bounce—and the tractor rolled over.

I ended up underneath, with gas and oil pouring over me, and shut off the engine. The roll bars or bucket frame had protected me, and I crawled out with only a couple of scratches. But I was pretty shaken as I walked the quarter mile back to my truck!

'Never Let Go Till You Win or Crash'

By Harlan McCall, Savanna, Illinois

MANY YEARS AGO, my Minneapolis-Moline Z and I nearly had a fatal wreck. I was pulling a New Idea two-row corn picker down a hill when one of the wheels on the picker hit a small hole.

That made the picker swerve back and forth behind me, causing the Z to zigzag out of control. With each zig, the Z got closer to a big ditch beside the freshly graded gravel road.

I'd wanted a Z ever since 1937, when Minneapolis-Moline began producing that model in prairie gold with red wheels and grille. My first tractor had been a nice, used Allis-Chalmers WC, but in 1944, I got a chance to buy the Z that I was looking for.

A friend was selling his farm...he offered me his well-cared-for '41 Z for a very reasonable price, and I bought it.

One of the things I used the Z for was filling silo. Back in those days, we cut corn with a binder, hauled it into the silo on a flat rack, then fed it into a belt-driven ensilage cutter. The cutter chopped the stalks into pieces 1/2 inch or so long, blowing the ensilage up into the silo.

There were always two men on the cutter, and for fun, they often tried to kill the engine on the tractor running the belt by overloading the cutter. If they succeeded—which they frequently did—they would gloat over their accomplishment.

No one ever managed to stop my Z when it was on the belt. One time a man who owned a Farmall F-12 and his friend tried all day to get the Z to conk out. They would shift gears on the cutter to change the length of the stalks and force more corn into the cutter than it could handle.

They finally did manage to throw the drive belt off...but the Z never quit. The next day, the owner of the F-12 had his tractor on the belt, and two different men were working the cutter. When they got the F-12 to sputter and die, it really angered the Farmall's owner...he couldn't stand the idea that he and his friend hadn't been able to kill my Z.

Vision of Landing in Ditch

As you can see, I was mighty proud of my Z. When I was pulling the New Idea corn picker down the hill, I was pretty cocky and going too fast. Once the picker and tractor started swerving, it was all I could do to stay in the seat and hang onto the steering wheel.

I had a sudden vision of crashing into the ditch with that big corn picker right on top of me. My Z and the corn picker would have ended up in the junk pile...and I'd have gone to the Hereafter.

The only thing I could do was pray. The Lord must have had an angel nearby, because somehow my hand slipped and hit the throttle, closing it down completely. That's what it took to get the rig under control. When I came to a stop, one of the Z's rear wheels was teetering on the edge of the ditch. I got off the tractor and was shaking so hard I could hardly stand for at least 5 minutes.

From that experience, I learned to respect horsepower and speed, and to never let go till you either win or crash. If my faith was ever shaky before that day, it hasn't been since.

By the way, that Z and I are still together...I've owned it for 52 of its 55 years.

LONGTIME PALS. Harlan McCall and his Minneapolis-Moline Z have been through a lot together, including a near-accident that could have put both man and machine permanently out of commission.

Driving Tractors Uphill Tested Operators' Skills

By Frank Austin
Cedar Springs, Michigan

I DID odd jobs around the sawmill for my Uncle Joe in the late 1940's. One job was moving sawdust to the swamp out back with a Farmall F-12.

Before the job was done, Uncle Joe came home with a small Allis-Chalmers tractor with an electric starter for me to use. All went well until I decided to take a shortcut to the swamp, going straight up a big hill instead of around it.

When I got to the steepest part, the wheels started to spin and I made the mistake of touching the clutch. The next thing I knew, the load of sawdust was pulling the tractor down the hill—and it went down a lot faster than it went up.

Somehow everything stayed lined up until we reached flat ground, but I'd learned my lesson. Shortcuts weren't always best.

For a while, Uncle Joe used a steam tractor to run the mill. He later replaced it with a Rumely OilPull, which had plenty of power and ran very efficiently once you got it started—but that could take 2 or 3 hours.

The OilPull soon was replaced by a McCormick-Deering 15/30 tractor. It took a little more fuel, but at the end of the day, there was a lot more lumber cut, because it always started easily.

One day, Uncle Joe decided to move the old steam tractor out back. The mill yard was full of logs, and the only path to the back was between a pile of dirt and Uncle Joe's new house. He'd been working on the house for some time and hadn't gotten around to backfilling the basement.

Uncle Joe built just enough fire in the tractor to move it and started around the end of the house. It had just rained, and the dirt pile had turned to clay. As soon as the back wheels hit the slippery slope, they slid down toward the house, while the front wheels stayed high on the pile.

This tractor was designed to turn around where there was lots of room, and a slippery dirt pile wasn't such a place. So Uncle Joe ran the tractor up the pile as far as he dared, then cranked the steering wheel as the tractor rolled back down. It was a tricky maneuver—if he went back too far, the tractor would go right through the basement wall.

He went back and forth for what seemed like 10 minutes and finally worked the front wheels off the pile. I seem to recall the dirt pile was moved not long after that.

TEEN ESCAPED INJURY AFTER BEING THROWN TOWARD PLOW

By Ed Gompf, Marion, Ohio

I WAS IN my early teens when Dad bought a 1937 John Deere B on steel, plus a two-bottom plow with a rope trip and adjusting handles behind the seat. We later put the tractor on rubber, which gave it more ground speed.

One wet spring day, I was finishing a dead furrow and reached behind to adjust the plow while on the move. Just then, the tractor hit a hole and I was thrown off.

I still was holding the lever, so I pivoted off that with one hand and landed on my feet beside the plow. My guardian angel was with me that day.

Of course, the tractor kept on going, and I had to run over plowed ground to hop back on and stop it. Then I just sat there, out of breath and scared.

Soon afterward, we got a plow with handles that were much safer to operate.

Early Equipment Exposed Drivers to Many Dangers

By William McGaughey, Denver, Colorado

OUR FIRST TRACTOR, a Fordson bought in 1928, had a habit of rearing up in front whenever it was involved in a hard pull. Many times I had to push in the clutch to keep it from going over backward.

The Fordson had to be cranked to start, and it frequently refused to turn over. There were many times I spent 3 or 4 hours cranking before it would start. The tractor had the same vibration coil for ignition as the Model T, so we rigged up a switch and used a "hot shot" battery to start it. Then we'd switch back to the magneto.

In winter, we'd put a small amount of gasoline in a pan, place it under the engine and light it to heat the oil so the tractor would start easier. The Fordson had no flammable material, so this wasn't quite as dangerous as it sounds.

But there were other dangers to farming with tractors. The wheel lugs could catch a person walking alongside and knock him down. The open power shaft to mowers, corn pickers and other machinery also posed serious risks.

My worst scare was when I upset my Farmall F-20 as I crossed an empty irrigation ditch. The tractor went over sideways, and as I jumped off, one of the lugs hit me in the back. It could have been much more serious if I hadn't thought—and moved—quickly.

Farm equipment in those early days was a far cry from today's dual-wheel, front-and-back tractors that can easily pull a 10-bottom plow, or the equipment that can combine eight to 12 rows of corn or beans at once. But in those early days, tractors provided relief from the drudgery of farming.

Cutting Radiator's Water Supply Wasn't a Hot Idea

By Charles Mann, Laveen, Arizona

PAPA HAD a tractor in the early 1930's that was a real bear to handle—a McCormick-Deering 15/30 with iron wheels front and back and a cast-iron steering wheel. Our 119° Arizona summers didn't make things any easier, either. I called that tractor "the iron beast".

One day, Papa sent me with the beast to plow my uncle's 40 acres. "You may hit a couple of mesquite stumps," he warned me. In the early days, our whole valley was a forest of mesquite. Dad had removed all the stumps on our farm, but my uncle hadn't.

I hit not one stump, but three, and each time the impact pulled my three-bottom plow in half. I would look back, and there, a block or so behind, was the other half of the plow.

This meant getting three new bolts, backing up with the front half of the plow, lining it up with the back half and jacking it all into place so I could line up the bolts. Have you ever tried backing a tractor—without power steering—with half a plow behind you?

But that wasn't the worst of it.

One trip around the 40-acre field was about a mile, and each time I completed a loop, I'd stop to fill the beast's heavy cast-iron radiator. It was bolted to the engine at the top and bottom and had a cast-iron cap 6 inches in diameter, with a wing nut on top.

As I worked my way around the field inward, each circuit became a little shorter. On the fourth day, the loop was much smaller, so I decided to drive around the field twice before filling the radiator. It didn't work.

I made it around the field one time and got about halfway through the second loop when the radiator cap blew like Old Faithful. I jumped off and ran out into the field, waiting with folded arms while the tractor spewed steam. Then I had to catch it before it tore the fences down.

In the meantime, that heavy-duty radiator cap crashed down right on top of my head. If I hadn't had a heavy straw hat and a big mop of hair to cushion the blow, I wouldn't be here today.

Prospect of Skittish Mules Terrified Young Driver

By John Vitt, Bartlesville, Oklahoma

DAD and my uncles owned an Aultman & Taylor tractor they used in the 1930's to power a Superior grain separator that was fed from both sides. At 10, I was the "water boy", taking jugs on my pony to the bundle-pitchers in the field.

One day, Dad was one driver short and asked me to drive a team of mules pulling a bundle wagon. I agreed—as long as I didn't have to be on the belt side. I'd seen teams run away when the belt came off, and that possibility absolutely terrified me.

When it was my turn to unload, if the side being unloaded was on the same side as the belt, the men would lead my team past the belt. Luckily for me, the belt never came off.

As for the Aultman & Taylor tractor, it's now in a museum in Fort Scott, Kansas.

He Shut Off Fuel Line To Stop Runaway Deere

By Ward Derhammer
Kalamazoo, Michigan

ONE DAY IN the 1950's, I was using my old John Deere D to pull a three-bottom plow. When I got to the end of the field, the tractor wouldn't stop. A pin had fallen out of a clevis on the end of the clutch lever, so the clutch wouldn't work.

I drove the tractor over the fence-row—wire fence, stones and all—and into the next field, dragging two rods of fence behind the plow. I said, "You went over, you'll go back." I turned around in the hay field and headed back toward home.

As I approached the gate, the only way I could shut the tractor off was by climbing out on the fuel tank, reaching under and shutting off the fuel line.

Tractor Talk

AN 800-MILE WALK

In the "good old days", a farmer walked 8 miles per acre behind a walking plow at a speed of 2 mph (reduced to a 1-1/2-mph average when you consider turnarounds and rests, which the farmer needed as much as his horses).

An average farm worked with horses was 100 acres. So multiply 100 acres by 8 miles per acre, and you see that a farmer had to walk at least 800 miles a year behind a horse just to plow!

Small wonder that during those 800-mile walks, farmers thought of faster and better ways of getting the job done.

OilPull Was A Little 'Squirrelly' At First

By Robert Young, Bear Creek, Wisconsin

WE HAD quite a surprise when we tried to start the old Rumely OilPull 20/40 that Dad bought in the early 1960's…and then we had an accident that put the tractor out of commission again.

To get the 20/40 running, we belted it to a Farmall M. We could get the old tractor to fire a few times, but then it would quit.

For a while, Dad thought the crank shaft was broken, then he decided to pull a head off and take a look inside. That's when we got the surprise. It seems a squirrel that needed a place to store its hickory nuts had gone down through the carburetor and filled one of the cylinders.

When the engine turned over, nuts were forced into the valve, keeping it open and preventing the engine from ever running.

After taking all the nuts out of the engine and putting the head back on, the tractor started right up. In fact, it started so easily that from then on we just cranked it by turning the flywheel by hand.

We ran the Rumely a few times every year after that just for the pure fun of it. About 6 years ago, we had a little mishap. I was driving the 20/40 to a parade along with a Nichols & Shepard steam engine and an Aultman & Taylor 30/60 gas tractor.

Headed for Restoration

Just as we reached the top of a steep hill, the Aultman & Taylor's clutch began to slip. We shut it down and adjusted the clutch, but then had trouble getting the old tractor started again.

I hooked my 20/40 to the Aultman & Taylor and pulled it along the side of the road. That did the trick, but unfortunately I spun the wheels just as the 20/40 was coming back on the blacktop. Before I could pull the clutch lever back, the tow chain got a couple of good hard jerks.

As a result, the cooling pans in the radiator scraped against the angle-iron frame, splitting them open along the entire left side. Of course, we couldn't run it like that, so I had the 20/40 hauled home.

I fully intended to fix it up to drive in the same parade the following year. But you know what can happen with the best of intentions: For several years, the OilPull sat outside in the yard, then in the shed.

A BRIGHT PAINT JOB, a flag and some ribbon turned this Rumely OilPull 20/40 into the "best tractor around".

In 1995, my brother John and I decided it was time to pull that old beast out of the shed and fix the radiator. We also decided that we might as well do a little cleaning and painting, too.

We stripped down the 20/40 and took everything off the main frame except the engine and transmission. I sandblasted all the parts with a handgun, so the task took a long time. Then we filed, primed and painted each part.

I am not a body man, so some of these parts had to be sanded and painted a number of times before we figured out how to get it right, mostly through trial and error. I had no idea the amount of work and number of hours a project like that could take!

John didn't keep track of his hours, but I kept track of mine—around 850 by the time we were finished. I know John put in at least that much.

Maybe the restoration isn't the best job in the world, but John and I are proud of it. To us, our Rumely OilPull is the best old tractor around!

Scooping Dirt Leads to a Big Mess in The Kitchen

By Darlene Pair
Jacksonville, Florida

MY FAMILY bought a small farm in Indiana in 1947. After we got settled, Daddy purchased a used Farmall.

Because he didn't have a hired hand, I helped out whenever I could, even though I was only 11. When Daddy decided to finish digging out the partially built basement, he called on me to lend a hand.

He shoveled the dirt out one of the windows, and when he had a big pile beside the house, I got the Farmall. We had a slip-scoop on the Farmall, and as I drove, Daddy operated it.

Unfortunately, at one point, something caused the steering wheel to jerk out of my hand and the tractor caromed off the pile of dirt and into the side of the house. Of course, Daddy was upset. He wanted to make sure I was all right and that neither the house nor the tractor were damaged.

As it turned out, I was okay and so was the tractor...but the house had a hole in the siding. That wasn't the end of the trouble, however.

As Daddy was straightening things out, Mother came running out the back door. It seems that when the tractor hit the house, the bobber flew off the pressure cooker and plastered boiled potatoes all over the ceiling.

Well, eventually we got the kitchen cleaned up and the dirt hauled away from the side of the house. I didn't stop driving the tractor...but from then on, I only drove in the field far from any obstacles.

HUMILITY AND RESPECT. Old black-and-white photograph shows Lloyd Hamm's dad, Ed, driving the Minneapolis-Moline U on which Lloyd learned humility and also gained some new respect for his father.

Dad's Foresight, and a Bit Of Rope, Saved Boy's Life

By Lloyd Hamm, Upland, California

I HAVE many fond memories of growing up on our Illinois farm, but none more vivid than one bitterly cold Saturday morning in November 1954. After I ran my trap line and finished my chores, Dad loaded me into our old pickup to go to a farm sale. He wanted to look at a tractor to replace the Farmall F-20 we'd had for years.

It was exciting for a 12-year-old to go anywhere in those days, so you can imagine my excitement when I heard where we were going. When Dad suggested this new tractor would be mine to drive the following spring, I was beside myself with anticipation.

At the sale, we stood in the cold for what seemed an eternity until the tractor Dad wanted came on the auction block. The bidding went up and up. Finally, the auctioneer said, "Sold!" and pointed to Dad. Our prize was a used Minneapolis-Moline U.

Too Short to Drive

When I asked Dad how we were going to get it home, he looked at me and said, "Well, I guess you'll have to drive it." I was too short to see over the engine, so I had to stand on the platform behind the wheel, with the seat swung out of the way. I drove "my" new tractor the 17 miles home, with Dad following in the pickup.

When the fields dried out the following spring, I could hardly wait to start disking. I had never been turned loose in the fields alone to plow or disk. This would be my very first solo journey.

When we got to the field, Dad took a piece of rope from his pocket. He attached one end to the clutch handle, which was to the right of the steering wheel, and tied the other around my waist. He explained if I fell off the tractor, the clutch would disengage and I wouldn't be run over by the disk.

I was devastated. I couldn't believe Dad would even consider that I might fall off "my" tractor. After all, I was 12 years old and knew everything there was to know about driving it.

But I swallowed my pride and took off on my first trip alone. I can remember no other moment in my life when I was so excited.

You can probably guess what happened next. The minute Dad disappeared, I hit a large hole with one of the rear wheels. The lurch threw me backward off the platform, leaving me hanging precariously from the rope— right between the tractor and the disk, but the tractor had stopped.

I gathered myself up, crawled back on the platform, tightened the rope and proceeded on my way. Had it not been for Dad's humiliating rope, I would have died that day.

I had a lot more respect for Dad's wisdom after that, although he never knew why. I kept my experience a secret for 30 years and never shared it until after Dad had passed away.

After Flipping, Steam Engine Was Repaired Along Highway

By H.V. Longley Jr., Elkton, Virginia

IN THE EARLY 1930's, my grandfather owned two farms in Virginia's Shenandoah Valley. One, known as the "valley farm", had a rock quarry; the other, in Albemarle County, had a sawmill.

A steam traction engine was used to run the heavy equipment on both farms. The farms were about 65 miles apart, with the Blue Ridge Mountains in between, so moving the engine from one farm to the other took about a week.

On one occasion, the engine was needed at the valley farm to pull the rock crusher. My Uncle Sam drove while another man walked next to the left front wheel, carrying a lantern. They took Highway 29 out of Charlottesville, but the road was so new that the shoulders hadn't settled enough to support such heavy equipment.

The shoulder gave way under the right rear wheel, and the engine flipped over onto its back. Uncle Sam stepped off, unhurt. It was the first time anyone around these parts had heard of a steam traction engine being flipped upside down,

I went to the scene with Dad. He and Uncle Sam decided to right the heavy engine by leaving the large rear wheels on the ground and pulling the front end over backward with a "chain fall".

The cab was torn off, the flywheel was broken, and the smokestack and all the lines were torn up. With the engine still sitting alongside the road, Uncle Sam and some farm employees repaired the lines, installed another flywheel, fixed the smokestack and made other repairs. Then they fired it up and backed it out onto the road.

When they rounded the turn about a quarter mile from home, Uncle Sam pulled the steam whistle wide open and didn't let up until he turned into the lane. He was smiling from ear to ear and puffing so hard on his cigar that it was hard to tell what was throwing more smoke, his stogy or the smokestack.

Bucking 10/20 Cooled His Interest in Potato Farming

By Sam Brass
Star Lake, New York

I'D ALWAYS heard it was impossible to raise the front of a 10/20 off the ground. I didn't set out to refute this claim, but that's what happened.

I wasn't raised as a farmer, but when I got out of the Navy in the 1950's, I decided to try growing potatoes. With an acre of land and a 1921 McCormick-Deering borrowed from my brother-in-law, I set out to plant my crop.

At harvesttime, I found an old horse-drawn potato digger in the toolshed. My brother-in-law discovered the hitch would fit on the tractor if we used a hole in the platform under the seat, way above the proper drawbar.

The digging went well...until I hit a shale ledge underground. The old tractor gave a snort and raised a good 3 feet off the ground. I had to push the clutch pedal way down, beyond the end of the fender, so it would hook and I could yank it out of gear. (We later discovered that more than half of the disengaging pawls on the clutch were broken.)

The machine came down with a crash that shook my bones. It was getting dark, so I disconnected the digger and headed for the barn. My brother-in-law took one look at me and asked if I'd seen a ghost!

We looked the tractor over and found no damage—not even a blown tire, and those were the oldest tires I've ever seen that held air.

The next day, my brother-in-law returned to the field with me to rescue the digger and look at the tracks. "From what I see, you must have taken some ride," he said.

I finished harvesting the crop, but after that, I had no more interest in shale ledges, 10/20's or potatoes.

The old 10/20 ended up in a collector's barn and was lost in a fire before it could be restored.

Tractor Talk

HENRY FORD AND "HORSE CENTS"

The Ford Tractor Co., formed in 1915 in Minneapolis, Minnesota, had no relationship to Henry Ford's Ford Motor Co. in Dearborn, Michigan. The Minnesota company used the name to gain market share, and actually conducted a search for anyone named Ford just so it could use the name.

When Henry Ford started his own tractor company in 1917, he called it Henry Ford & Son and began producing the Fordson tractor. The first full year of production was 1918, and 34,000 Fordsons were sold, garnering 26 percent of the tractor market. Henry calculated that it was cheaper to plow with his tractor than to use horses.

When Things Go Wrong, They Sometimes Go Really Wrong

By Cecil Schneider, Bakersfield, California

WHEN I WAS in the eighth grade, in 1942, I attended a church school 8 miles from our farm. The school was on about 5 acres, and church members used the ground to plant "victory gardens".

Water from a nearby canal was used free for irrigation, and my father brought our Farmall tractor to help out. On a flatbed trailer behind the tractor, he hauled a plow, disk and furrow puller. All this equipment certainly made planting the garden much easier.

After the ground was prepared, my father asked me to drive the tractor and equipment home. A friend who lived on a farm about 2 miles away and always rode his bike to school asked me to give him a ride.

He put his bike on the trailer and off we went up Highway 99, the main north-south route in the state in those days. After we'd gone several miles, my friend wanted to drive. He climbed up on the tractor and I got on the trailer.

As we crossed the Kern River bridge, my friend hit the sidewalk with one rear tire. That pulled the front end around and for a second, it looked like we might be headed for the river 25 feet below.

Luckily the metal railing prevented that...but it also knocked the tractor over on its side. My friend was thrown off and injured his hand slightly. The trailer was fine...I jumped off and turned the magneto on the tractor off. Till the engine quit, the tractor crawled along the ground on its side like a snake, wiggling back and forth.

My friend was in good enough shape to ride his bike home. A car stopped and gave me a ride back to Bakersfield so I could call my house. No one was there—Mom was in town for my sister's piano lesson, and Dad was out in the field.

I stood beside the road with my thumb out and got a ride home. When Dad saw me coming, he rushed over to see what had happened. Together we got our truck and a big tow chain and headed back for the bridge.

We'd only been there a few minutes when there was another wreck. Two cars were approaching the bridge from the same direction—the one in front was a fancy new one, and the one behind was an old jalopy.

The guy in the jalopy was looking at our tractor instead of watching where he was going. At the last minute, he swerved to miss the newer car, glancing off it and into the front fender of our truck.

Two fenders from the newer car and two from the jalopy were knocked off onto the bridge. For a while there, traffic was blocked in both directions.

Somehow the two drivers got their differences worked out, picked up their fenders and drove off. Dad and I were able to straighten out the fender on the truck so that it wasn't a problem.

Just then, Mom and my sister came along. Dad asked them to pick up a block and tackle at a nearby dairy farm. By hooking the block and tackle to the bridge railing and using the tow chain and truck, we got the tractor upright.

The only damage on the tractor was the battery, which cracked. As we were hitching the tractor and trailer to the truck, the highway patrol finally arrived.

When asked what the problem was, Dad just said that we were taking the tractor home and had had a little problem. The patrolman looked around, then drove off.

I learned that day more than 50 years ago that when things go wrong, they can sometimes go really wrong! ☞

Cleats Scarred Shed Wall

By Mabel Stamler
Lincoln, Nebraska

WE HAD a tractor with cleats on the wheels when I was growing up in the 1930's. It was the first tractor we'd had on the farm, and one day, Dad asked me to pull a wagon in the field with it.

I was to go back and forth across the field while the men loaded sheaves onto the wagon. When the wagon was full, Dad told me to take the tractor to the shed.

I didn't realize that I had to leave plenty of extra room between the wheels and the wall for the cleats, which stuck out quite a way to the side. When I drove into the shed, the cleats hit the wall, pulling the front end around so that it hit the wall, too.

Before I could get the tractor stopped, it knocked over several large barrels of livestock feed...and the cleats badly clawed the side of the shed. Dad told me to back the tractor out, then drive it back in again the right way.

Recently I returned to the old farmstead in Ohio, where my niece now lives. There on the wall of the shed were the old cleat marks I'd made 56 years earlier!

They were a reminder of how easy it is to get into trouble on farm equipment if you aren't using your head. In a way, those cleats scarred me as well as the wall—it took a long time for me to feel confident driving either a tractor or a car. ☞

Boy Rode Out Twister By Clinging to Farmall

By Ramona Lehar
Granby, Missouri

ONE DAY when he was a boy, my dad was plowing a field in western Kansas and saw a tornado approaching. He was driving an older Farmall F-12 that didn't move very fast.

There was no way he could drive to a safe spot...so Dad got off, wrapped his legs around the back spoked wheels and then began to pray that he would stay put when the twister blew through. And he did!

Luckily, both he and the tractor were unscathed. ☞

Cockshutt Taught Him a Lesson He Was 'Lucky to Live Through'

By John Chisholm, Levant, Maine

WE CAME TO farming late, and the equipment we bought was used but affordable. Our first tractor was a Cockshutt 30, and buying it was one of the very few things I did correctly in learning how to farm.

Originally, the Cockshutt did everything I didn't do by hand myself. Now we both have an easier time of it, but my respect for older equipment, and the farmers who ran it, comes from hardwon knowledge. The Model 30 taught me one such lesson that I was fortunate to live through.

This tractor has a five-speed transmission, with four forward speeds and a reverse gear. But it also has a transfer case, and in the upper range of top gear, it's capable of speeds exceeding 12 mph. That may not sound like much, but for a tricycle tractor with 38-inch rear tires and no suspension, that's clipping right along.

The operator's manual includes a specific and clearly worded precaution for using the top range: "CAUTION— Always lock brake pedals together by means of the sliding pin when traveling on the road in fourth speed." It's very

POTENTIAL DANGERS. This Cockshutt 30, still in use on John Chisholm's farm in Maine, taught him a valuable lesson about the potential dangers of operating old tractors.

good advice, and I took it one very cold morning in January 1988.

We have a woodlot that's about a quarter mile from our house, down a dirt road, and I was heading there to haul home some heat. I locked the pedals together long before shifting into top gear, high range.

When I reached the woodlot and hit the brakes, the left brake drum sheared off, so only the right side of the tractor was slowed. The result was an immediate, violent and unforeseen hard right turn at top speed.

The right rear wheel came up well clear of the ground, and only the torque of the wood cart behind me prevented the tractor from rolling over. Instead, the tractor—now at a 90-degree angle to the road—shot out into the alders, pussy

willows and deep snow, where it became thoroughly mired. A very shaken operator climbed down to examine the brakes.

Now, I had completely rebuilt those brakes because I wanted to be safe. There were new linings and properly adjusted rods, too. But the temperatures were below zero, and the brake drums were then 40 years old.

As you can imagine, I had a devil of a time getting that tractor out. It gave me plenty of time to imagine what might have happened, and to figure out just what I would do to ensure that it didn't happen again, ever!

Well, I haven't used top gear, high range since. But what I—and everyone who loves old tractors—must remember is that they are old, and the most careful restoration doesn't make them any younger!

Missing Clutch Pedal Made Heavy Tractor Unstoppable

By Layman Morrison, Camp Verde, Arizona

BEFORE World War II, I was working for a cattleman near Griswold, Iowa and packing silage in an open pit with a heavy McCormick-Deering 15/30 on steel wheels. At noon, I drove a quarter mile down a lane to gas up and eat.

During one rough ride down the lane, the clutch pedal fell off—but I was not aware of that until I pulled in front of the gas shed and couldn't stop. I took off the corner of the shed and ran into an old hayrack before the McCormick stopped. If I'd ruptured a gas barrel in the shed, I wouldn't be here.

When the boss came home, he was rather put out—until his son admitted he'd had trouble getting the McCormick stopped once before. The culprit was a pin that had fallen out of the clutch pedal.

Tractor Talk

JOHNNY POPPER FADES INTO HISTORY

In 1960, John Deere stopped producing its two-cylinder "Johnny Popper" engines for its tractors. Other manufacturers had not used two-cylinder engines for decades. The race for more horsepower had already begun.

Remarkable Recovery Results in Restoration

By Ruby Reese, Watsontown, Pennsylvania

1946 JOHN DEERE B, shown below with Cleon and Helen Reese and their son Lawrence, nearly cost Lawrence his life when he was 13. In 1992, he became the tractor's owner and restored it to like-new condition (above).

MY HUSBAND'S PARENTS, Cleon and Helen Reese, bought a new John Deere B in October 1946. They farmed 57 acres in Northumberland County, Pennsylvania, land which had been in their family for more than 125 years, and they milked dairy cows and grew all of their own feed and produce.

It took Cleon quite some time to get used to farming with the tractor, and oldest son Duff never did get the hang of it. But another son, Lawrence (who eventually became my husband), and his brother Skip often fought over who got to drive the B. Because Lawrence was the youngest, he usually lost the fights.

He occasionally did get to drive the tractor, however, and one day when he was 13 and spreading manure on a hay field, the stop bolt pulled out of the tractor's steering. The B upset, pinning Lawrence underneath.

He struggled to free himself and was found by his grandmother about 150 yards from the scene of the accident. A neighbor rescued Lawrence from the field, and he was rushed by ambulance to the Geisinger Medical Center in Danville.

There the doctors discovered Lawrence had suffered a fractured skull, several crushed ribs and numerous dislocated bones. He was given a 50-50 chance of survival.

With lots of determination and many prayers, Lawrence did survive his ordeal. In 1992, nearly 45 years after the accident that almost killed him, Lawrence's parents gave him

the B, which was in need of restoring and repainting.

Lawrence did much of the restoration work himself, and he now proudly drives and displays the B for family and friends. Now 68, he occasionally remarks, "Once we ironed out our differences, that old tractor and I became pretty good buddies!"

Stranded Tractor Operator Longed for Open Flywheel

By David Berger, Vienna, West Virginia

ABOUT 20 years ago, I was working in a plant, running a high-pressure water cleaner in a basement area I called "the dungeon". It was a little dangerous, but it paid 13¢ more an hour. With a wife and child, I needed every penny.

One Thursday, another worker told me the company needed someone to mow the grounds with a tractor for the summer. The pay was the same as my "dungeon" job. Would I be interested?

"Do cows like grass?" I said. "Sure I'm interested. Can I start now?" The next morning, I was mowing on a later-model Farmall Cub. It was almost as if my prayers had been answered. I found myself singing "Back in the saddle again, out where a friend is a friend."

When Monday rolled around, I found myself wanting to go to work. No dungeon for me today—just sun, fresh air and the fumes from one of those machines that made American agriculture great.

I went over the tractor, greased everything and turned the key. The starter began to grind and smoke. This was not supposed to happen.

The engine maintenance man said the starter had died. When I told the foreman, he went into a rage. That tractor had already put him $800 over budget.

The foreman led me back to the tractor, told me to get on, and he and the

mechanic gave it a shove. I let out the clutch and the tractor started.

From then on, that's how I operated the tractor. When I came to the plant for breaks and lunch, I parked on a slope so it would start. Once in a while, someone would remark that we must still be about $800 over budget. I just nodded. I had no complaints.

Watched the World Go by

The best spot to mow was right along the Ohio River. Mowing that stretch took a glorious 4 minutes and 54 seconds from one end to the other. Occasionally a riverboat would go past, shoving barges. Other times pleasure boats went by, and they were interesting to look at, too. I could put up my feet and watch the world go by.

After 3 weeks, a woman was assigned the mowing job, but she refused to drive a tractor without a starter, saying it was a safety hazard. When the foreman asked me if I'd continue

Fall from Fender Nearly Canceled Their Wedding

By Marie Perrine, Jackson, Michigan

I WAS ABOUT to get married, and to be near my boyfriend, I sometimes rode on the fender of his family's new Ford tractor while he did fieldwork. Before buying the Ford, my future father-in-law had worked his farm with a "doodlebug"—a homemade tractor built out of an old Dodge car.

The new Ford was a big improvement, and my fiancee, Leonard, and I enjoyed both it and being together. One feature of the new Ford: It had a plow you could raise or lower attached right to the tractor.

One day as we were plowing, the tractor hit a stone…I fell off right in front of the rear wheel! Luckily, the stone was big enough to stall the tractor, or there might not have been a wedding.

That incident scared Leonard and me so much that I never rode on a fender again. But nothing could diminish our appreciation for that great little Ford tractor. In fact, on behalf of our Ford dealer, Leonard often went around to local farmers to demonstrate tractors.

He also entered many plowing contests like the one about to begin in the color photo (at right). I'm proud to report that Leonard won many of those contests!

NEVER AGAIN. The tractor Marie Perrine fell off is shown (with plow attached) at far left in the black-and-white photo. After her fall, Marie never rode on a tractor fender again. The color photo, also taken in the early '40's, shows a plowing contest about to begin. Marie's husband, Leonard—a frequent contestant—is on the second tractor from the left.

driving it, he was so angry I could feel the heat radiating from his face.

My position was precarious. I wanted to drive the tractor, but I didn't like going against a fellow worker. I rubbed my chin a minute, then said it wasn't really a safety hazard. "I guess I can keep on driving it," I said. And I did.

I enjoyed mowing that summer. The plant manager said the lawn looked really nice, and with the help of the engine mechanic, the tractor was running better all the time. After a while, I didn't even remember that it had no starter. That changed in mid-August.

I'd mowed all along the river and was finishing up around a couple of large propane storage tanks. I didn't need much power there, just enough to get through some loose gravel at the base of each tank. I cut the throttle way back, stopped and started to back up. The engine died.

I started to reach for the starter switch and realized I didn't have a starter. I'd really goofed.

I had to get that tractor started. Every day, the foreman asked me if I could keep that thing going. The thought of facing him—or the woman who'd refused to drive it—was enough to fire me up.

Nothing Seemed to Work

I shoved the tractor out of the gravel and pointed it toward the river, about 200 yards away. I tried shoving it in gear. No luck. I held down the clutch with a stick and shoved. That didn't work, either. If the tractor had only had a crank or an open flywheel, I could've started it.

I shoved real hard and pulled the gearshift into third while the tractor was still moving. It almost started. By then, I'd moved the throttle lever back to about three-quarters. I was covered with sweat and getting very tired, so I took a short break.

After my break, I tried again. This time it was do or die. I shoved with all the "umph" I had, then reached up and was just able to grab the gearshift and pull it into gear. The tractor almost stopped, but I managed to keep it moving. It popped a couple of times, then started.

The tractor took off, and I dropped to my hands and knees, exhausted. I'd done it! Then I realized the tractor was running toward the river on its own. The tractor had a big head start, but it still had 100 yards to go. I caught up with it, ran around to the side, jumped on the mower and grabbed the steering wheel.

When I finally got the tractor turned, I was about 15 feet from the riverbank. I shifted out of gear and leaned over the steering wheel. Now I could die, and I had that right. Had the tractor gone into the river, my fate would've been worse than death.

Chapter Four

Memorable Tractors

From youthful rites of passage
to a grandpa's sunset years,
family milestones frequently
involve tractors.

SO LONG. Sheila Bedi's grandfather takes his Case tractor for one last drive around his Vershire, Vermont farm.

Photo Preserves Grandpa's Last Ride on Case

By Sheila Bedi, West Hartford, Vermont

MY GRANDFATHER'S weathered face creased into a smile as I climbed out of my car.

"Hi, Grampa," I greeted him. "Gram told me you sold the tractor. I came up to take a few pictures."

His smile faded, and I sensed a little remorse in his voice as he said, "It's down in back."

He waited outside while I ran into the house. When I told Gram I was going to take some pictures of the Case, she asked if I could take a few for her, too. "I'd like to have a few of Grampy with it before it's gone," she said wistfully.

The Case was down the knoll, next to the garden. Grampa was making his way toward it with a gasoline can. I crouched and snapped a photo as he poured gas into the tank, freezing the moment on black-and-white film.

Grampa explained that, until recently, the Case hadn't been started in over 2 years. He'd dismantled and cleaned the carburetor and got it running long enough to move it out of a tangled nest of weeds. "I came this far with it and it quit," he said. "It might not be getting gas through the filter."

With a finger, I traced the brown hose of the gas line. That soft caress transformed me into a freckle-faced 7-year-old, standing on the lawn as Dad and Grampa backed a loud blue monster off a flatbed. The large tractor frightened me with its menacing sounds and foul-smelling black exhaust.

Dad and Grampa spent the next 6 months buying new parts, tinkering and painting the Case. The choppy sounds were tamed, and a new muffler of gleaming beige and orange made the Case seem friendlier, like a true member of the family.

Grampa finished pouring in gas, then settled into the metal seat and turned the key. The Case made tired, whining noises, fired twice and caught. I walked ahead. Grampa, trying to find first gear, let the Case roll backward a few feet. With a sudden jerk, the clutch engaged and the Case lurched forward, crawling up the knoll toward me. All four tires were cracked and low; one in back was nearly flat. Yet Grampa and the Case moved on with determination, past me and around the side of the house.

I remembered riding the Case with Grampa at haying time. I'd lean on a fender, grasp the back of the seat for dear life and plant my sneakered feet firmly on the orange steel beside Grampa's left foot. It was the best seat in the house, and I was proud to come along and give Grampa what little help I could.

Sometimes I would just sit on the Case, pretending to plow and cut hay, making tractor sounds as I turned the wheel. The memory brought a lump to my throat. I could never turn back time and be a child, and Grampa would never again be 20 years younger, except in my memory.

Grampa parked the Case across the road where it could be plainly seen from the living room. He switched the key off, and the tractor emitted one last, fiery grunt and fell silent. Grampa grabbed the steering wheel and swung down carefully. We stood there for a minute, watching the heat waves rise from the hood.

"The guy who bought it said he's going to restore it," Grampa said, rubbing his chin.

"I hope he gets it done," I said. "I'd like to see it in all its glory again."

Then Grampa and I crossed the dirt road together, stepping over the tire tracks the Case had left behind. As we walked toward the house, I realized that this had been Grampa's last ride. ✂

"OLD EBBAS". This scene was photographed in 1922, when Ansel Dean's father was separating oats with his International Harvester 30/60 12-ton Mogul. "I was born in 1931, and the tractor was 18 years old then," says Ansel, of Mauston, Wisconsin. "Dad called it 'Old Ebbas' and used it for plowing and belt work until 1948. By then, most of the roads were paved, and we couldn't take the tractor from farm to farm, so Old Ebb went to the scrap yard," Ansel recalls.

STARTING JOHN DEERE D WAS A RITE OF PASSAGE

By Philip Barenberg, Parker, Colorado

IN WINTER, our John Deeres stood in stark contrast to the snow, hibernating like huge green bears awaiting the first stirring of spring.

As a child trudging past these behemoths to do chores, I found both comfort and challenge in their presence. Even at a young age, I understood the important role they played in our life. These were the D's, Dad's pride and joy, the mechanized wonders we used to wrest a living from 600 acres of Kansas farmland.

The D's were simultaneously the most dependable and the most cantankerous of inventions. Our "Johnny Pops" were our workhorses, with a sound so unique I can still hear it in my mind almost 30 years later.

Every spring, I'd contemplate the D's, wondering if this would be my year. The rite of passage on our farm was simple. When you were big enough to start the D, you were old enough to drive it and responsible enough to work in the field.

The challenge of the 1938 D was formidable. Pistons the size of coffee cans, placed inside two gigantic cylinders, generated so much power that petcocks were installed to bleed off excess pressure and allow the engine to start. The distinctive hiss would blow up clouds of dust while you struggled to turn the massive flywheel.

The most important rule was: Be sure to let go. Otherwise, you would be tossed forward if the tractor started, and backward if it didn't. The numerous myths and horror stories of injuries to youths who were careless always weighed heavily

SEMI-RETIRED. Since he bought it new in 1948, Max Simpson hasn't let this John Deere M out of his possession. After deciding to "semi-retire" the tractor, Max had it cleaned and painted in 1995. "It looks just like the day I bought it," says Max, of Sharpsville, Indiana.

At Threshing Time, Dad Was on Top of the World

By Merton Wilch, Tecumseh, Kansas

WE HAD a John Deere D and a threshing machine in the 1930's. When I was just old enough to sit on the tractor and operate the clutch, I got to work with those big threshing crews.

Dad's pay was determined by the number of bushels threshed. Though times were hard, I believe that one of Dad's favorite moments was standing atop the thresher, arms folded, watching as wheat bundles were pitched into the machine. In those moments, he was on top of the world.

on my mind each time I challenged the legend of the D.

I'll never forget the day I finally passed that first test of manhood. The engine sputtered, snorted, kicked and finally rewarded me with the resonant sound that would ring in my ears until fall. The days passed rapidly that summer as I circled the fields, the captain of my D.

I know that time has tempered my memories, so the look back is golden and perhaps not very realistic. But I also know I learned lessons on the seat of that tractor that will serve me the rest of my life.

I learned the necessity of preparation, the anticipation of planting, the rewards of the harvest and the disappointment of crops destroyed. I grew to understand that there is a time, a season and a purpose to most things.

Like the D, the sum of my parts and the strength of my heart are what matter most. My family, my heritage, my home, are all a part of me, wrapped in the memories of a green and yellow tractor. Today, just as back then, I cannot think of any better custodian.

Huber Emerged From Shed Only at Grinding Time

By D.M. Stephenson, Hanna, Indiana

OUR OLD Huber tractor was used for only one thing—grinding feed for the livestock and chickens. Our plows, planter, cultivator, mower, rake and wagons were all powered by horses.

On feed-grinding days, the tractor was moved out of the equipment shed to within about 50 feet of the grinder. A wide belt was rolled out and attached with a twist at the center around the flywheels.

Dad would feed grain into the grinder, then scoop the powdery meal into the gunnysacks my sister and I held—our least favorite job. The sacks were just wide enough for the scoop shovel, so tiny fingers were easily pinched. We weren't fond of the dust, either.

When we were done grinding, the belt was rolled up for storage, and the tractor was backed into the shed until the next time.

Logger Accepted Tractor As Payment Of $100 Debt

By John Ryan
Whitewood, South Dakota

A 1925 McCormick-Deering 10/20 came into my life when I was about 5 years old...that's when I was finally big enough to crawl up on the old tractor that had been parked beside our chicken coop for a number of years. I played on that old tractor throughout the rest of my childhood.

Dad was a logger, and an acquaintance gave him the tractor to clear a $100 debt. We didn't have a farm, but Dad figured he could use the tractor to plow snow.

That didn't work too well. We had a very steep driveway, and the tractor could go down it but couldn't get back up. The spiked wheels would spin on the ice. Dad cut off the iron wheels and replaced them with truck tires and chains, but the tractor still couldn't make the hill. So finally he just parked it next to the chicken coop.

Once my brother and I asked Dad to start the tractor, so he told us to pump up the tires and oil the controls. We didn't know what the primer cups on top of the engine were, so we filled them with oil. After showing Dad our

GOOD AS NEW. A fresh coat of paint glistens on Wayne Ryan Sr.'s 1925 McCormick-Deering 10/20. Wayne, of Lead, South Dakota, restored the tractor in 1992. Son John says that as a child, he spent hours standing on the crank to turn it, hoping the engine would start. "Of course, it never did," he says.

work, he laughed and said there was no use trying to start it now!

By the time I was 30, Dad was retired and had already restored several old outfits. He decided to make the McCormick his next project. After cleaning the sludge out of the oil pan, replacing the cork float in the carburetor and doing some minor adjustments and brake work, he had a drivable tractor.

The body left much to be desired. The radiator and fuel tank were faded yellow, the beat-up hood was blue and the rest was red, accented by solid-rust fenders. Dad went to a small farming community, where he easily acquired a full set of good iron wheels and other parts. After many hours of work, he had an immaculate tractor.

Now I'm 33 years old, and on any given day, you can find my 5-year-old daughter beside my storage shed, sitting on my 1947 Case VAC. 🚜

Dad Talked to Deeres to Keep Them Running Well

By Leslie Hess, Millersville, Pennsylvania

IN THE MID-1950's, we lived on a dairy farm in central Pennsylvania. The farmer Dad worked for had nothing but two-cylinder John Deeres, and Dad was a natural at running them.

There's just something about the sound of a two-cylinder motor. When they started working really hard and the rpm's slowed, the sound was like a heartbeat. It still gives me a thrill to hear them run.

I often heard our neighbor Mabel talk about my dad and the Deeres. She said they worked so well for him because he talked to them. I can't say I ever saw him do that, but I know he loved them very much.

Today, my wife and I own a small farm of our own, and we have two Deeres, a 60 and a B. Dad's been gone for almost 20 years, but I think of him a lot, especially when I'm on my tractors. I inherited a lot of his skill in running them— and every once in a while, I even talk to them when they do a good job! 🚜

Sisters Picked up Slack When Dad's Hired Hands Went to War

By Gaynobelle Reed-Fischer
Palmdale, California

ONCE WORLD WAR II was in full swing, most of Daddy's hired hands had enlisted or been drafted. The farm was 10 miles from our home and a tenant lived there with his family, but he wasn't able to handle all the work alone.

I was home from college, and my sister Genny was waiting to begin college, so we decided to become "farmerettes". Daddy sold Ford Ferguson equipment, and we were delighted when he gave each of us a new tractor with plow, disk and harrow.

Our first season, we put in 160 acres of corn and soybeans. It was a wet spring, and we worked many nights to catch up on plowing and planting. Sometimes our farmer friends would come out on moonlit nights to ride with us or spell us.

Genny and I also grew 15 acres of hemp for the Navy to use in making parachutes and rope. When government officials told Daddy his hemp was the best in the region, he proudly told them his daughters raised it.

Part of the farm was right off Route 66, and Daddy would bring his tractor customers to watch us work. "See there," he'd say, "my daughters can skillfully run those tractors, and so can your women." People marveled at how straight our rows were, and we loved showing off.

We did have a few adventures and mishaps, though. Daddy equipped our tractors with umbrellas, but one day I decided I needed a deeper tan and removed mine. That night, I had such a bad sunburn that my arms were stuck in tractor-driving position! I was in bed for 2 weeks, and our doctor came by daily to re-dress and wrap the burns.

Wash, Set...Work

Another time, looking forward to a dance date, I washed and set my hair at the farm. That night, dressed in a pretty formal, I took out the curlers and found my hair was full of mud! Through my tears, I heard Mother telling Daddy, "Lloyd, I do not want those girls doing that farm work anymore. They'll ruin their complexions and their hair." But there was no stopping us.

It was a struggle, but Genny and I got up every day at 4:30, sometimes after only a few hours' sleep. I'd doze while Genny drove to the farm. The farmhouse had a screened porch with cots,

"FARMERETTES". Gaynobelle Reed-Fischer (above) and sister Genny helped work the family farm during World War II. Their father, a Ford Ferguson dealer, provided brand-new tractors and equipment.

and sometimes we took naps there.

One morning, Genny and I went right to work when we should have taken advantage of those cots. We were working a few rows apart when I looked up and saw Genny weaving all over, plowing up our 3-foot-tall corn. I screamed at her, but she couldn't hear me over the noise of the tractor.

The tractor plowed through a wire fence and started down a ravine before Genny woke up. By the time she got the tractor stopped, she was on Route 66. Thank goodness there was no traffic—and Daddy wasn't standing there with his customers!

We returned to the field and got on our hands and knees, trying to replant the corn, but it was useless. We should have prayed instead. The rows were never straight again.

After that, Daddy made us promise to stop and take naps whenever we got sleepy. You can imagine Mother's reaction! But Genny and I wouldn't quit. We farmed for 2 years.

When the news came that my pilot boyfriend had been killed in the war, I decided to enlist. Mother, Daddy and Genny came with me to Chicago for my 3 days of written and physical tests, and watched as I was sworn in. That was the first time I saw Daddy cry.

During my time in the service, I often reminisced about our good old "tractor days". And I still do. ✦

HAULING BEANS. Orville Howland photographed this tractor as it hauled lima beans to the Charles J. Haines Warehouse in Santa Monica, California in 1916. "The beans were grown in the northeast section of the city, before any houses were built there," says Orville's son, Donald. The make and model of the tractor are unknown.

MARTIN HAGEN HAD A 'B'...

By Harold Hagen, Joice, Iowa

IN 1938, my father, Martin Hagen, went to the John Deere dealership run by Lester "Cootie" Larson in Northwood, Iowa. There, he traded two horses and a corn binder for a new John Deere B tractor, a two-bottom 14-inch plow, a two-row cultivator and a 10-foot single disk.

The B's serial number was 52621. We used that tractor until 1950, when it was traded in for another B. My four older brothers—Eldon, Raymond, Irvin and Marlin—and I all spent many hours in the seat of that 1938 B, which we always referred to as "Dad's tractor".

In the mid-1970's, I began collecting vintage tractors. I wanted to add a John Deere G to my collection, and I finally located one near Northwood, along with an old model B. The owner didn't want to separate the pair, so I bought both.

I later sold the B to a good friend, Arden Midgaard of Fertile, Iowa. I'd occasionally see the B when I visited Arden, and I always felt there was something familiar about it.

One day while talking with Cootie Larson's son, Jack, I asked if there were any sale records that might show the serial number of the B my dad bought back in 1938. To my surprise, Jack was able to locate the paperwork and that's how I learned the tractor's serial number.

I ran an ad in the Northwood newspaper describing the tractor, explaining that it had been traded in that community and asking for information about its whereabouts. I got no response. Then I remembered the B I'd sold to Arden. I asked him to check the serial number, but he kept forgetting. This went on for over a year.

During that time, I also purchased an IH W-4, a real beauty, in North Dakota. Arden really liked the looks of the W-4, so I told him, "Check the serial number on that old John Deere B, and if it's Dad's tractor, I'll trade you even up." Arden told

EXCEPTION TO THE RULE. "My dad, Billie Tuder, has always had orange tractors on his farm," reports Pamela Key Tuder, Whitestown, Indiana. "The fifth generation of our family is now living on this farm, and all but the first have been lovers of Allis-Chalmers tractors. Now Dad has the restoration bug, and the farm has even more orange tractors! There is one exception—a 1948 Ford 8N that belongs to my mother, Phyllis. In the late '40's, Mom's dad used to borrow this same 8N from a friend to plant corn, and it's the tractor Mom learned to drive on. She got married in 1949 and didn't drive the 8N again...till we managed to buy it in April 1992 and restore it. Now we have 15 orange Allis-Chalmers and one gray Ford. Three generations are involved in restoring these tractors, and at a recent parade, Mom and Dad and each of their kids drove one. We took grandkids along for the ride in wagons. Restoring and showing old tractors is a family affair! The photos (above) show the 8N and Mom and Dad next to our 1937 WC."

me to come on over and check the serial number myself. Sure enough, it was Dad's tractor! Turned out Arden had known all along and was just having some fun with me.

Dad's original John Deere B is now back home where it belongs, fully restored, and all five of us brothers recently had our picture taken with it.

One last point: Dad never did come to believe that tractors would completely replace horses for farm work. In all the years we had "Dad's tractor", he never drove it! ☠

HAGEN BROTHERS Eldon, Raymond, Irvin, Marlin and Harold recently posed with the John Deere B their father, Martin, acquired in 1938. The tractor was later owned by a friend and relocated by Harold, who traded an IH W-4 for the B to bring it back into the family.

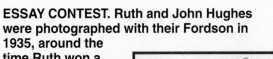

ESSAY CONTEST. Ruth and John Hughes were photographed with their Fordson in 1935, around the time Ruth won a *Capper's Farmer* essay contest on how tractors eased the farmer's work. "She won a Briggs & Stratton washing machine with a gas engine," writes her daughter-in-law, Mrs. Charles

Hughes of Amery, Wisconsin. "After rural electrification, the engine was replaced by an electric motor. She used that washer for many years for her family of 10. She drove the tractor, too!"

Teen and 'Little Allis' Handled Fieldwork Together

By Sally Kurtis, Niles, Michigan

EVEN THOUGH Granddad preferred farming with horses, in the spring of 1951, when I was a teenager, he bought a used Allis-Chalmers C that we called "Little Allis". Granddad was happy to leave the tractor-driving to Dad and me…I was happy, too, because I loved the little tractor and all the work I did with it.

Daddy worked off the farm on weekdays, so I did a lot of manure spreading, plowing, disking, dragging, cultivating, mowing, raking and hay-hauling. Daddy and I planted corn together, often into the wee hours. He drove the tractor while I operated the planter behind him.

My fieldwork usually wasn't too exciting, but there were a couple of exceptions—like the times I nearly tipped Little Allis over backward.

The first time, I was plowing and hooked a big rock. The plow didn't come unhitched, and the front of the tractor tipped upward. Dad started yelling, "Clutch! Clutch!" I shoved in the clutch, and the front end slammed down with a bounce, knocking my foot off the pedal. Up went the front again, but this time the plow unhitched.

The second time, I was plowing up a slope and the front end just kept rising. I remembered the clutch that time.

One of my favorite memories is of driving Little Allis to school in Edwardsburg, Michigan on brisk fall mornings, pulling a wagonload of corn. My younger brother, Warren, would ride on top of the corn, and we'd leave the tractor and wagon on a side street near school during the day.

After school, we'd go to the lumber company to have the load weighed, then head for home. It was often quite dark by then, and while the tractor had lights, the wagon didn't. Warren would sit in the rear of the wagon, holding a flashlight to warn motorists on Highway 12 of our presence. We made that trip many times, chilled to the bone, but proud we were helping to sell the corn.

Warren says those were "the good old days", and I heartily agree. I'd willingly do it again.

Little Allis finally had to be retired and used for parts to restore another C, which my brother owns. So part of her still lives on.

Widow Bought Tractor For Transportation

By Doris Schmidt, Elgin, Nebraska

WHEN MY father passed away in March 1950, Mother wanted to stay on their farm, but she couldn't drive the car. So she bought a new Ford 8N for her transportation. With the tractor, and the help of a hired man, she was able to remain on the farm for another 19 years.

Our son—Mother's only grandchild—was born in 1953. Mother would drive the tractor the 12 miles to our house at least three times a week to spend time with him. She didn't have a phone, so she drove here when she needed to call a veterinarian.

The route she followed to our house wasn't a road, just a seldom-traveled trail. If she'd ever had trouble with the tractor, she would've been a long walk from the nearest farm.

Mother was a rugged individual, a hard worker with strong values. She respected the land and all that walked upon it. A former schoolteacher, she taught her grandson much about life.

Mother departed this life in February 1974. We later restored her tractor and still have it in our garage. Needless to say, that 8N is very important to our family.

WHEELS FOR WIDOW. Roy and Doris Schmidt restored this 1950 Ford 8N after the death of Doris' mother, Dora Bergman. The tractor was Dora's sole mode of transportation after she was widowed.

COMPACT FORD WAS THE 'BEST TRACTOR I EVER HAD'

By Maurice Fellers Genoa, Nebraska

I LOVED my little Ford 8N. I could do everything with that tractor except milk!

I bought it in 1944, when I purchased a farm near Columbus, Nebraska and had too many acres to farm with horses. Tractors were rationed then because of the war, and you needed a permit to get one. They put everyone's name in a hat, and if yours got pulled out, you got the permit!

The day I drove the tractor home from the Ford garage, I was one proud farmer. Unfortunately, I didn't have any machinery to use with it, and equipment was hard to get.

I took a dozen hacksaw blades and shortened my horse-drawn gang plow. When I finished, I had a plow that worked like new. I had a blacksmith make a cultivator out of a two-row horse-drawn cultivator. At haying time, I turned a horse sweep into a hay sweep, and it worked to beat the band. By golly, I was farming 240 acres with that little Ford tractor!

Once the wind hardly blew for 2 weeks, and the stock tank went dry. I jacked up the little Ford next to the windmill, rigged a connection between the axle and windmill pump, and we had water again. That little Ford was the best tractor I ever had.

Warming Closet Kept Fordson's Coils Dry

By Lloyd Everett, Broken Arrow, Oklahoma

THE 1928 Fordson Dad bought in 1941 had a four-cylinder engine, no distributor and four wooden coils. The engine started quicker if the coils were warm and dry, so we kept them in a warming closet above the cookstove.

The Fordson had a 1-gallon gas tank and an 18-gallon kerosene tank. You crank-started it with gas, then switched to kerosene when the engine got warm. The brake and clutch were on the same pedal, so you had to come to a complete stop to shift gears.

In 1942, I took a job with a farmer who had a 1940 Ford 9N. It sure was a treat to use a tractor that had rubber tires, lights and, most of all, a starter.

At harvesttime, we used the Ford to pull an Allis-Chalmers combine. My job was riding the combine and sacking the grain, tying a miller's knot in each sack. The first six sacks I pushed off the platform came untied. I had to clean up all the wheat and got docked a half day's pay—25¢.

BIG IMPROVEMENT. Lloyd Everett, at age 15 in 1942, was happy to drive this "modern" Ford when working for a farmer near Dundee, Ohio. He viewed the Ford as a big improvement over the 1928 Fordson he was used to driving at home.

AC's Toolbox Provided Ideal Perch for Farm Girl

By Jeannine Homburg, Warsaw, Indiana

AS A young farmer's daughter, I spent many hours riding on Dad's bright orange Allis-Chalmers. That toolbox on the side fender was just the right size for a seat.

Finally Dad decided I was big enough to take the Allis C and one-row cultivator to the cornfield and dispose of the weeds. My excitement waned as the day progressed, but I stuck to it and finally finished that 7 acres.

The next year, Dad sent me to the field with a two-row cultivator. Things went just fine until I looked back and discovered I'd plowed out a row. But when I showed Dad, we discovered he had gotten off course when he'd replanted that row by hand. I was redeemed!

I also drove the Allis WD at hay-baling time. Those were enjoyable days, because we always knew the neighbors would be there in the evening to load and mow hay, and we kids would have lots of time to play hide-and-seek.

After Lots of Haggling and a Bad Fire, 8N Is Still in Use

By Lewis Schleter, Princeton, Indiana

I WAS 16 when my father, Wilfred Schleter, bought a 1951 Ford 8N. It took a week for Dad and the dealer in Vincennes, Indiana to agree on a price.

Whenever they'd get together to haggle, I'd sit on the tractor in the showroom and wonder what it would be like to drive such a machine. When we finally got the tractor, my brothers and I were thrilled.

Dad ended up paying $2,175 for the tractor, a plow, an 8-foot disk, a harrow, a grader blade, a cultivator and several other implements. At the time, we were farming 80 acres with horses, and all that equipment made life a whole lot easier!

Two years later, Dad also purchased a one-row Case corn picker to pull with the 8N.

Then one day, my older brother, Gerald, borrowed the 8N to plant his garden. When he was finished, he put the tractor in his garage to keep it out of the weather.

Unfortunately, trash was being burned nearby and sparks set the garage on fire. Despite quick action, the tires, steering wheel, electrical wiring, headlights and gauges on the tractor were destroyed. The paint was scorched, and heat from the fire expanded the gas tank without causing an explosion.

The insurance company said that the 8N was a total loss. That upset us—not only had it been a great tractor, it had taken on sentimental value.

After lots of discussion, we got the insurance company to change its mind and pay to have the tractor repaired. However, the 8N never quite looked or ran the same. In a few places, fresh paint had been applied over rust that eventually showed through.

When Dad passed away in 1972, Mom gave me the tractor. One of my favorite hobbies is restoring old John Deeres and entering them in shows. The 8N became a high-priority project for my son, Steve, and me, and we finished restoring it in 1990.

This time around, we did the old tractor justice. We take it to antique tractor shows and still use it on our 200-acre farm for light work…and now Steve looks forward to the day when the 8N Dad bought after a week of hard bargaining will be his.

JUST LIKE NEW. Restored 1951 Ford 8N is now doing light work on Lewis Schleter's farm, and also is showing its stuff at numerous Old Iron shows.

Driving Restored Farmall Is 'Something Like A Miracle'

By Virginia Lough
Bryant, Indiana

MY HUSBAND worked for the local Allis-Chalmers dealer during the early 1960's, leaving me to run our 160-acre Ohio farm, milk 20 cows, and tend to the hogs, calves and our six children.

I did all the farming with a Farmall MD and a Farmall C—and I did a good job. It was fun. I especially loved my MD because we worked so well together.

One night I took the MD and two wagonloads of beans to the mill, with the kids loaded on top. My husband met us there on his way home from work, and he stayed with the beans while the kids and I went home to milk.

By the time he started home with the tractor, it was dark and he hit a parked car. My tractor—my friend—was literally broken in two. When I got there and saw it lying in the road, my heart lay there with it. My father-in-law managed to fix it, but we quit farming soon after that. Still, I never forgot "my" tractor.

I later saw another MD at a farm auction near here. It had been in a barn for years and was covered with dust and hay chaff. It looked so pitiful that my heart just melted. I bought her and took her home.

Some 33 years later, my son Chris completely restored her. When he finished and I drove her around, something happened that was kind of like a miracle. I felt so at ease with her, just the way I remembered feeling with my old MD all those years ago.

I am very, very proud of the gift that my son gave me when he fixed up this old tractor. ◆

JUST LIKE THIS ONE. Virginia Lough's Farmall MD waits on a trailer for the trip to an equipment show in Portland, Indiana. Virginia used a tractor just like it as a young farm wife and bought this one at an auction after she'd stopped farming. Her son restored the MD 33 years later.

Dad Traded Mule Team For New John Deere B

By Larry Engle, Urbandale, Iowa

ON A WARM sunny day in the spring of 1940, a new John Deere B was delivered to the farm my parents rented near Cumberland, Iowa. I was only 5, but I'll never forget that grand event. The arrival of the bright green tractor with yellow steel wheels was a highlight of my young life.

Dad also had another tractor, but I was so impressed with the Deere that to this day, I don't remember what it was. He also had a team of horses and a team of mules. In those days, farmers could trade in a team as partial payment on a tractor, and Dad traded his mules. I remember him leading them from the barn to be loaded onto the dealer's truck.

When Dad started the new Deere, it was music to my ears. I bounded into the house as fast as my legs would carry me, eager to tell Mom how wonderful it was to have that new tractor.

I found her at the stove, preparing dinner and looking out the window. To my surprise, tears were trickling down her face. I couldn't imagine why she'd be sad. This was one of the greatest days of my life. What could be more thrilling than having a new green and yellow tractor delivered?

When I asked Mom the reason for her tears, she said quietly, "I sure hate to see those old mules go."

As I grew older, I began to realize how easy it was to become attached to special farm animals.

I became attached to the John Deere, too. It was the first tractor I drove. When it was traded for a bigger tractor 4 years later, I was sad to see it leave the farm.

It's been over 5 decades since the day that beauty was delivered, but it remains as vivid in my memory as if it were yesterday. Most of the time I smile when I recall that day. Occasionally I shed a tear. ◆

A HIGHLIGHT. Larry Engle (above left) and his twin sister help their father fill the gas tank on their John Deere B in 1943. Larry recalls the tractor's arrival as one of the highlights of his childhood.

Poem Honors Grandpa And His Tractor

By Yavonne Bagwell, Jacksonville, Arkansas

MY GRANDFATHER, Clark Lewis Field, was born in 1924 and farmed in Illinois all of his life. I remember visiting him and Grandma when I was a little girl, playing with my cousins on a huge uprooted tree in one of the pastures.

Later, my grandparents moved to another farm with a 10-acre peach orchard. To this day, the scent of peaches brings a smile to my face as I recall the many good times there.

I have many vivid memories of Grandpa, like seeing him walking with a bale of hay on his shoulder, and, of course, driving his beloved old Farmall tractor.

Grandpa passed away rather suddenly in 1994. To honor his memory, I wrote this poem (right), told from the point of view of my twin sons, Quinton and Zachary. I framed the poem and gave it to Grandma for Christmas, along with these two pictures. 🚜

Great-Grandpa's Tractor

We were only 3 years old
When Great-Grandpa passed away.
Much too young to remember him,
Or the sadness of the day.

But Mommy says we'll know him still,
Through her we'll know his style.
And through her films and photographs
We'll come to know his smile.

Great-Grandpa had some favorite things,
Chocolate cherries and mincemeat pie.
He played croquet and Ping-Pong
And liked to yodel...what a guy!

But Great-Grandpa had one special thing,
He liked more than all the rest.
He was a farmer and so, you see,
He liked his tractor best.

The classic big red tractor,
On it he sat with pride.
Day in, day out, so happily,
He'd sit each day and ride.

So here we sit upon his tractor
As Mommy smiles through her tears.
She hopes this picture that she's taking
Will keep him close to us through the years.

And as we sit in his favorite spot,
In his seat...so big and tall,
We feel his love flow through us
Atop his old red Farmall.

TO HONOR the memory of her grandfather and his cherished Farmall, Yavonne Bagwell wrote a poem and photographed twin sons Quinton and Zachary in their great-grandpa's favorite seat.

She Fell for Tractors While Still a Toddler

By Ruth McCauley
Brookville, Pennsylvania

I RODE OFTEN with Dad on our tractors, starting when I was just 1-1/2 years old. I was always excited when he started the Eagle tractor by turning a big wheel on the side.

When I was about 10, Dad got a more modern tractor with a crank on the front. He would start it, then I'd get on by myself and drive it to harrow and roll the level fields. That was a real thrill for me.

We got our first Fordson several years later. It was smaller, and I could

LOVED RIDES. Even as a toddler, Ruth Mc-Cauley loved going on tractor rides with her father, R. Wilson Hamilton. They were photographed on this Waterloo Boy tractor in 1917 at their Home, Pennsylvania farm.

drive it anyplace on the farm that the men could. I also drove our neighbor's Farmall to haul hay.

Later, we owned a John Deere. I was always scared driving it down the hill with a big wagonload of loose hay or grain sheaves. The Deere had a brake pedal on each side, and I had to stand up on them as I descended the hill to keep the speed down.

In 1935, I started teaching at a one-room school and drove the tractor only on evenings and Saturdays. I married in 1942 and continued driving tractors until we sold the farm in 1970. I'm now 80 years old and still think back on those farm years with fond memories.

Steel Wheel Lugs Turned Fence Posts into Kindling

By Donavon Pfenning, Scottsbluff, Nebraska

WE WEREN'T allowed to drive our John Deere B on the public roads when we first bought it in 1941—it had steel wheels front and back and the lugs would tear up the roadbed. We traveled from field to field along the ditch banks.

One day, we got the tractor stuck in a gopher hole in an alfalfa field, and Dad sent me to get fence posts to throw under the wheels. To our amazement, those steel wheels worked just like a saw, chewing the posts into little pieces!

It was hard to get rims and rubber tires during World War II, so we had a blacksmith cut off the lugs and weld on new rims. Then we could drive on the roads. But the new rims didn't work out very well in the field—during plowing or disking, the welds would break loose.

After about 2 years, we were lucky enough to get rims and rubber tires. In 1944, we finally got brand-new wheels without spokes.

DRIVING THE 'A' WITH DAD WAS A THRILL

By Les Parker
Arvada, Colorado

MY DAD often gave me rides on his 1935 John Deere A, but one of my happiest memories occurred when I was 6 years old and he let me drive the tractor myself.

Back on our farm in eastern Kansas, the barn was across the creek and we had to go down a gravel road to get to it. I would stand on the platform behind the steering wheel, and Dad would sit on the seat with his arms on both sides of me so I wouldn't fall off.

One day, we had gone over to the barn in this manner to work in the adjacent field. Dad climbed down to open the field's barbed wire gate, leaving me standing on the platform with the tractor idling.

When he'd pulled open the gate, he hollered to me, "Drive 'er on through!" He had left the tractor in gear with the clutch lever pulled back, and from watching him many times, I knew just what to do.

I gently pushed the tall clutch lever and then carefully eased the tractor through the gate in low gear. I immediately got that warm fuzzy feeling from knowing that Dad now trusted me to drive the tractor by myself. How proud that made me!

Dad passed away the following spring, and a few years after that, Mother was unfortunately forced to hold an auction and then move the family into town. Several years ago, I went back to ask some of the old neighbors whether they could recall who had bought the old A, but no one could help me.

Even though I was unable to locate the A's final home, I still cherish the memory of the first time I got to drive a tractor.

Farmall Mishap Led Couple to Foster Son

By Henry Roper, Clanton, Alabama

MY WIFE and I moved to my hometown in central Alabama in 1954. We planned to "get rich" on our 140-acre farm, even though we knew very little about farming. One of my first purchases was an International Farmall tractor, which my neighbors helped me learn to operate.

Three years later, I bought a rotary cutter. It took much longer to stop the Farmall with the cutter attached, but I didn't know that—until I ran into a big pine tree.

The steering rods were bent, so I took them to a repair shop in town. While I was waiting, a 17-year-old named Perry Dalton came in with a letter from the man he'd been staying with. The letter said this fine young man needed a home and the opportunity to finish high school.

The shop owner knew that my wife and I had hoped to adopt a child, so he introduced me to Perry. We'd been thinking of adopting a small child, but this one was 6 feet tall! Perry and I talked for a few minutes, and I invited him to come work with me on the farm that afternoon.

After getting to know Perry and talking with his mother, we asked him to live with us as our foster son. He enjoyed farm life, and he operated the tractor and other machinery as if he'd been doing it all his life. We also found that he could repair anything that needed fixing.

Later, Perry's mother, three brothers and sister joined our family, too. They moved to a little house on our farm, and we all worked together. Perry's mother is deceased, but she seemed to like our relationship with her children.

Perry is now a minister in Pensacola, Florida, with a family of his own. In addition to raising two daughters of their own, he and his wife have served as foster parents to at least 35 children and young adults.

I still use the Farmall that brought us all together, and Perry recently restored it. We all feel sentimental about that tractor. We feel God used it as a connecting rod, answering our prayer for a child with a very special son and his family.

SPECIAL OLD FRIEND. Henry Roper's Farmall A still ran well enough but needed a face-lift, so foster son Perry Dalton provided one. The tractor brought the two together nearly 40 years ago. That's Henry on the seat in both photos …and Perry standing next to the spruced-up tractor.

Old Photo Helps Remind Him of Chores Done by Case 'RC'

By Bob Coleman
Easton, Maryland

ONE DAY several years ago, I opened up our local newspaper and got a big surprise. There on the front page was a black-and-white photo of a tractor that looked very familiar indeed.

The tractor was a 1938 Case RC, and the reason I recognized it immediately was that it had a wooden skid rigged up under the front wheels. My dad and I had owned just such a tractor, and one winter, I'd made a skid to help it get through deep snow.

As I looked more closely at the photo, I suddenly realized that it was not only our tractor, but me driving it! Turns out the photo was taken for the newspaper after a big blizzard during the winter of 1939-40 ...and I didn't even know it.

I was 19 at the time and pulling a sled filled with cans of milk being delivered to folks in town. The man on the sled is Clarence Chance, a neighboring farmer. Clarence's son now lives on the same farm and is a neighbor of mine.

Dad and I bought the RC in March of 1938. We paid $900 for it, a set of rubber tires and a two-row cultivator.

I still have the RC. It's in good condition...I take it to tractor shows and parades. Even after all these years, it has most of its original parts—only the radiator core, air-cleaning stack and tires have been replaced.

I don't have any trouble remembering my RC...seeing that black-and-white photo helped remind me of the many chores the old tractor did for us over the decades. 🚜

THEN AND NOW. Two snapshots of the same tractor—a 1938 Case RC—show it ready for a recent show and delivering milk back in the winter of 1939. The black-and-white photo was taken for the newspaper by professional photographer Robbins Hollyday.

Dad Willed MM to Daughter Who'd Worked Alongside Him

By Barbara O'Neal, Okarche, Oklahoma

DAD DID ALL of the work on our farm near El Reno, Oklahoma with a 1949 Minneapolis-Moline tractor. We had lots of fun working together to bale hay, plow and drill wheat.

One day, we had to move two tractors from El Reno to Mustang to bale hay. Dad drove the big John Deere, and I followed on the MM. We caused quite a few stares because I was only 8 years old—and so small that no one could see me driving the tractor!

One summer, Dad paid me $65 to plow 65 acres. I was able to buy school clothes for my sister and me, a watch and a pair of shoes—and I still had money left over. Wow! Those were the days.

When Dad passed away in 1977, he willed the tractor to me. We used it until we moved to Oregon, and then my brother-in-law took it over. He used it for a couple of years, but then the MM was left sitting in a field.

The tires went flat, the smokestack was left uncovered and water got into the pistons. It was disheartening to see the tractor so deteriorated.

Then along came a gentleman who was looking for an old MM to restore. He bought my tractor, and about 6 months later, he sent me a picture of it, showing it completely restored. 🚜

He Won Tractor For 50 Cents!

By June Holmes, Nye, Montana

OUR FAMILY enjoyed a rare bit of good fortune during the Great Depression when our dad, Lawrence Erickson, won a tractor in a raffle.

Dad purchased his raffle ticket for 50¢ in Minot, North Dakota. The winning number was drawn at a fund-raising event in Minnewaukan, about 75 miles away. Apparently the drawing must have been held around midnight, because Dad got a phone call at 2 a.m telling him he'd won.

The tractor was a 1935 Co-op, and Dad used it to farm that entire season. The following year, he traded it for a 1936 Co-op 3.

The 3 was the first tractor in our community with an electric starter and rubber tires, and it could reach road speeds of more than 30 miles an hour. This tractor was used in operating our family farm until 1980.

IT'S A KEEPER! Lawrence Erickson, shown here at age 89, acquired this 1936 Co-op 3 by trading the Co-op tractor he'd won in a raffle the previous year. The 3 may well be the oldest such tractor still running, according to Lawrence's children, Larry Erickson, June Holmes, Jeanne McNea and Bonnie Irwin.

A few years ago, we discovered that this may well be the oldest Co-op 3 still running. Over 5,000 were built between 1935 and 1952. The serial number of our tractor is 124, meaning it was the 124th one to come off the line.

The Co-op was completely reconditioned in 1988 by a talented neighbor, Dan Tuchseherer. Nowadays, we drive the tractor in parades throughout North Dakota. It has also been displayed at the North Dakota State Fair and the Makoti, North Dakota Threshing Bee.

Tomboy Fondly Recalls Fordson

By Joyce Marschke, Gold River, California

GROWING UP on a farm near Alden, New York, I was a tomboy and followed my dad around everywhere.

Some of the fondest memories of my time spent with Dad were from the early spring, when I would ride along on our old Fordson tractor while he did the plowing. I rode with him for hours, and one of our neighbors once had me pose atop the tractor while he snapped a picture (below) prior to our starting for the day. I was about 10 years old at the time.

In the fall, I also helped with the harvesting, tramping down the loose hay that Dad pitched up onto the wagon. Later, I learned to drive an old flatbed truck as the men loaded it with bales.

When I tended our livestock with Dad, I wore boy's overalls and work shoes. I couldn't have guessed that one day such an outfit would be fashionable as girl's wear!

Those were wonderful times and I often find myself recalling them as I ride around the field on the old Fordson.

LIKE FATHER, like daughter. Joyce Marschke has fond memories of keeping her dad company when he plowed with the family's Fordson.

Tractor Talk

RUMELY OILPULL

One of the most popular and reliable tractors to emerge after the turn of the century was the Rumely OilPull. The OilPull had a high-compression engine that was cooled by oil instead of water. The oil-cooled system worked so well that it enabled kerosene and other low-grade fuels to be used, and it was advertised as "guaranteed to burn any fuel at any speed." By 1910, engines produced 24 percent of the horsepower used on farms.

Grandfather's OilPull Saw Rise in Price

By Paul Lawrence
South Bend, Indiana

MY GRANDFATHER, Enos Maxam of Decatur, Michigan, bought a new Rumely OilPull 25/40 tractor in 1928. He used it to power a thrashing machine, clover huller and silo filler, and for other jobs.

From age 11 to about 16, I went along with Grandfather at thrashing time. My job was to keep fuel and water in the tanks, and to help Grandfather oil the bearings when we had downtime.

Grandfather's health wasn't good, and the tractor was rough to ride over the gravel roads. He bought some truck tires made of hard rubber, cut the rubber from the wheels and mounted the pieces in short strips on the Rumely's wheels for a smoother ride.

Grandfather also owned a 1927 Chevrolet roadster that he used for hauling supplies. When I was 11, he taught me how to drive the car from job to job. When I was 13, he taught me how to drive the tractor. My mother was very upset with him for teaching me to drive the car, and Grandmother was upset when he taught me to drive the tractor!

When Grandfather died in 1952, the tractor was sold at auction for about $350. I never knew what happened to it until about 5 years ago.

Our local paper ran an advertisement about a Rumely tractor collection being sold at auction in Dowagiac, Michigan. Out of curiosity, I went to the auction to see if Grandfather's tractor might be there.

It didn't take long to find it, because Grandfather's old OilPull still had the rubber tire lugs on the rear wheels. And it sold at that auction for $12,750!

EASY TO IDENTIFY. Paul Lawrence found his grandfather's old Rumely OilPull tractor at a collector's auction in Michigan. Identifying the tractor was easy—the rear wheels still had the rubber tire lugs his grandfather had attached for a smoother ride.

IMPORTANT AS A KING. Mark Burns, shown with son Mitchell, has loved his grandfather's 1949 Case since he was a toddler. "I probably rode it a thousand miles while sitting on his lap," recalls Mark, of Stewart, Mississippi. "One day when I was about 11, we were disking a hay field. Suddenly he jumped off, turned and waved and sat down under a shade tree. No king ever felt more important than I did that day. I disked until quitting time." Here Mitchell is seen sitting where his dad used to...except now Mitchell only sits there when the tractor is stopped.

He Found Dad's Old Farmall in Fencerow

By Robert Fager
Murphysboro, Illinois

COULDN'T RESIST. Robert Fager's father bought this Farmall H in 1939 and sold it in the 1960's. When Robert ran across it several years later, he couldn't resist buying it back. "I was 14 years old when Dad bought it," he says. "We grew up together."

AFTER MANY heated discussions at the breakfast table, my dad finally bought a new Farmall H in 1939.

My brother was convinced that a used F-30, available for about $450, would be no bargain compared to the pretty new H listed for $795 in the *Prairie Farmer*.

Dad finally agreed to visit the dealer in Murphysboro and ask about the H. The dealer had never had one but arranged to have one sent out. Of course, Dad bought it, and although he never admitted it, he was very proud of that tractor. It was the first H in our neighborhood, and possibly in the county.

The H had no hydraulics, lights or starter. The most advanced features were the rubber front tires. Dad bought a hand-lift mower, planter and cultivator, a one-bottom, 16-inch pull-type plow and an 8-foot disk. He later added hydraulics so we could get rid of all the levers.

The tractor served us very well from 1939 until the mid-1960's, when Dad traded it for a newer H. A neighbor bought our old one, added lights and a starter, and used it to plant and cultivate for the next 12 years.

Around 1975, I found that tractor, "retired" in a fencerow. I bought it, took it home and put it in storage. When I retired in 1990, I began restoring it, and removed the hydraulics and lights.

The tractor had only minor problems. The motor had already had one complete overhaul, and the pistons and sleeves were still in good shape. I put in new main and rod bearings and new rings, and now it runs like new.

When Cranking Didn't Work, He Pushed Deere Down a Hill

By John Russel, Lowell, Indiana

MY MOTHER used to work for the local John Deere dealer, and when she and Dad married in 1941, she bought him an A. I think she paid about $950 for the tractor and a two-bottom plow.

One day when I was about or 9 or 10, I was told to put gas in the A. When I finished that task with an old hand-crank pump, I tried to start the A, but I was too small to turn the flywheel fast enough.

There was a slope just a few feet away, so I somehow pushed the A to the edge of the slope and got it started down. Then I jumped on, shoved in the clutch and got the A started.

Shortly after that, Dad bought an Allis-Chalmers WD with an electric starter. But the A is still in our family, awaiting restoration.

A Missing Shoe, an Old Tractor and Peace

By Lester Finger, Phoenix, Arizona

IT WAS July 1944, and I was on leave from the Navy. I decided to go to Cashion, Oklahoma to help my sister and her husband harvest wheat on their farm.

They always tried to plow the wheat fields as soon as they were harvested—that way they could be replanted before the fall rains.

My brother-in-law had a two-cylinder John Deere with a two-bottom plow, and he asked me to drive that. His goal was to keep the old tractor going 24 hours a day.

I drove the tractor after dark, using the single headlight my brother-in-law had rigged up to see where I was going. The first night, my feet got so hot from the engine that I took my shoes off.

When I was relieved, I found one shoe without any problem…but not the other. The next morning, I had to go buy another pair—an expensive proposition in those war days.

When my leave was up and I returned to the Navy, I felt richer for having spent many hours on that one-lunger…but poorer for having lost a shoe. The following summer, my brother-in-law was plowing the same field when he found my other shoe!

By then, it was 1945 and the war was ending. Finding that shoe was like finding something that had been missing from the world during those years of terrible conflict.

It made me feel hopeful that peace would last a long, long time!

SISTERS Nancy Blower (left) and Cindy Porter enjoy hearing tractor anecdotes shared by their dad, Donald Weeks. Donald uses the 1947 H they're posing by for odd jobs. While pulling stones off a hillside, Donald once had a teeth-rattling experience with the F-20 shown above being driven by his father.

Father Recalls Favorite Farmalls

By Nancy Blower, Milford, New Hampshire

MY SISTER and I recently visited our dad, Donald Weeks, in New York State, and we asked him to share a few tractor memories with us. Our mother passed away last year, and having Dad reminisce about tractors proved to be the perfect way to temporarily take his mind off his loss—his enthusiasm as he recalled tractor anecdotes was like that of a small boy on Christmas Eve.

Dad grew up near Auburn in New York's Finger Lakes district, a beautiful area of gently rolling hills. His father was the resident caretaker of a 265-acre farm named Buck's Point. Dad first drove a tractor in 1935, when he was 9 years old, but it wasn't the farm's steel-wheeled IH F-14.

"Pa wasn't about to let me drive the IH with those dangerous steel wheels," Dad recalled. "I had to sneak up to Burl Butler's place and drive his tractor, an orange Allis-Chalmers with real rubber tires!"

Eventually Pa did allow Dad to drive the F-14, and later they upgraded to an F-20, again with steel wheels. Then in 1943, the big event finally occurred.

"That was really some deal when we got rubber tires," Dad told us. "They were used, but they were real rubber, and what an improvement! I think that's why my back is the way it is, after all those years of riding over stones on steel wheels."

This reminded Dad of the time he was using the F-20 to pull stones off a hillside and pile them on an old wall at the foot of the hill. With the winch mounted on the rear of the F-20, he picked up one huge stone and started backing down the hill with it.

"Suddenly, the weight of the stone caused the front end of the tractor to rear up like a wild stallion," he said. "Luckily, when that huge stone hit the ground behind the tractor, it allowed the front end of the tractor to drop back to earth, but with a real teeth-rattling jolt. Needless to say, I never told Pa about this incident!"

An H model was also added to the farm's inventory, and Pa and Dad used this tractor to plow snow during upstate New York's severe winters. In 1960, they purchased an IH 350 with three plows and a two-point hitch.

He Saved the Day

"Our farm was really equipped," Dad said. "Then came that dreadful Thanksgiving Day in 1964, when the barn somehow caught fire. I ran into the barn, jumped on the 350 and drove it out. The tractor had a canvas cab, the top of which was already engulfed in flames. We hosed it down as soon as I got it outside, and someone then pointed out that all of the hair on top of my head was singed!"

Dad later left the farm and started his own business, but he took the 350 along with him. He continued using it for a variety of tasks, everything from loading the boat and hoisting it into the lake to driving the tractor in parades. Then, tragically, in September 1971, it was destroyed in another fire.

Today, Dad enjoys the company of a 1947 H he bought to replace the 350. He says he's in the market for a newer model, or else he'll have to rebuild the H's engine. "Wouldn't be the first one I've rebuilt!" he jokes.

We know he may well have a new tractor to show us the next time we visit him in Auburn. But there's something else we're a bit curious about.

Dad spends his winters in Florida now, and we can't help wondering if he also keeps a tractor down there, parked alongside the swimming pool under the palm trees!

RUNS JUST AS WELL. Herman Renschler makes no apologies for not restoring his 1939 Keck-Gonnerman ZW. "I bought it, gave it a valve job and fired it up," says Herman, of Mount Vernon, Indiana. "Call me lazy if you want to, but it runs just as well without being restored—and I don't have to worry about someone scratching it." Since the tractor is on steel, he doesn't drive it long distances, but he does take it to the Keck-Gonnerman Antique Machinery Association show each June in New Harmony, Indiana.

He Traded 'Pretty Car' for a Tractor

By Rachel Rhodes, Farmington, Missouri

I WASN'T HAPPY when Daddy first drove his 1954 John Deere tractor home...he'd traded his 1953 aqua and white Plymouth for the tractor, and I loved that car!

I was 8 years old at the time. Now, thousands of "putt-putts" later, that old John Deere is still in the family. It has plowed and disked our fields, dragged logs from the wood-lot and generally helped us make our living off the land. It didn't take me long to understand why Daddy had given up his pretty car for a tractor, and after that, I had a special place in my heart for "Old John"!

Eventually, I got married, moved off the farm and started my own family. One day, I was sitting by myself on the porch and feeling a little low when the phone rang.

It was Daddy. He said that Mom had left him alone to go shopping, so he'd been going through some old letters. One was from a former girlfriend.

"In it, my girlfriend told me how disappointed she was when I traded my Plymouth for a tractor," he said. I realized with a smile that he was talking about me...the summer he'd gotten the tractor, I'd written him a little note telling him how much I missed his pretty car.

He'd kept my letter through all these years, showing how much he treasured it. That really lifted my spirits. Once again, the old John Deere was showing me just how much it had become woven into the fabric of our lives.

Now my brother has the tractor. He is restoring it and plans on keeping it in the family, where it belongs. Recently when I heard a John Deere putt-putting in a field, the sound took me all the way back to 1954—a good year for tractors!

WHEAT THRESHING. "This photo from the 1930's shows my husband operating a Rock Island tractor his father owned," writes Melba Wehmeier of St. Charles, Missouri. "They threshed wheat and oats at eight or nine farms."

Tractor Talk

AS BOLD AS GOLD

During the late 1930's, Minneapolis-Moline pioneered the use of LP gas as a tractor fuel. It had limited success, but the company became known for innovation. By the end of the decade, Minneapolis-Moline had introduced the enclosed cab, five-speed transmission and high-compression engine.

Chapter Five

In Pretty Sorry Shape

Restoring a 60-year-old tractor
is no easy task—especially if
there's a tree growing up
through the frame!

SUPER
44

Master 'Tinkerer' Works His Magic on Old Fordsons

By Tom Walker, Merrimack, New Hampshire

MY FATHER has always loved to tinker. If something's broken, chances are he can fix it. I marvel at his ability to take anything and make it work like new.

I felt that same excitement all over again when I visited my folks last fall and Dad asked if I could help bring my grandfather's 1926 Fordson home to restore. I faintly remembered this tractor, probably from seeing it in old pictures and "super 8" movies. The last time it was used, in 1971, I was 2 years old.

Grandfather put the Fordson in a corner of the garage and forgot about it. Over the years, many things had been piled on top of it. If you didn't know it was there, you'd never have guessed a tractor was sitting beneath all that stuff.

But my father knew, and he wanted to run it in the parade to celebrate his town's 200th birthday. With Grandfather's blessing, we went over to save the Fordson.

We spent the better part of a morning moving lumber, motors, boxes and everything else Grandfather kept in the garage. When we finally uncovered the tractor, it had one flat tire and not a speck of paint. My father immediately ran over and turned the crank.

Had His Work Cut Out for Him

I said, "Dad, you don't honestly think you're going to start that thing, do you?" He replied, "No, I was worried the motor might have frozen up, but it hasn't. So it won't be long before it'll be up and running." I thought even Dad had his work cut out for him this time!

We pulled the Fordson out with Grandfather's 1959 Ford 600 tractor. Dad's creativity showed from the start, when he fashioned a tow bar to bring the Fordson home. After putting some air in the tires and checking other essentials, we were ready for the 6-mile journey to my folks' house.

Dad asked if I wanted to drive the pickup or steer the tractor. I took the tractor and got quite a ride. The rear tires had flat spots, and it took a while for them to round themselves out. Even at 5 mph or slower, it was like riding a bucking bronco.

The Fordson didn't look like much on the road, and we got some funny looks all the way home. But that didn't discourage Dad. He could see past the rust to the tractor's potential.

When I went home again about 6 weeks later, I was amazed when Dad told me about the problems he'd encountered and the solutions he'd devised. He said he'd even had the Fordson running a few times. My brother, brother-in-law and I wanted to see that for ourselves.

It had snowed that morning, so Dad filled the radiator with hot water and my brother-in-law began to crank. After he lost his breath, I gave it a try. A couple minutes later, it fired, and after just a few more cranks, it started and ran. We

all took turns taking it for test drives around the yard.

A few months later, two more Fordsons, a 1918 and a 1920, followed my father home. With hard work and cleverness, he's gotten the 1920 and Grandfather's 1926 repainted, ready to show and running as well as they probably ever did.

In a day when high-tech computers run almost every facet of our lives, I'm amazed by the simplicity of these tractors every time I see them run. I think it's that simplicity, and restoring a little bit of history, that makes Dad so excited whenever he talks about his Fordsons.

My son Tommy is only a few months old, and I sometimes wonder what will happen to him in such a complex world. I pray that he'll learn to appreciate the simple things in life, just as my father has.

OLD GRAY PAIR. The 1926 Fordson that belonged to Tom Walker's grandfather stands unpainted and partially restored (below)...above it's on the left with a 1920 Fordson on steel wheels.

Little 'Betsy', the 1939 Case R

By Harry Cruchelow
Portland, Oregon

EVEN THOUGH my wife and I live in the city, I collect old tractors. My backyard is big enough to hold all 11 of them…and our neighbors don't seem to mind as long as I don't make too much noise.

My collection includes a 1946 Farmall W-4…a rare 1929 IHC 10/20 tracktractor…a 1920 Cletrac F…an Oliver-Cletrac HG…a 1929 Caterpillar 10 (the smallest "Cat" ever made)…a 1948 Perrin crawler…a 1945 John Deere BO …and four Cases—a 1946 SO…a 1937 L Wheatland Special…a 1936 C…and a 1939 R.

This story is really about the little Case R. In 1991, I already owned the L—the largest Case made in the 1930's—and the C—the middle-sized model from that decade. I really wanted an R, the smallest Case built in that period.

But I hadn't been able to find one anywhere. Then I had to go into the hospital for some surgery. The admitting nurse spotted a sore on the back of my hand and asked me about it. I told her it was a burn from a hot manifold on a 1926 Graham Brothers truck that I was restoring.

That led to a discussion of old tractors. Turned out the nurse, Karen Compton, knew where I could get ahold of a Case R. Her father, Leland Barklow, had bought one new in the late 1930's to replace a team of horses on his dairy farm down on Catching Creek near Myrtle Point, Oregon.

Was It Worth Restoring?

She explained that the tractor had been sitting out in the weather unused for at least 15 years. When I got out of the hospital, I drove down to take a look. It was in pretty sad shape—maybe not worth restoring…except that I really wanted an R.

I decided to buy it, and took a friend, Don Lewellen, along to pick it up. Well, that R really made Don and me work for our supper. (We're both in our late 60's, and by the time we got the old tractor on the trailer, we were feeling our age.)

It had rained all day, and the R was down a hill covered with blackberries. First we tried pulling the R up the hill with the four-wheel-drive power wagon…but all four of the tractor's tires were completely shot and the wheels wouldn't turn. You can see in one of the accompanying photos (lower right) how the rear wheels plowed the dirt.

Next we eased our tandem-axle trailer down the hill a ways, unhooked it and, using come-alongs, turned it to a better angle. We placed a jack under the drawbar of the R, raised it up and turned the tractor 90 degrees to go on the trailer.

Finally, with winch and chain, we pulled the R onto the trailer. The winch and come-alongs were "Armstrongs"— Don and I supplied the power by cranking and ratcheting. We didn't get home till midnight…but I had my Case R.

Just how bad a shape was the little tractor in? All four pistons were stuck…the magneto was beyond repair…the carburetor was rusted solid…the radiator had bullet holes, a very large staple and a No. 20 spike in it…the sheet metal was rusted out…the front wheels couldn't be used…the stamped round tops were all of the rear fenders that could be saved…

A friend of mine who is a body man went to work on those fenders. He put new metal on the insides and made

'ONCE WE LEARNED ALL HER TRICKS, SHE GOT US THROUGH TOUGH TIMES'

By Ruth Barklow

AFTER my husband, Leland, recovered from a logging accident, we moved to the family homestead near Myrtle Point, Oregon and started farming. Leland used a team of horses for a few years, then in 1939, he bought a Case R.

I don't remember exactly how much we paid for the tractor, just that the price included the team, some pigs and a couple of cull cows. We decided the team was too expensive to keep and that by getting rid of it we could make room for more dairy cows.

Once we got the R, we also had to buy a plow and disk and convert the hay wagon to pull behind the tractor. It took a while to learn all the R's tricks. For instance, when the engine quit, you didn't have any brakes…so you had to keep your wits about you on hilly ground.

Also, I broke my arm before figuring out how not to crank the R. But after we got to know her, we fell in love with her and started calling her "Betsy".

Even knowing a tractor well didn't keep you from having mishaps. One day when I was baling hay with a big Minneapolis-Moline baler, I accidentally killed the engine on the R by trying to go up a hill in too high a gear.

The whole rig started to roll backward toward the creek. The only thing I could think to do was swing the R around so that one big tire hit the drawbar and stopped turning. Luckily, that worked…but as I cranked up the R again, my knees were really shaking.

Another time, Leland was hauling a load of hay up a steep hill and I was driving our 1-1/2-ton truck right behind him. The R had plenty of power left, but suddenly the front wheels started coming up off the ground.

I jumped out of the truck and climbed onto the front of the tractor. There was a piece of baling wire looped around the radiator that I held onto because the radiator itself was so hot.

With both feet on the axle, I leaned back as far as I could. My 138 pounds was enough to keep the wheels on the ground, but it was nip and tuck for a while there.

Yes, I remember that little Case R very well…it helped us through tough times. Now I'm happy it has a home where it will be treated with the respect it deserves.

62

braces to replace the old ones since they had been completely rusted out. My brother Carl, who still lives back in Iowa where we both grew up on a farm, went out and found one front wheel for an R in a junkyard.

Brotherly Love

He then took another off his Case RC so I could keep my R as original as possible. That meant he had to go looking for another wheel for his tractor—a real example of brotherly love! (Carl does about the nicest job of restoring tractors of anyone I know.)

My brother also got me another gas tank, some brake covers, a carburetor, a magneto, a dipstick, a belt pulley and an original hood. Thanks, Carl!

Now I finally have a "Papa" Case L...a "Mama" Case C...and a "Baby" Case R. I also got to know Karen Compton and her mother, Ruth Barklow. They were kind enough to share with me their memories of their little Case R (see the stories below).

Just having their stories about the R makes all the effort that went into restoring it worthwhile. I thank the Lord for giving me a nice, clean hobby and for introducing me to all the good people who love old tractors as much as I do.

And, of course, I thank my neighbors for letting me keep my tractors in the backyard. ⌗

SHARED MEMORIES. Karen Compton and her dad, Leland Barklow, enjoy a moment with "Betsy", the family's 1939 Case R (above). That's Betsy below, over half a century later, being loaded onto a trailer for the trip to her new home...and after having been completely restored by Harry Cruchelow and his friends.

'MY ONLY REGRET—DAD CAN'T TELL YOU ABOUT HIS TRACTOR HIMSELF'

By Karen Compton

WHEN MY DAD, Leland Barklow, traded our workhorses for a 1939 Case R, I was upset. I was about 7 and didn't want to say good-bye to those fine old horses.

The first time I rode the tractor with Dad, I was afraid of it. I was sitting on his lap and he asked me if I wanted to steer. "No!" I hollered...but Dad said someone had better steer or we'd go in the creek.

A few seconds later, I grabbed the steering wheel. Tentatively, I turned it in one direction, then the other. Soon I was driving the tractor...and Dad had another helper.

Besides working the farm, Dad had a full-time job at the Coquille Mill. He would come home in the evening, milk the cows, then run the R in the field till after dark. Both my parents worked very hard to make ends meet, so it was a big help when I learned to drive the R.

Dad did the plowing himself, but when he was at the mill, I disked, then ran the clod masher over the field. When he was home on weekends, he ran the tractor during the day. I took over while he milked, and between us, we kept the Case R going day and night for most of the spring and summer.

I liked haying season best—that was when Dad and I worked together. He would drive the tractor while I operated the hay rake behind him...or I would pull the hay wagon while he and the crew loaded it with loose hay.

Eventually, however, my father developed a bad heart and went blind. He had been building a shed for the little tractor but couldn't finish it. So the R stayed where Dad last parked it—out in the weather, forlorn and abandoned.

One day, the farmhouse burned down...by then, I'd moved away to become a nurse and raise a family. Later, the barn collapsed from old age and disrepair. All that was left of the home I once knew was the empty land, a partly framed shed and the little 1939 Case R.

To this day, I can't believe how Harry Cruchelow and I got to talking about Case tractors that morning in the hospital...but I'm grateful that we did! Thank you, Harry...you rescued "Betsy" and gave her a home!

My only regret is that Dad isn't around to tell you about his tractor himself. He would have loved nothing better than to talk about little Betsy. ⌗

Cranking Didn't Bother Him, as Long as Tractor Was Green

By Stephen Pousardien
Harrodsburg, Kentucky

ON OUR SMALL subsistence farm in southern Indiana, Dad considered antifreeze a luxury. He insisted on dealing with freezing temperatures by draining the radiator and block on our old International Harvester Farmall F-14.

As you might guess, the day came when the temperature dropped even lower than the weatherman had predicted, and the result was a cracked block.

Now we had to make a decision: Should we repair the F-14 or buy a new tractor? We weighed three options—repairing the F-14, buying a recent model Farmall Super C or buying a 1939 John Deere A. The options quickly narrowed to the latter two.

The Deere was rather basic, with no starter or power lift, while the Farmall C was more modern, with an electric starter and full power lift—and a higher price tag.

My older brother recommended the Farmall, arguing that its greater efficiency would offset the higher price. Dad favored the Deere, primarily because of the lower price.

Then Dad asked my opinion, making sure I understood the attributes and drawbacks of both tractors. "You know the green tractor would have to be started by hand," he reminded me.

Having already begun a love affair with John Deere tractors, I replied, "I don't care, as long as it's green!"

Dad bought the John Deere, and I was in hog heaven.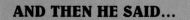

AND THEN HE SAID...

"My restored 1939 John Deere H always starts on the second turn—if there isn't a crowd around!"
—*Craig Rhodes, Gilman, Iowa*

SIGHT UNSEEN. "I bought this 1938 Allis-Chalmers B sight unseen over the telephone in 1994," reports Bob Coleman, Easton, Maryland. "You can see what shape it was in when I found it in a clump of bushes. It took lots of work, but it's like new now. One unusual thing: The manual says the serial number should be on the left side of the engine flange, but it's on the back of the engine. I understand that the B was first built in 1938, starting with serial number 11000. The serial number on the engine is BE11319G. There's another serial number on the transmission housing: B11318. Either way, it seems the B was one of the first off the line."

'The Fenders Looked Like Swiss Cheese...the Gas Tank Had Holes'

By John Hall Jr., Bahama, North Carolina

THE TRACTOR my father and I restored—a 1923 Case Cross-mount 12/20—sat under a cedar tree for 36 years before we bought it. The owner parked it there because the engine had locked up.

You can't believe all the problems with that tractor—the steering was frozen...the clutch and gear shift were stuck...the engine was not only rusted tight, but the crankcase had 7 gallons of water in it...the manifold was broken into several pieces...the entire bottom of the gas tank was rotted away, and the kerosene tank had holes the size of a fist in it...several steel spokes in one of the front wheels had rotted out...the oil pump had frozen and busted...the hood had several holes in it...the fenders looked like Swiss cheese...the toolbox had nearly rusted into nonexistence...and the carburetor and magneto were a mess.

My father and I restored the tractor in 10 months and 2 days, putting in 475 hours of work. At the time, I was 18 and attending a technical school to be a mechanic.

Only the fenders and toolbox were made new...everything else was repaired to keep the tractor as original as possible. We even used the same piston rings...though, of course, we had to take them out and rework them first.

Other than making the toolbox, fenders and cover for the spark plug wires, my father and I did all the work. We enjoy collecting and restoring old tractors and have four of them. Sometimes we start them up and run the thresher or silage cutter—it's not only fun, but a good way to maintain your skill at operating such machinery.

After all, one reason for restoring antiques like the Case 12/20 is so that future generations will be able to see how previous generations worked and lived.

IN PRETTY BAD SHAPE...that's how John Hall Jr. and his dad found this 1923 Case. It had been sitting unused for 36 years.

Oliver Returned to Farm After Years as Snowplow

WORKHORSE. Before its restoration, this Oliver Row Crop 70 had been battered by years of plowing snow and skidding logs. Gregory Aldrich now uses it on his small family farm, where he grows sweet corn and pumpkins.

By Gregory Aldrich, Amherst, Massachusetts

MY OLIVER Row Crop 70 was in pretty poor shape when I found it. It had no nose grille, only one fender and three of the six gears didn't work. The owner had been using it to plow snow and skid logs for years. But the Row Crop 70 is a farm tractor, so I brought it home to mine.

The Oliver required over 100 hours of cleanup and painting, and the search for missing parts is ongoing. I found most of the parts—including the two-row cultivator, which makes the Oliver more useful and handsome—at Willard Equipment in Willard, Ohio.

The important thing wasn't to have a showpiece, but to have a working tractor—and "Ollie" is just that. The six-cylinder engine will run smoothly all day. Sure, it burns some oil and leaks some more. But that's not bad for an engine that's 50-something.

My 1944 Ford 2N actually does most of the work around the farm, but the Oliver is a rare part of American history. I find myself starting it just to hear the engine run.

Work on Ailing Farmall Rekindled An Old Flame

By Jane Lynes
Dillsburg, Pennsylvania

OUR SON Eric needed something to mow his nearly 3 acres of lawn. So when my husband, Carl, saw an ad in the local paper for a used Farmall, he encouraged Eric to buy it.

He did, but the tractor quickly became a source of discouragement and frustration. Every time Eric used it, something broke or needed to be replaced, and he was working on it more than he wanted to.

Carl decided to buy it from Eric and restore it. In the next 6 months, working a little at a time, he overhauled it completely. When he was finished, the 1947 Farmall A looked like it had just come off the assembly line.

Now the Farmall has a new life—and Carl does, too. He has since bought several other old Farmalls, each a different year and type, and plans to restore them all. We've attended many tractor shows, where we've found needed parts and met lots of nice folks and fellow tractor lovers.

It's been nearly 40 years since Carl drove his grandfather's old Oliver around on their farm, but that one project was all it took to rekindle his passion for tractors. Now he has a hobby that's interesting and rewarding for both of us.

HOPELESS SITUATION. Restoration partners Chuck Whitcomb and Richard Wolff found the 1951 Case DO below abandoned in a Vermont cow pasture. They'd already restored a Case LAI and wanted another to compete in lighter tractor pull classes. "When we found the DO, we knew it was time to bring home 'Little Brother'," says Chuck, of Woodbury, Connecticut. The restored DO is shown above left next to the larger 1942 Case LAI.

CONSTANT FRUSTRATION. When this 1947 Farmall A discouraged Carl Lynes' son, he bought it and restored it to its former glory (right). Now he's hooked on restoring Farmalls.

He Turned a 'Pile of Junk' Back into a Great Tractor

By Gene Robbins, Angelica, New York

THE FIRST TRACTOR my wife, son and I ever restored was in the worst shape of any we've worked on since. We have now restored 15 tractors plus an 1894 shingle mill, an 1870 clapboard maker, an 1890 wood splitter and a 1936 gas engine.

That first tractor was a 1929 Huber R made in Marion, Ohio. We bought the tractor when an 88-year-old gentleman I'd known most of my life asked if I'd be interested in it.

I told him I would be—when I was a boy, the gentleman had let me ride on the tractor with him when he worked his fields. He also used the tractor to thrash.

When a friend of mine and I went to pick up the tractor, we found it half in and half out a barn, with the roof of the barn caved in on top of it.

The tractor had been that way for 30 years and was pretty well rusted out. It took my friend and me 7-1/2 hours to get the old Huber out of the rubble.

When we got the tractor home, my wife asked what in the world I was going to do with that "pile of junk" loaded on my trailer. "Restore it," I said...and restore it we did.

It took my wife and son plus my brother and a friend 13 months to turn that pile of junk back into a beautiful tractor. When we were finished, I asked the elderly gent I bought the Huber from if he'd like to come see it and take a ride on it.

When he arrived, he couldn't believe his eyes! He said that he never dreamed he'd see it running again, let alone looking like new. We went for a ride and he kept exclaiming "Oh, boy! Oh, boy!" over and over.

That made it all worthwhile. Needless to say, the old tractor is our favorite. We've since bought a second Huber, a 1935 HK. We take them both to county fairs, and recently they were chosen to represent our county at the state fair. ⚡

WIDE FRONT END was a distinguishing characteristic of the John Deere BW, like this one owned by Marvin Ball.

DEERE COMES HOME

By Marvin Ball
North Ferrisburg, Vermont

BACK IN 1935, a new John Deere BW—the W standing for wide front end—was shipped to the dealership in North Ferrisburg, Vermont and purchased by a farmer in nearby Charlotte. My uncle bought the tractor from him at the outset of World War II.

My folks also had a farm back then, so Dad often borrowed the tractor. When I was about 5, I got to steer it. Dad sat on the seat and I stood between his legs to steer.

After we sold the farm, we still occasionally used the tractor, as did other nearby farmers, to saw wood, haul the manure spreader and run the corn blower.

In the late 1950's, the tractor was sold again and became what was known as a "hired hand special". It was used for a variety of tasks by quite a few people, and it suffered some pretty rough treatment for a number of years.

Finally, in 1969, when the B's latest owners retired from farming, I was able to buy it back. Our family's old John Deere is now home where it belongs, and that's where it will stay.

I've known that B all my life, so to me it's a lot more than a funny-looking old farm tractor. ⚡

"THIS TRACTOR, a 1954 Massey-Harris Pony, was sitting in a yard I passed every day on the way to work," says John Zullig of Odessa, Missouri. "It was in very poor condition, but temptation finally got the best of me and I stopped to see if it was for sale. I ended up buying the Pony, and that was the beginning of a long but rewarding restoration project. Now I enjoy driving the Pony in parades and exhibiting it at tractor shows—I guess it's true what they say about every 'kid' wanting a pony!"

THAT'S THE 1929 Huber R on the left that spent 30 years under a collapsed barn roof. Jackie and Gene Robbins sit proudly between it and their 1935 Huber HK.

John Deere 40 Crawler Was 'Screamin' For Help'

By Richard Frombach
Burton, Washington

WHEN I SEE an old dead tractor, I get a sorrowful feeling. The old gal probably had a good life when she was young, doing her job just fine. Then a string of abusive owners got hold of her and wanted her to do more than should've been expected.

That was certainly the case when I found a 1953 John Deere 40 crawler. This thing was just screamin' for help.

Many of the bolts had fallen out, and most of the rest were loose. Bearings and brushings were worn out, the steering clutches and brakes were shot, teeth were broken off the gears and the track frames were falling off. The housing that holds the engine to the transmission was broken, bending the main shaft and stripping out the drive spline.

She was dead in her tracks, so to speak. But unbelievably, her engine purred like a kitten.

To most people, that thing was just a 6,000-pound pile of scrap. But I only hesitated for a moment before offering the owner $600 for the carcass. I was smilin' the whole time, knowing that block of steel already was warming up to me. I had a feeling that as I restored her, we'd become close friends.

That's not to say I didn't lose patience with her, but I was quick to forgive. It wasn't her fault my welding and mechanical skills were pushed to the limit.

My father, who had me on a late-1920's Toro B Junior at age 8, was a great help and inspiration on this project, and our newfound friend brought us closer. We spent hours and hours welding, brazing, bolting, machining, fabricating, hunting parts and painting.

My sister-in-law found this "male bonding" quite amusing. She tried not to listen while Dad and I hollered back and forth over the roar of two brazing torches.

I just love that piece of Old Iron. Now that the restoration is finished, I don't know who's more proud—Dad and me, or the old gal. 🚜

REMOTE CONTROLS. When Harold Radandt found this 1930 Massey-Harris GP at a farm auction, it wasn't a pretty sight. Since retoring it, he's installed remote controls that he can operate from a wagon or implement behind the tractor. Now he drives it in parades near his home in Manitowoc, Wisconsin. "It gets quite a response from the crowd," he says. Harold also owns about 50 pieces of antique earth-moving equipment.

EARLY YELLOW. Richard Frombach freely admits that his crawler isn't painted traditional John Deere green, but he notes that several of the company's early industrial implements were painted yellow.

Chapter Six

Decals, Paint and Pistons

One problem with trying to make an old tractor "like new" is not knowing exactly what it was like when it was new.

After 60 Years of Neglect, Twin City Has Its Day in the Sun

By Harold Tillman, Bella Vista, Arkansas

PLENTY OF HELP. This Twin City 17/28 was battered by the elements for nearly 60 years before Harold Tillman started restoring it. He says he got plenty of help with the project, especially from hobbyists he found through antique tractor magazines. "Every person I contacted tried to be helpful," Harold says. "That's the way people who love old tractors are."

I HAVE ONLY one old tractor, a restored 1928 Twin City 17/28. My father-in-law bought it in 1936 to work his 640 acres near Durango, Colorado. He hated it from the start.

The tractor was already well-worn when he bought it. A bad front end made steering difficult, it leaked oil from every possible place and the clutch was bad. Dad finally got sick of his "bargain" and let it sit outside, idle, from 1936 until 1946, when I was discharged from the Navy. My task was to clear 180 acres of virgin land.

Dad gave me the 17/28 and a small disk plow, and I started pulling red cedar, pinon trees and 6-foot-tall sagebrush. What a job! Every tree had to be pulled at least three directions before the taproot could be severed. The beast has two forward speeds, 2.2 and 2.9 mph, but I usually ran in high gear, so its speeds were essentially "slow" and "stop".

Late in 1947, with the clearing done and the first wheat crop drilled, I drove the beast into a grove of pinon trees and returned to Kansas with my wife and new son. The tractor was forgotten by everybody.

When my father-in-law died in 1964, hunters started trespassing on the place. They found the tractor, and things began disappearing from it. A neighbor pulled it to his house for safekeeping, but the magneto, mounting plate, toolbox, gas tank cap, wiring harness and copper tubing were gone.

After retiring, I realized the Twin City might be a worthy restoration project. Son John and I went to Durango in 1985 to collect the beast. We took along a modern magneto, hoping it would enable us to at least start the tractor for loading and unloading. It worked, but just barely. We had to cobble up a temporary coupling.

Drew People Like a Magnet

We took off the gas tank and cleaned it the best we could, then put on new copper tubing. When we filled the radiator, the water ran out almost as fast as we poured it in. The bottom plate, we later discovered, was like a sieve. The radiator had been perfectly good when I put in "in storage" in 1947.

We pulled it around with a big John Deere and got a few firings, but we were guessing at the timing. It sounded more like a one-lunger than a four-cycle. Still, we got it loaded onto the trailer under its own power.

That night, we stayed at a motel, and that old tractor drew people like a magnet. It was a sorry sight, with fenders flying in all directions, the front wheels trying to lie down and everything one color—rust. But we were answering questions about it until after dark.

Back home, a friend had a Bosch magneto, the exact model used on the 17/28. But it had been rebuilt for a generator, so most of the guts were missing, and what was there was useless to us. We eventually found the missing parts, got new coupler plates completed, aligned everything and timed the engine.

The engine still had a lot of "slap", and the rods needed re-babbitting, but we decided to overhaul the engine last. I drained the 40-year-old oil, dropped the pan, removed about 10 pounds of Colorado silt and made a new pan gasket.

Fenders and Hood Couldn't Be Saved

Antique tractor magazines helped me find shops that fabricate and repair sheet metal, and that was a good thing. The fenders, hood and deck plate were beyond saving, the gas tank was dented, and the air cleaner looked like it had been used as a battering ram.

Radiator shops told me the template for the bottom plate—the leaker—had been destroyed years ago, so I'd need a new radiator. That hurt; the rest of the radiator was good. The new one weighed about one-fourth as much as the old brass one and had about half as many tubes, but seems to cool efficiently.

When the engine was overhauled, we learned the crankshaft, camshaft and valves were good. It needed one piston and a set of rings, so we substituted those from 1947 and earlier Minneapolis-Moline U's. I asked Chester Anderson of Smolan, Kansas to re-babbitt and bore the rods; he was 85 years old, but he agreed to do it. His work was perfect.

The governor housing had been die-cast from pot metal, and after 60 years' exposure to the elements, it was crumbling like an eggshell. We were holding it together with friction tape. I designed another housing out of 4-inch solid aluminum round stock, and the machinist got all the details exactly right. To my surprise, it works like a new one.

There were many people who helped me get this old beast restored. Without them, this project never would have been completed, because I'd bitten off more than I could chew myself.

I'd really like to have a KTA and a 27/44, but I don't think I could stand it.

GRAND CHAMPION. After restoring this 1944 Farmall H in 1994, Patrick Skiba (on tractor) won a grand champion ribbon at the Minnesota State Fair. Patrick was 14 years old when he completed the project, which took about 8 months.

It Was a Jewel, Not a Pile of Rusted Junk

By Chris Cummings
Winfield, Kansas

EVER SINCE I was a boy and got my first toy tractor, I've wanted to be a farmer. While I was growing up in town, I always took whatever job I could get on nearby farms.

Unfortunately, in this day and age, if you aren't born on a farm, it's pretty hard to become a farmer. I eventually did the next best thing—bought an old tractor and restored it.

For many years, all I could do was attend tractor shows and dream about owning one of those beauties. My dream finally came true when I bought a 1936 Farmall F-20 at an auction for $90.

As you can tell from the accompanying photos (at far right), the F-20 may not have been much to look at in its deteriorated condition, but to me it seemed like a vision. I could look at it and imagine it coming off the assembly line new.

But finding a tractor and getting it home were just the beginning. When my wife first saw the F-20, I had a hard time convincing her it was actually a jewel, not just a pile of rusted junk. On the other hand, the kids thought it would be a great thing to play on and imme-

diately began climbing around on it.

The first thing I needed to know was if it would still run. I grabbed the crank and gave it a good turn to see if the engine was stuck. It wasn't, so I went to work setting the gap on the points in the magneto, and adjusting the valves.

After several hours of tinkering, I put gas in the tank and gave it a crank—then another...and another...and another. Finally it fired a few times and started to run.

It sounded rough, as if the valves weren't seating. I shut it off, pulled the head and gave it a valve job. While the head was off, I figured I could get the tractor up on its wheels. (The tires were next to nothing, so I just wanted the tractor on the rims.)

Next I started looking for tires and parts...my "$90 jewel" was quickly going to get more expensive. I had a friend sandblast the wheels, and I painted them their original red.

Then I got the tires mounted. Even though the tractor was obviously far from being completed, having black tires on red wheels made the tractor look like I might really have something.

The fun part came when I began scavenging through area farms for parts. I needed a hood and a number of other

items. Not only did my search turn out to be educational...it helped me relive a little of the past.

Whenever a farmer heard what I was up to, he wanted to talk about how things were done—and how the machinery worked—in the old days. I wouldn't trade that experience for anything—it gave me such a warm feeling just to see the old-timers' faces light up. Mention a piece of machinery they'd worked with long ago, and they'd take you back in time with their stories.

After I'd found all the parts I needed, I began scraping off the grease and rust with a putty knife. Then I sprayed the whole tractor down with an aerosol can of Graffiti Remover, letting it sit for an hour.

Finally, I washed everything with a steam cleaner turned up to about 900°. After about 30 minutes of washing, the tractor was nearly spotless, and the metal looked like shiny new cast. I let the tractor dry off in the air, then blew it with an air hose.

After replacing some leaky seals, I was ready to start painting. To restore the F-20's rich gray, I used Ditzler paint. Once the paint was dry, I put on the gas tank, hood, air cleaner, wheels and tires.

Sitting there in the sunlight, she was

By Patrick Skiba, North Branch, Minnesota

I PLAYED with toy tractors and began collecting models as a little kid. After going to an antique tractor show with my dad, I began to dream of buying and restoring a tractor of my own and started saving up for one.

In the fall of 1993, after 4 years of saving my 4-H premium money, I began looking for an older Farmall. I looked in the paper for a tractor I could afford and went to several auctions. I saw tractors I liked, but they went for too much money.

I kept watching the paper and finally saw an ad for a 1944 Farmall H. After calling for more information, I asked my dad to drive me to the seller's place to check it out. The price was right—$650, less than any of the tractors I'd looked at. Dad and I picked it up October 25, 1993.

The Farmall ran, but not very well. It was going to need a lot of work. When I started tearing it down, I had a good laugh over the Massey-Harris fenders that had been welded on. I took those off. The lights were also in the wrong place, and an aftermarket distributor had been added.

I tore the tractor down to almost nothing, then started to overhaul the engine. I ordered new piston rings and a gasket kit, then ridge-reamed the sleeves and honed them out. When the gasket kit and rings came, I started putting the engine back together, then assembled the rest of the tractor.

The next step was sandblasting to remove all the old paint and rust. Then I primed it and assembled the tractor some more for the final coats of paint.

The hood had quite a few dents. I pounded them out, filled in the nicks and wet-sanded the hood smooth. After painting the hood, battery case and small parts, I put on the final parts and mounted the battery case. It was finally time to see if the tractor would run. Was I ever happy when it did!

Then I put on the hood and decals, and I was finished. I waited until just before the Isanti County Fair to paint the tires. It was named grand champion there and went on to win grand champion at the Minnesota State Fair. I'm very proud of my tractor. ●🚜

---

alive with sparkles. Now I replaced all the old grease zerks and put on a new belt. Of course, I had to add red pinstripes and new decals.

As I stood back and looked at this beautiful piece of machinery, my heart swelled with pride. It had taken me a couple of years to get it to look this great, but it was worth it.

Now for the trial run (and the chance to show others what I had accomplished). I cranked it up and right away it began to hum. It not only looked great, it sounded great. I hopped up in the seat and took it for its first spin in decades.

My buttons were popping…I was actually driving my dream tractor!

I am sure this is only the beginning. As I search for a second—and maybe a third or fourth—tractor to restore, I know I will hear many more stories about American farming from those who lived and worked in the old days.

And when I take my Farmall F-20 to tractor shows, I'll sit and watch for a twinkle in an old farmer's eye as he glimpses a part of his past and comes up and tells me about the time he had a trac-

tor like mine…or knew someone who did. There is no generation gap when it comes to this hobby, and there are no strangers! ●🚜

LOTS OF POTENTIAL. Even before it was restored, this Farmall F-20 looked like a jewel to Chris Cummings. Of course, now that it's restored, the tractor is a jewel.

Do the Work Yourself, and You'll Get to Know Every Nut and Bolt

By Paul Desmet
Ludington, Michigan

I WAS BORN and raised a "city slicker". When I moved to the country several years ago, I quickly noted that rural folks are judged not by what they own, but by what they can do.

Most of my neighbors seemed to be working on some kind of project, especially building or rebuilding machinery. One of these neighbors decided that I wouldn't be much of a country boy till I'd seen a tractor pull, so he took me to one.

Truth be told, I was kind of bored by it. I did find all the old tractors fascinating, however. Most were still used daily on the farm and looked like they were only a step or two away from being junk.

When the PA announcer called out their names, I thought they had a nice ring—"Waterloo Boy"…"Happy Farmer"…"OilPull"…"Titan". The one I liked best was "Farmall"…I decided it might be nice to have one of those.

Well, living in the country has finally caught up with me—I now own a 1950 Farmall C. I found it—or it found me—behind an old fence at a sawmill. It had been dumped there years ago by a guy who needed to get it out of his yard.

I bought the tractor even though it was in a sorry state…but the engine still ran in a halfhearted sort of way. Suddenly I had to decide what to do with that stove-up old C.

Had I ever driven a tractor? No! Did I even know the slightest thing about tractors? No again. I didn't even know that you couldn't shift gears while moving and wondered why the gears kept grinding whenever I tried.

Of course, despite my ignorance—or maybe because of it—I went ahead and started restoring the old tractor. The only thing I can say about rebuilding a tractor is that it is a true learning experience.

Unless you find someone who has restored the same kind you're working on, no one will know what you're talking about when you look for help or information. Here are some of the things I've learned about how to restore a tractor without losing too much sleep over it:

● Buy three books: the I.T. shop manual for the model tractor you're restoring; *How to Restore Your Farm Tractor* by Robert N. Pripps; and the color history of your make, published by Motorbooks International.

● Ask yourself: Do I just want it to run well…or do I want my tractor to run and look great? There's a big difference. Most folks with a little mechanical skill can get a tractor to run…but much more skill and lots of money are needed for a complete restoration.

If you do the work yourself, you will become intimate friends with every nut and bolt. You will need to get good at working with machinery, and you'll have to have some good tools.

Don't forget: Your tractor will need to be totally stripped down, with all the paint, rust and dirt removed to the bare metal. (I hope you know how to spray-paint and can get ahold of the necessary equipment—having each piece painted commercially will be very expensive.)

Also, any part that can't be repaired must be replaced…that, too, is expensive—as are good rims and tires.

● Any parts you find on your tractor may be the wrong parts. Just because you find them there doesn't mean they belong. Forty or 50 years ago, a farmer may have used whatever part he could find just to keep the tractor running. (My Farmall C had the wrong carburetor …electrical parts…clutch…)

● Ignore the old saying about how, before you take something apart, you'd better be able to put it back together. Wrong! How do you know someone who owned the tractor before you put it together the right way?

You need to use your reference books to learn how to get it back together. Watch out for the word "similar". Sometimes, your model may look similar to the one in the book, yet not be the same.

One reason: The company that made the tractor may have had some extra parts lying around from another model and used them instead of the ones that should have been used.

Restoring an old junk-of-a-tractor can get mighty confusing!

● When you finish your project— which you will (eventually)—ask yourself: What it is that I hope to accomplish with my tractor now?

Part of the answer is, of course, "Drive it!" But if you actually use it for anything like cutting wood or hay—or to compete in one of those tractor pulls— all those clean parts and that nice paint job will soon get dirty.

So…the real answer may be that, while you're working with your restored tractor, start looking for another old junker—you can fix that one up just for show.

My Farmall C is looking great. It still needs a front grille, but all that DuPont RED paint is sooo beautiful!

What will I do when I get that grille on and my Farmall is really finished? Take my own advice and start another restoration…and maybe attend another tractor pull—it's possible I didn't give that first one a chance.

Best of luck with your restoration project!

Tractor Talk

JOHN DEERE

John Deere was born in Vermont in 1804. By 33, he was a blacksmith looking for opportunity. Heading west, he decided Grand Detour, Illinois would be a good place for a blacksmith shop. He arrived there with $73.

Farmers of the day had many of their tools made by the local blacksmith. That's how the young John Deere learned that the sticky soil of the Mississippi valley watershed stuck to cast-iron plows, making it necessary to stop and clean them frequently.

At first, Deere tried to solve the problem by redesigning the plows. Then a broken steel saw blade at a mill caught his eye. Deere fashioned a prototype plow out of the blade and took it to a farmer to test. The farmer was so pleased he ordered two on the spot…and Deere & Co. was on its way!

Brothers' School Project Revives Grandpa's Farmall

By Josh and Derek Miller
Marengo, Iowa

WHEN WE NEEDED a project for an agriculture class, we decided to restore the Farmall M our grandfather had bought in 1946. It had been used regularly until 1987, then sat in a shed for the next 5 years.

The tractor had been switched to liquid propane in the 1960's, so our first decision was whether to leave that in place or restore the gasoline system. Since we still had the original gas tank, we decided to use the gas system.

In August 1992, we hauled the tractor from our uncle's farm to the ag mechanics shop. For the next 2 years, whenever our ag classes met in the shop, we worked on the tractor.

We started by removing as many parts from the main frame as possible. One thing quickly became obvious—in 45 years, a tractor that's been used accumulates a great amount of grease, dirt, rust and just plain "gunk".

We cleaned and sanded the smaller parts by hand and took the larger parts and frame to a metal shop for sandblasting. We used as many of the original parts as possible, then cleaned, sanded, primed, painted and reassembled the tractor with some much-needed help from our FFA adviser (and veteran tractor restorer), Andy Rowe.

The Farmall is not exactly as it was when our grandfather purchased it. He made several additions to better suit his needs, and we decided we wanted to keep the changes he'd made. His modifications included a live hydraulic system and an overdrive.

We spent 310 hours on the project.

Our costs were $599.10 for parts, $89.92 for materials, and $186.10 for sandblasting and labor.

BLUE-RIBBON WINNER. What a difference a few hundred hours of work can make! This Farmall M, shown before and after restoration, was a class project for Josh and Derek Miller. The project won first place at the Iowa County Fair and a blue ribbon at the Iowa State Fair.

Fixing Farmall Was Easy For Former IHC Employee

By George Roberts, Boise, Idaho

I BOUGHT MY 1949 Farmall M from a friend in Oregon. He'd bought it from an elderly neighbor who wanted to clear some old stuff out of his machine shed. It looked pretty rough when I got it, and it wouldn't run. In fact, some people said I'd never get it running.

But restoring the Farmall was no problem. I knew IHC tractors from A to Z. I started working for International Harvester in Idaho Falls, Idaho in 1936 and had worked on many of the company's tractors. I was foreman of the shop in Caldwell, Idaho for some time and later worked for the company in Boise.

I did run into a few problems, though. One was getting all the varnish from old gas out of the gas tank, carburetor and gas lines. It took me days.

Another problem was finding rubber grommets for the seat, so I bought some and made them fit. Then I couldn't

A REAL SNAP. Restoring this 1949 Farmall M was a snap for George Roberts, a longtime IHC employee who'd worked on many of the company's tractors. "Some people said I'd never get it running, but it was no problem," George says.

find a shock absorber for the seat, so I went to an auto parts store and searched until I found something close, then made that fit. Now the seat arrangement feels like new.

The restoration took 2 months. I painted it with a gun and compressor, just as I'd done many times at IHC.

They Kept Detailed Account of Fordson Major's Restoration

By Crispin Kangas, Dousman, Wisconsin

I CALL IT my "Book of Restoration". It's nothing fancy, mind you—just a blue loose-leaf binder with about 100 pages of notes and photos showing the restoration of the 1957 Fordson Major that belonged to my father-in-law, Arnold Wundrow.

After he died and his farm was sold, my two boys, Shaun and Tyler, another relative named Christopher Gilbert and I picked up Arnold's tractor and began working on it. That was August 11, 1991. It took more than 2 years, but we finally got the Fordson back into great running condition in October of 1993.

Truth is, if it hadn't been Arnold's tractor, we wouldn't have restored it…it was in pretty sad shape when we got it. I always respected and loved Arnold, and getting his old tractor fixed up was a way of paying tribute to him.

Now it's a symbol of Arnold's love of farming …and instead of doing farm work, it can take life a lot easier, going to tractor shows and parades.

The book I made is a complete record of all the interesting things that occurred during restoration and afterward. I add material whenever we do more work on the tractor, or if we pack it up and haul it all to a show or parade.

Took Notes and Pictures

We started the book for two reasons. When we checked the tractor over and saw all the work that had to be done, we realized we needed a record of how we took things apart so we could get them back together again.

We were also afraid that we would never remember all the details of the project. A lot of our free time and savings would go into it, and we wanted to accurately recount those details in the future.

So each time we worked on the tractor, I took notes on whatever we did and added them to the book. We also took lots of pictures, and I sometimes made drawings showing such things as the wiring of the voltage regulator.

The first thing we did when we picked up the tractor was make a list of its problems—"right front tire missing"…"rear tires don't match"…"no oil, water or antifreeze"…"grille and radiator shroud severely damaged"…"right fender in bad shape"… "right brake doesn't work"…

As soon as we got home, we started taking things apart. The fenders, three-point hitch, grille, old loader-supports and toolbox all came off right away.

Luckily, Christopher found an I.T. Service Manual at a flea market, so we had some documentation to follow.

As I mentioned, the long process of restoration lasted till October 1993—ironically, the same month the Fordson originally came off the assembly line 36 years earlier. Now, it was again emerging into the world as a bright blue tractor with orange wheels.

On the day we planned to start the old tractor, I picked up the new keys we'd had made from a dealer…but then the engine wouldn't turn over. We swapped the two 6-volt batteries we were using for one 12-volt.

That got the engine turning over, but now it wouldn't fire. When we checked things over, we found that although fuel was reaching the injector pump, it wasn't coming through the injector lines.

Disassembled Injector Pump

After talking it over with two of the many friends who helped on the project, Dale Brushaber and Norm Knoll, we decided that the injector pump must be defective. That night, a Saturday, we went over to Norm's shop and disassembled the injector pump.

The cam followers were stuck in the up position and we decided that electrolysis must have occurred between the aluminum body of the pump and the hardened steel of the followers. To get the followers loose, we used a brass drift and some rust penetrant. After a lot of effort, the pump started working.

On Sunday, we put the pump back in the tractor, then filled the fuel lines again. Finally, we bled the lines from the injector pump to the injectors.

Suddenly the engine started running…but only on one cylinder! Amazingly, it kept running that way, so we quickly bled the remaining injector lines. As each line cleared, that cylinder would kick in.

Soon all four cylinders were running…and Arnold's 1957 Fordson Major was back in business!

After a few minor adjustments, the engine sounded smooth and powerful. We checked out the other systems—generator…oil pressure…water temp— everything was A-OK. The engine, slow to warm up, was running at a cool 170°.

Later in the week, I re-sanded the hood and painted it with spray cans. After that, we put a final coat on both the hood and the fenders, then drove the old tractor out into the bright fall sunlight and took its picture.

It was quite a moment—at last, Arnold's tractor was ready to go to shows. I think he would have been as proud as we were!

FROM THE TIME Cris Kangas got his father-in-law's 1957 Fordson Major home till the time it had been restored and was driven out into the fall sunlight, over 2 years had elapsed. During the project, sons Shaun and Tyler worked on the rear wheels, and the crankshaft, once stained by water marks, was repaired. Cris kept a book detailing every aspect of the restoration.

Dad's Deere Stories Led Him to Restore 1936 B

By Paul Singer, Windsor, Missouri

FOR $600 and the trade-in of a mule, my dad bought a 1938 John Deere B and a two-row mounted cultivator in 1939. It was one of the first tractors in our county with rubber tires, which made fuel consumption much more efficient. At the time, all Deeres burned low-grade "power fuel"—kerosene or distillate that sold for as little as 6¢ a gallon.

When the dealer brought the tractor out for a demonstration, Dad had 35 acres of corn to cultivate. The dealer deposited a 60-gallon fuel drum at the edge of the field and said, "If that tractor won't cultivate this field on this much fuel, I'll give you the tractor."

By the end of the day, Dad had drained the drum but could still touch fuel in the tank.

Soon afterward, Dad's cousin Alfred bought a similar B on steel wheels, with a lever for raising and lowering the cultivator. At the end of each row, you pushed the lever forward to raise the cultivator. After turning, you grasped the lever again, released the latch and tugged to lower the cultivator. With practice, you could develop such a rhythm that you didn't have to stop at the turns.

One day, Alfred and his neighbor were cultivating in adjacent fields. The neighbor had a Farmall F-20 and had to move four levers to raise and lower his cultivator. His view was partially obscured by trees, so he couldn't figure out how Alfred could turn so quickly at the row ends.

Turned with Cultivator

The neighbor apparently thought Alfred was turning with the cultivator still in the ground—and figured he could do that, too. On the next round, he turned without working his four levers. The left side of the rig went right under the tractor and joined its mate on the other side, bringing his fieldwork to an abrupt halt.

After hearing such stories over the years, I decided I wanted an unstyled B like Dad's. I found a 1936 model in November 1993, in the shop of a friend from my tractor club. He'd bought it in 1985, torn it down and overhauled it, then had to stop due to illness. The tractor had been sitting, disassembled, for 8 years. When I offered to buy it, my friend said, "It's all here. We just have to dig for it."

Over the next few months, I hauled home the loose parts, restored them and brought them back to put on the tractor. I bought a new carburetor, magneto, tires, tubes and gauges.

New rims were welded on the cutoff spoke front wheels, and the wheels were sandblasted and painted.

My brother and I hauled the B home in June 1994. During that 30-mile trip, three different people offered to buy it. We parked it behind a neighbor's auto repair shop, out of sight of potential buyers.

In the weeks that followed, I added fuel lines, new spark plugs and wires, changed the oil and filter, and added an-

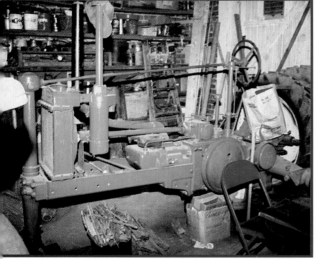

SITTING IN PIECES. After restoring his 1936 John Deere B, Paul Singer attached a 1945 Deere No. 5 sickle mower for use on his farm. When Paul bought the tractor, it had been sitting in pieces in a friend's shop for 8 years.

tifreeze up to the leak in the radiator. On August 16, I talked my brother-in-law into helping me try to pull-start it. He'd never been on a farm tractor before, so I knew this would be interesting.

I showed him how to operate the pulling tractor, my dad's old 1952 B, and we hooked up. "Okay, go!" I hollered. Yank. "Whoa," I yelled. "Take it easy!" Apparently operating a hand clutch is an acquired skill!

We made one lap around the 5-acre lot with everything turning, but only an occasional faint "putt" from the exhaust. We stopped, and my neighbor, an ace mechanic, came out and asked if I'd put gas in it.

I stared at him. "I put some in it," I said. "Not a whole lot."

He peered into the tank. "Must not be much. Get some more and we'll try it again."

I poured in a couple of gallons, climbed back on and signaled my brother-in-law. Another 10 feet and the '36 putted to life, amid wisps of blue smoke, for the first time in years. We immediately found the governor wasn't working right—the engine was running far too fast, and when I throttled it back, it would quit.

Couple Unusual Features

I spent several weeks taking apart and cleaning the governor, freeing up its weights and soldering the radiator. Then I drove it home, hooked it up to my sickle mower and started breaking it in. Getting it up to running temperature did wonders for the engine operation.

The tractor now has great compression (the valves were sticking). It takes a good tug or two to start, but it will start on the first pull. Taking the tight new engine into consideration, I once gave the flywheel a mighty heave. The engine fired immediately, and I nearly fell down from the momentum.

This tractor has a couple of unusual features. At one time, the hydraulics were converted to operate with a hand lever on the right side, and it has a one-way remote cylinder outlet on the rear. According to John Deere archives, these features were available in a factory kit sometime in the 1950's. This is the only unstyled tractor I've seen with these modifications.

I hope to have both my model B's around for quite a few years. Dad is now in a nursing home, but as long as I have the old John Deeres, there will always be a part of him working on the farm.

QUITE A CHALLENGE. A friend told Larry Kritchen, shown above with one of his grandsons, that he'd never get this old Case tractor running again. Larry persevered, and now the Case is a family favorite.

Perseverance Pays Off

By Larry Kritchen, Cordova, Alaska

I'VE ALWAYS enjoyed reading other folks' stories about restoring old tractors. A couple of years ago, I got the chance to restore one of my own.

A neighbor dropped by to visit and asked if I was interested in an old tractor that had been sitting in the nearby woods for several years. It had been out there so long, he said, that its vertical exhaust pipe was rusted away, its engine was stuck and full of water, and it might have a broken drive shaft.

I was restoring two old Harley motorcycles at the time, so I didn't really think I needed a rusted-out tractor with a frozen engine. But after thinking about it for a few days, I asked a friend to go with me to take a look at it.

When we found it in the woods, we discovered it was an old Case, probably from the mid-1950's or early '60's. After one look, my friend told me to forget it. "You'll never get this thing running!" he said.

I had to admit it looked pretty bad. But his remark seemed like a challenge, so I decided to haul the old tractor home to save it from the local landfill.

My son, Lyle, helped me tow it to my warehouse. I began by taking off the head and putting a mixture of penetrating oil, kerosene and other solvents into the cylinders.

I let it sit for a month, then tried to turn the engine over with a 48-inch pipe wrench on the end of the drive shaft. No luck.

The next day, I sopped all of the oil out of the cylinders, heated the tops of the pistons with a torch, then tapped them lightly with a hardwood dowel and a hammer. I did this every morning for a week, alternating oil, heat, hardwood and hammer.

Finally, to my surprise, I saw a piston move slightly. I rebuilt the starter, put in a new battery and—lo and behold—when I pressed the starter button, the engine turned over!

The next step was to take the engine apart and rebuild it. I did almost all of this work myself, and I finished the job by repainting the tractor in Case orange.

The tractor now runs well, and my grandkids enjoy sitting on my lap and "steering" when we take it out for a drive. I'd still like to find a Case medallion for the front of the tractor to make the restoration complete.

My son is using the tractor to clear some land next to his family's cabin in McCarthy, Alaska. I'm now rebuilding a 1930 Ford Model A coupe, and I hope when I'm finished, it will run as well as that old Case tractor!

He Adapted Automobile Carburetor for Fordson

By John Rosenogle, Wawaka, Indiana

MY DAD had Fordson tractors as soon as they were available after World War I, and he continued using them until the early 1930's. One big drawback to the Fordson was the troublesome ignition system—the same one used in Model T automobiles.

In 1975, I bought a Fordson that had escaped the World War II scrap drives. I found all the parts I needed, except for the carburetor, so I adapted an automobile carburetor for it. The Fordson starts easily now, thanks to a Fairbanks-Morse magneto add-on. 🔧

Untold Time and Money of Restoration Were Worth It

By Gene Timberman, Newfield, New Jersey

MY FATHER was raised on a farm but moved into a small town when he got married. Even so, he had a large garden where he grew all kinds of fruit and vegetables.

That's probably where I got my love of gardening. Recently, I bought a home in the country where I now have room for my own really great garden.

But to manage the garden, I needed a small tractor. The one I found was a tired old 1948 Ford 8N with a 72-inch mower deck. I fell in love with the tractor and soon learned to enjoy all the tinkering that was necessary to keep it running.

Love at First Sight

By Dick Fenley, Port Townsend, Washington

"DO YOU KNOW anyone who wants to buy an old tractor?"

This question was put to my wife and me by the UPS driver on our route. He told us his father had a 1949 Minneapolis-Moline for sale.

We had been to many antique tractor shows over the years, and I had always thought it would be a lot of fun to have one of those wonderful old machines to restore and play with. Now was our chance.

We tried not to sound too eager as we told him we'd come up to his dad's place on Saturday "to take a look". After he drove away, we decided that just in case we couldn't pass up the tractor, we should go ahead and rent an equipment trailer and take it with us to bring the MM home—after all, it was a 60-mile round-trip, and we wanted to be prepared.

I think I already knew that we'd be bringing the tractor home with us, regardless of how it looked. When we got to

our destination, the UPS man's father took us out to see the old MM. It was sitting in tall weeds and had berry vines climbing all over it. It still bore some of its original golden-yellow paint but was badly rusted and liberally dented and dinged. I thought it was beautiful.

Someone else had already been there to see it, so it had fresh gas in its tank. We hooked up an old 12-volt battery to turn over its 6-volt starter, and it started right up. The tractor ran well enough to be driven up onto the equipment trailer we'd brought…except that the trailer was too small!

We made a quick trip to another rental facility a couple of miles away and picked up a larger trailer. Then we returned and got our MM—my new toy—and hauled it home.

Like a little boy, I couldn't wait to start working on it and taking things apart. But first I had to return the large trailer and pick up the smaller one we'd originally rented and bring it back to our local rental yard—another 60-mile round-trip. I thought it would never end.

Finally, however, I got all of these obligations out of the way. We booted my wife's car out of the garage to make room for me to scatter tractor parts all about, and at last, I was ready to begin. The date was October 23, 1993.

It took nearly 6 months to completely restore the old MM. Every night after work and every weekend, I could be found out in the garage doing whatever was necessary to bring the tractor back to life.

Some nights I would tell my wife, "I'm just going out to

IT WAS THE START of a beautiful relationship when Dick Fenley and his wife hauled home this 1949 Minneapolis-Moline tractor. Six months later, Dick completed the MM's restoration, and he now enjoys driving it on the streets throughout his neighborhood—and sometimes even to work!

Then one day, I got this crazy idea—why not buy a second Ford and fix it up so it would be like new? I'd still use the first in the garden…the second could be for fun and showing off.

It took more than 2 years, but I finally found the tractor I was looking for—by coincidence, another 1948 8N. It had been sitting in a barn unused for better than 25 years.

At first glance, it looked pretty rough under all that dust, grime and rust. Upon closer examination, I realized the tractor showed few real signs of wear and tear. All the sheet metal was in good condition, and it still had its original tires.

I bought the tractor then and there. When I got it home, it started easily, but there was a strange sound in the engine.

I traced the noise to the cylinders and discovered that while it was in storage, the rings had rusted into the sleeves, etching deep grooves. That allowed the pistons to slap.

I rebuilt the entire engine, replaced the tires, wheels and brakes, then checked the transmission, rear end and hydraulic system. As I worked my way through the tractor, I discovered

CRAZY IDEA. Gene Timberman bought his first 1948 Ford 8N to work in his large garden. After constantly tinkering with the tractor to keep it running, he says he got the "crazy idea" to buy a second '48 8N and fix it up strictly for show. Here is the result.

there was even less wear and tear than I'd expected.

The engine was very clean, with almost no sludge—unusual for any machine nearly a half century old. The knurled surfaces of the brake and clutch pedals were like new, as were the dimples used for friction under the throttle lever.

Every piece of the tractor was sandblasted to remove rust, paint and grime. After I put on a coat of primer, the tractor was sprayed with Ford red and gray enamel. A new wiring harness was installed and a set of decals added.

Much to my surprise, the tractor sputtered to life as soon as the starter switch was engaged. Now I had two 8N's, one for work, the other for pleasure. The untold hours—not to mention money—that went into restoration were all well worth it!

---

check on that 'whatizzit' part so I'll know what to order tomorrow. I'll be back in about 15 minutes." Three hours later, she'd come out to the garage to tell me it was almost bedtime.

Through it all, she was very encourgaging and supportive. As though giving up her car's garage space wasn't bad enough, she found out that the top of our stove was now being used to dry the paint on some of the smaller parts I was refinishing.

I'd discovered that the gentle warmth of the three pilot lights hastened the drying process so I could hurry and spray on another coat of paint. I also used the oven to bake the paint on certain parts.

Any Excuse for a Drive

A retired machinist friend, Ed, was happy to fix up the MM's badly worn distributor shaft and bushing. His payment was a big bag of my wife's fresh-baked cookies. I delivered them by driving across town on the MM.

The restoration was finally completed in March 1994, and now I look for any excuse to go for a drive. I've even driven the MM to work a few times, and since it will reach 19 mph, the trip only takes about 12 minutes.

On some cool mornings, the heat from the engine and the tall muffler helps keep me warm. I notice that people look at us and grin a lot when they see the brightly painted machine cruising through residential neighborhoods and along country roads.

The exhaust note of the MM's long-stroke engine turning over slowly under load is music to my ears. Whether we're going up or down a grade, the engine's governor works the throttle as needed to keep a reasonably steady speed. All I do is steer and listen to that engine operate itself and play different tunes from its exhaust.

This tractor will be here long after I'm gone, and that's partly why I restored it. Did I spend too much time and money on it? Of course. Would I do it again? Absolutely—in fact, I already have.

My second restoration was a 1953 Farmall Super C, and now I'm getting started on a Farmall Cub. I guess I probably don't have to tell you that we still can't get my wife's car back into the garage!

After Restoring Ford 850, He's Eager for New Project

By Wallace Lawrence, Sebastian, Florida

IN A SHED near Vero Beach, Florida, I found a 1955 Ford 850 that hadn't been used in years. The sheet metal was nearly rusted away, and the gas tank and carburetor were in bad shape.

I cleaned the tank and installed a rebuilt carburetor. With new points, condenser, battery and distributor rotor and cap, the old iron horse came back to life. The hydraulic system didn't work, so I replaced the fluid and the O-ring on the cylinder. The hunt for sheet metal took quite a while, but I finally found what I needed in Missouri.

Sandblasting and painting took lots of time, too, but I was so pleased to bring this hardworking Ford back to a useful life.

Now I'm looking for a new project. I'd like to find a Ford 600 to restore next.

LITTLE EXERCISE. Wallace Lawrence started restoring this 1955 Ford 850 to keep himself busy and provide a little exercise. He enjoyed himself so much that he's now hunting for another restoration project.

Restoring 'Gruesome Green' Posed Plenty of Problems

By Dave Berger, Vienna, West Virginia

ONE FALL, I was visiting a retired friend and noticed his old John Deere in the field beside his house. I asked if he ever ran it anymore. He hadn't for a couple of years…would I like to buy it?

Bill knew I liked old tractors, but I didn't know much about Deeres. I had an old Farmall M that I used with a rotary cutter at my dad's farm, and I worried about getting stuck in the creeks and gullies—with only Dad's Farmall Cub to pull me out. That Deere could be a practical piece of machinery.

Knowing Bill, I figured the tractor just needed new points and timing, and I could just see it in my backyard in town. As a shift worker, I didn't get out to the farm much anymore. It would be like having a touch of the farm in town. I agreed to buy it for $550.

Two weeks later, I returned to pick it up. The closer I got, the more gruesome it looked. The box-type seat had a pile of rags for a cushion. The tires were all about flat, and the pipe from the exhaust manifold to the muffler was nearly rusted in two. I tried to look at it as having a lot of potential.

I pumped up the tires, tore into the seat, mounted a new battery, checked the spark and tried to check the timing. I blew out the gas line, put air through the carburetor, checked the air cleaner and oil and put gas in the tank.

We spent the rest of the afternoon trying to start the tractor. When I put gas or ether in the air cleaner line to the carburetor or into the cylinders, I could get a pop or two, but that was it. Bill pulled me with his truck, but still no luck.

It was clear Bill wasn't feeling too good about how things were working out. He tried to be a fair man, and I could tell this bothered him. To be honest, I wasn't all that happy myself. I told him, "Bill, it's got to be in the carburetor."

The first thing I noticed was a wire that went down the carburetor bowl and twisted around some pipe threads at the bottom, then up the other side. Inside was the biggest pile of crud I'd ever seen in a carburetor. The float was fine, but gas wasn't getting into the bowl.

Looked Better When It Ran

I unbolted the carburetor and told Bill to step on the starter. When I sprayed ether into the intake manifold, it started right up. We were both so happy that whenever the tractor started to die, I gave it another squirt. The tractor didn't look good, but when it ran, it looked a lot better.

Nobody could seem to fix the carburetor. I finally shelled out a couple hundred dollars for a new one, plus points and condenser, and the tractor started right up. One of the biggest thrills of restoring a tractor is starting it up and driving it after bringing it back from the dead.

By November, I'd flushed the gas tank time and again but still had fine rust in the fuel bowl. Sometimes the tractor lacked power, and I couldn't get the hydraulic system to run.

A mechanic at work said that if the power takeoff worked, the hydraulics would, too. Every day he asked me if I had the hydraulics running, and every day I said no.

One evening, I had the cutter bar running, and by chance I leaned on the hydraulic lever. It worked. The PTO had to be running for the hydraulics to work. I'd never experienced this on a tractor before. I felt stupid, but I also thought Deere must have had some dimwit engineers back in 1949. I told the mechanic the hydraulics were working now, but it was a long time before I told him the whole story.

I still hadn't figured out why the Deere sometimes lacked power. It was even hard to start. One day my father came by with a retired mechanic. He put a wooden stick against his ear, with the other end against the engine block. He looked up and said, "You've got a bad plug." I retorted, "I just put new plugs in about a month ago."

"Most people can't hear a misfire in an old John Deere," he explained. "In fact, the tractor probably sounds better to them." I got another spark plug, and it cured the problem.

Nothing But Black Smoke

I shut down the project for the winter, and when I started "Gruesome Green" the following March, there was nothing but black smoke. I tore into the carburetor and found a collapsed float. The only explanation I could think of was moisture in the gas line.

I shined a flashlight inside on a broken piece of mirror and found where my rust and water were coming from. The top of the tank was practically rusted out.

I couldn't find another tank anywhere. A parts man out west had one for a John Deere 50 that would work "with a little alteration". It worked, but it took more than a little alteration. The final cost for the tank was about $225, and I can't let the gas get too low, because it won't drain out at the lowest point.

Eventually, I drove the Deere about 50 miles to Dad's farm—a long trip with a top speed of 11 mph—and gave it a paint job. I used it there for several years with a rotary cutter. Now it's used only for tilling gardens, and it does a good job, even though it struggles at times.

If the day ever comes that it's no longer needed at the farm, I just might haul it back to my place.

TILLING GARDENS. It took a lot of doing, but Dave Berger eventually got the old John Deere that he found in a friend's field to not only run like new, but to look like new. Now he mostly uses the tractor for tilling gardens.

This Fix-up Turned into a 20-Year Project

By John Bunch
Mishawaka, Indiana

TIME WELL SPENT...that's how John Bunch feels about the 2-plus decades he put into restoring his father's 1937 Oliver.

IT TOOK ME more than 20 years to completely restore a 1937 Oliver tractor, but the time and effort were worth it.

The project began in 1971, when I took a correspondence course in mobile engine service. I was looking for something to work on to gain experience. My dad, Warren Bunch, owned a '37 Oliver and told me I could have it, but he reminded me that the old tractor hadn't been running for quite a few years.

When I removed the overhead valve cover, large flakes of rust fell down on the rocker arms. This was discouraging, but I kept going.

Several of the pistons were rusted to the cylinder walls. I freed them with penetrating oil—and a lot of elbow grease—and honed the cylinder walls smooth again.

I had the valves ground at the local Oliver dealer, who had most of the new parts I needed, including rings, bearings and a pressure plate. I also had the starter rebuilt.

I was working full-time, so it took me over a year to get all of this done. The Oliver ran just fine for several years, then something shorted out and I lost interest in my project.

I knew, however, that I wasn't finished with it yet.

I squirted oil in the spark plug holes and turned the crank every once in a while so the engine wouldn't freeze up again. Then a few years ago, my grandson, Troy Manges of Bremen, Indiana, restored an old John Deere A. And that was all it took to get me fired up again and determined to finish the job on the Oliver!

I removed the gas tank and had it steamed out, cleaned the gas lines and installed a new carburetor kit. I also installed all new wires on the tractor, and while doing so, I discovered where the short circuit had been and eliminated the problem.

Because I wasn't able to get the right ignition parts, I installed a new distributor as well. And I changed the electrical system to 12 volts, replacing the coil with one that had a resistor.

When I was ready to start the engine, I removed the number one spark plug to check for a spark. To my surprise, as I pressed the starter, the engine started idling on five cylinders.

I was really pleased. I'd done all the work as carefully as I could, but I still hadn't expected it to start that easily.

In the spring of 1995, I completed the job by repainting the Oliver and putting on new decals. To say that the tractor has a great deal of sentimental value is an understatement; Dad traded an old Fordson for this Oliver and I helped him farm with it for quite a few years!

Rubbing Alcohol Helped Him Free Stuck Engine

By J. Robert Morrison, Snellville, Georgia

THE FIRST TIME you buy an old rusty tractor with a stuck engine, folks ask your wife if you're feeling okay. They cock their heads to one side when talking to you, as if you're a few bricks short of a load. But when you buy a second one just like the first, they think you're onto something good and ask what those old tractors might be worth.

My dad and I have restored two steel-wheeled Fordsons, model years 1922 and 1924. With the first, we hand-sanded and steel-brushed the rust away, then painted it with a heavy zinc-based primer. With the second Fordson, we hired someone to sandblast it but found it very hard to get the sand cleaned off so we could apply the primer.

I wasted a lot of money and time on special products to pour in the spark plug holes to free up the stuck engines. One Sunday at church, an older man who'd retired from an equipment dealership said he'd heard rumors about my stuck engine. I told him what I'd tried.

ONTO SOMETHING GOOD. Robert Morrison says that folks look at you funny when you buy your first old tractor...then they think you might be onto something good when you buy the next one. Shown here is one of the Fordsons he and his dad have restored.

"That junk won't penetrate your skin, much less rust in a cast-iron block," he scoffed. He told me to pour rubbing alcohol in each spark plug hole, go do something else for 3 hours and come back to pull on the crank. It worked.

Chapter Seven

A Dream Come True

A seized-up engine…wheels that don't turn…rusted metal— repair those and you've realized your dream!

Seller Hand-Picked Buyer for His 1936 Unstyled 'A'

By Dot Hall, Broadwater, Nebraska

IN OCTOBER 1993, we were hauling a John Deere A home from Bassett, Nebraska and stopped in Valentine for the night. As we ate breakfast the next morning, a retired gentleman drove past and saw our trailer sitting there in the restaurant parking lot. When we came out after eating, he was waiting for us.

The man told my husband, Mike, that he'd been looking for a young fellow genuinely interested in restoring old tractors. He had several in a tree row and needed to get them out because he'd "sold the farm and gone' fishin'".

Well, Mike took off with this total stranger in a blue van full of fishing gear, leaving the kids and me to wonder if he'd come back. When they returned about an hour later, Mike was grinning ear-to-ear. The way his face was shining, you'd have thought he'd won a million-dollar lottery!

The next week, Mike went back to claim his prize, a 1936 John Deere unstyled A. When he got home and told me he'd paid $100 for it, I thought he'd lost his mind!

Mike spent that winter tearing the tractor down and rebuilding it, part by part. By February, he had it up on wheels. By March, he could start the engine. He completed his work at midnight May 27, 1994 and pulled with it in the antique tractor pull the next day at Camp Clarke Days in Bridgeport. He won first prize in the 4,500-pound class.

The Bridgeport paper ran a story about Mike. Our state senator saw it and sent Mike a note, saying how rewarding it must be to do such a superior restoration job.

Mike called the gentleman who'd sold him the tractor and told him about winning the pull. We also sent him pictures of the restoration process and a copy of the newspaper story. He was so pleased!

Now Mike's restoring another antique tractor for son Robbie, 5, to pull with in a couple of years. We travel to pulls with several of our neighbors, and it's become a real family sport. Some of the wives and kids pull, along with the dads and grandpas. I'm hoping to get started soon myself, as is Robbie. Daughter Beckie will be next—but right now she's only 3.

NICK OF TIME. Just hours after finishing the restoration, Mike Hall (below) won a pulling contest with this 1936 John Deer unstyled A. A chance encounter on the road led Mike to the tractor. His wife thought he'd lost his mind when she heard he'd paid $100 for it, but over the next 7 months, he turned it into a showpiece.

ESTATE SALE. Paul Bliss of Atlanta, Michigan bought this 1953 Ford NAA "Golden Jubilee" from the original owner's estate in 1986. "This design was a big departure from the earlier 8N's and 9N's and celebrated Ford's 50th year of production," Paul relates. The restoration involved replacing dozens of leaky gaskets, repainting the chassis and sheet metal, installing a new battery and wiring and replacing the tires.

Rumely OilPull Tugs at His Heart

By Tom Hoose, Fenton, Michigan

I SLAMMED on my brakes and put my truck in reverse. Something had caught my eye as I drove past a barn I had built for a man at Byron, Michigan. I came to a stop to take a better look.

It was an old tractor sitting out in the middle of a field. I studied it carefully for a few minutes, then decided to find out what kind it was. The owner, Bill Graves, was at home and happily consented to show me the tractor.

It was a Rumely OilPull 20/40 G, manufactured in 1923. That made her—after one look, I knew the Rumely was a "she"—nearly 70 years old!

My dad and I had recently attended the Steam Engine and Tractor Show at Buckley, Michigan. We enjoyed seeing all of the old tractors, especially the big babies like the Rumelys. Now, here was one right before my eyes. Bill said he'd consider selling her to me. The price he named was pretty hefty, but I knew she was worth that—or more. I had to think it over.

While I was doing so, I walked around Rumely—already we were on a first-name basis—and touched her big wheels. They were taller than I was.

Carefully, I climbed into her cab. What a feeling to be in the driver's seat! I asked Bill if she would run, and he said he thought so.

He cranked the big flywheel into position and, after several adjustments, I heard a loud huff and chuff, and Rumely shuddered to life. Big black clouds of smoke billowed skyward.

Bill and I went for a little ride. Rumelys don't move very fast, but then, you don't really want them to if you ex-

pect to keep control. It sure was some fun being at the wheel of such a big monster!

Well, I went home to ponder the deal. It was a lot of money, and maybe I wouldn't be able to handle the restoration. But I'd fallen in love with Rumely, so I went out again and took Dad with me. He liked her, too.

Almost before I knew it, I was making arrangements to come out and pick her up. I felt kind of guilty about the amount of money I was spending, but I wanted to prove to myself that I could make her like new.

I went back the next day and drove Rumely onto my flatbed trailer. All the way home, I could see heads turning to stare at us—we attracted quite a crowd.

Too Tall for Garage

After I unloaded her, I tried turning the 4-foot flywheel by hand…and immediately realized why they invented starters. After a while, however, she puffed to life again.

All of my neighbors wanted a ride, so Rumely spent her first evening at her new home going 1-1/2 mph up and down my long driveway. The kids ran along beside her. I thought she looked happy being useful again. That night, I covered her up with canvas since she was too tall for my garage.

Checking into Rumely's history, I found that Bill had purchased her from Mott's Hardware in Flint. Before that, she had reportedly run a sawmill in Sebawaing from her early years into the 1940's.

I could believe she had done mostly belt work, because her gears and drawbar were in excellent shape. Rumely had probably supplied the power that produced thousands of board feet of Michigan lumber—no wonder she felt depressed just sitting out in the middle of a field!

I really wanted to get Rumely into my workshop so I could begin working on her. That meant taking off her cab so she would go through the 7-foot door. I tried to get a handle on the entire job ahead—one that, as it turned out, would consume every spare moment of the winter of 1993-94.

Once I got her indoors, Rumely underwent a complete, down-to-the-frame disassembly. I removed her 3,000-pound engine from her frame with my front-end loader. I completely overhauled her engine, sometimes actually having to make tools to do a specific job.

She had a Secor-Higgins carburetor, which was very unusual, and could burn gas, water and fuel oil and kerosene mixes. I took the cylinders and pistons out to

HIS GAL RUMELY. Tom Hoose spent an entire winter restoring this Rumely OilPull 20/40 G, which he early on determined was a "she". Tom says the long hours spent on the restoration were worth it, and he now enjoys exhibiting Rumely at tractor shows, where she draws hundreds of admiring glances.

New York to be oversized, staying at Niagara Falls on the way home with my treasures. I had to remove and replace one of those pistons seven times to keep sanding it down, as it fit too tightly at first.

Perhaps the biggest job was scrubbing and cleaning all of her many parts. Dad and I steam-cleaned them and soaked them in acid and kerosene until they were immaculate and ready to spray-paint.

Taking her wheels off was another big job—and I do mean big! Each of the rear wheels weighs 1,200 pounds. If I had tipped either of them over, I'd have had a real problem getting it back upright. I took them to Davison on my trailer to be sandblasted.

The radiator had 27 sections to be cleaned, bathed and washed. We made new gaskets for them and then reassembled the whole unit.

The steering gears had to be rebuilt at Mason Kingman Engineering. I replaced the bearings and transmission and had steel rolled for new gas and water tanks. I fabricated the new fenders myself, using the original type of rivets that had to be hammered on. I tried to keep everything as original as possible.

When everything was repaired or replaced, I spent many hours painting her with coat after coat of the authentic Rumely dark green…with bright red wheels, of course. I then had a professional "detail man" pinstripe her in yellow.

I also made a new canvas top by spraying several coats of flat black paint on canvas. Finally, new decals were applied, and my 13,000-pound baby was ready to roll!

Maiden Voyage

It was a big day when we took her out for her maiden voyage up the driveway. We had to belt-start her with the big John Deere 80 diesel because with her new rings, I expected her to be hard to start at first. After a few tries, Rumely belched a few rings of smoke—in a very ladylike fashion, of course—and rumbled into action.

We made a few minor adjustments, then drove her proudly up and down the driveway at top speed—3-1/2 mph.

Rumely's cooling system contains 19 gallons of oil instead of water. Maybe that's why she's called an OilPull. At 450 rpm's, she can develop 20 horsepower on the drawbar and 40 horsepower on the belt. Rumelys can be used for threshing, plowing and other farm work. Mine has pulled an eight-bottom plow at a show.

I've now taken Rumely to lots of shows, where she proudly accepts the admiring looks and pats from hundreds of folks. At a couple of shows, she put on a hammer mill demonstration and ground corn into cornmeal. At another, she pulled a dump truck and trailer—with its brakes on—to show her tremendous power.

As you can tell, I've become totally smitten with Rumely. I had to build a new building to accommodate her, one with a 12-foot door. In the winter, she stays cozy in there, with my little Case to keep her company. But she always seems a bit anxious to get back outside and go to some shows when summer rolls around.

The 5 months and hundreds of hours, the aching muscles and icy cold hands from working late at night all seem worthwhile when I climb into Rumely's cab and she happily responds to my loving touch. She's my gal!

Luck, Persistence Helped Him Reclaim Dad's 1949 'B'

By Charles Leitner, Troy, Illinois

IN THE LATE 1940's, my dad and I were custom-baling with a 1935 or '36 John Deere AR. It seemed I spent as much time on the road as I did baling. We also had a 1943 A, but that was our cultivating tractor.

In 1950, our neighbor traded in his 1-year-old John Deere B for a bigger tractor. That same day, Dad was at the dealership, and the next morning, I had that B for baling. I was in hog heaven, picking corn in low gear instead of shucking by hand.

In 1952, I went to Korea. While I was there, Dad had a sale. Everything I'd dreamed of was gone.

In the early 1980's, I started looking for the B. Luckily, my sister had kept all the sale records, so she was able to find the buyer's name. I learned he was in a nursing home and went to visit him there. I showed him a picture taken of the B right before I went to Korea, but I didn't have the nerve to tell him I wanted it back.

Months later, the man died. After some time passed, I called his daughter to ask about buying the tractor. I kept calling for 3 years. Her answer was always the same: "Yes, but…" Finally she told me she was selling the farm—and the tractor was going with it.

Good luck struck again. A friend of mine bowled with the man who'd purchased the farm, and he told him I wanted the

CORRODED MESS. Charles Leitner's father sold this 1949 John Deere B while Charles was serving in Korea. When Charles finally saw it again decades later, he found a corroded mess. Vandals had punctured the tires, spraying the tractor with calcium chloride. Restoration took 13 months.

tractor. The new owner invited me out to look at it.

I hadn't seen the tractor since 1952 and could hardly believe my eyes. The new owner explained that some neighborhood kids had punctured the tires about 4 years before, and the corrosive calcium chloride inside sprayed the whole tractor.

If I hadn't had sentimental reasons for wanting the B, it would've stayed there. But I hauled it home and started dismantling the rusty mess.

I boiled 5 gallons of bolts and every piece in caustic soda. (This requires great caution, including protective clothing and eyewear.) Light sandblasting took off all the paint pigment. Then each piece was painted and the tractor reassembled. Thirteen months later, I had a new B again.

About that time, my son Mike suggested we take the B to EXPO-1, a tractor show in Iowa. I didn't think the B was old enough or good enough, but we went anyway. That was in 1987. We've since taken the B to three more EXPO shows, and now it's on tractor cards.

All this work was done for my own satisfaction, but it sure made me feel good when I got a call from a young man in Texas. He'd seen the B in *Tractors and Equipment* and wanted to know about the paint. It's John Deere paint, right off the dealer's shelf, with 3812S DuPont reducer.

ONE STUCK ENGINE! "I found this 1923 Fordson F in a barn, where it had sat for over 40 years," relates Gerald Golding of St. Petersburg, Florida. "All the parts were there, but the engine was sure stuck! It took me 5 weeks of soaking in NAPA Rust-Buster to free it up, then another 8 months of sanding and scraping before I could start painting."

AND THEN HE SAID…

"I run dozers that move 35 yards of dirt in one pass, but I have more fun turning over 24 inches of dirt with my 1929 McCormick-Deering 10/20 tractor and an old plow."
—*Bill Ackerman Mundelein, Illinois*

'It's Taken 47 Years to Look This Good!'

By Steve Gallick, Streator, Illinois

FOR A NUMBER of years, my grandpa, Robert "Ray" Negray, had been looking for a Farmall H or M. He had a small farm and always figured a Farmall would fit right into his operation.

Then in 1976—the year that I was born—a neighbor and his wife asked Grandpa to build a little shed on their farm. Naturally, he obliged. When he finished the project, he refused any payment because the neighbors were good friends.

However, the neighbors knew that Grandpa really wanted a Farmall. They had a 1948 H that had been retired after many years of hard work. It wasn't very pretty to look at anymore, but they decided to give it to Grandpa as a gift.

Well, Grandpa was overjoyed! He drove the tractor home and immediately put some Freeman lift arms on it for hauling big pieces of firewood. Then he had a snapshot taken of him behind the wheel (at left).

Some of my earliest memories are of Grandpa and his H. During the 15 years after he got the H, Grandpa used it to work the soil in his cornfields and to mow grass and split firewood.

As the years went by, the old H spent more and more time out in the weather, sometimes needing a jump start to get going on cold winter mornings.

Its "work attire" of faded red paint was peeling away and turning to rust. Then Grandpa and I started attending the annual Threshermen's Reunion near Pontiac, Illinois. All the tractors there had bright coats of paint gleaming in the sunshine...and I began to wonder whether Grandpa and I couldn't get his old H to look like that, too.

I asked Grandpa if we could restore the H because it had become an eyesore. What better way to repay it for all its faithful service than to make it look and run like new?

Finally in 1995, restoration began, 19 years after the H arrived on Grandpa's farm and I arrived in this world.

First we washed the H with a friend's high-pressure washer, removing the first layer of dirt, rust and old paint. Then we sandblasted it, getting rid of the more stubborn layer of grime that had been caked and baked on over 47 years of working in muddy fields and under a broiling sun.

Over the Fourth of July weekend, Grandpa, Dad and I painted the H. The weather was superb, and when we finished, we let it dry for a month. Then I buffed all the sheet metal—especially the rough spots—and applied the decals.

When I stepped back to look at the H, I could hardly believe my eyes. No longer just a rusty hunk of Old Iron, it looked even prettier than I'd imagined it would.

And the only thing that glowed more than the bright red tractor was Grandpa—he was beaming with pride. All our tinkering had really paid off!

Grandpa no longer farms, but he and I still use the H for chores like mowing several acres of grass around the house. We're more careful now, of course...there's no way anyone's going to put a scratch on the old H.

After all, it's taken 47 years to get the tractor to look this good!

WORK ATTIRE. "That's Grandpa on his Farmall H back in 1976 (below)...and me on the H just last year (bottom), after it had been fitted out in new work attire," quips Steve Gallick.

Moline Project Let Him Forge Special Bond with Grandfather

By Thomas Bickel
Parker, Pennsylvania

IN THE SUMMER of 1986, at age 18, I started restoring a Farmall C my great-grandfather had owned. That got me hooked, and I couldn't wait to get to work on his Minneapolis-Moline Z.

I started disassembling the Moline in 1990. The more I tore into it, the more I realized it wasn't worth the money or the effort. I decided to use it for parts and began looking for an identical Z to restore. At the time, I didn't know Molines were few and far between.

I think my fiancee thought I was crazy, but she got used to hearing me

"talk tractors". I made a lot of friends and heard some great stories, but my search wasn't getting anywhere.

One day, a gentleman told me he'd driven a Z in our area. As he described the tractor, my eyes grew wide. He was talking about my tractor!

I finally found a 1953 Z in a small town nearby. It looked rough at first glance, but on closer inspection, its true colors shone through.

The owner had been uncomfortable with the tractor's large size and hadn't used it much. There was only surface rust—no holes—and the tires were the original set from the factory.

Bringing home the tractor sparked many conversations with my grandfather, who let me work on the Z in his garage. He enjoyed watching my progress and was of great assistance on many occasions.

The tractor was painted the original "Prairie Gold", but I added touches of my own, painting parts other colors. It

wasn't painted this way at the factory, but it helps highlight the tractor.

I restored the entire tractor before I ever heard it run. The motor was in pieces when I got it, and fortunately it didn't take much to put it back together. When I started it for the first time in February 1993, it was a big event—the moment we'd all been waiting for!

Unfortunately, Grandpa wasn't there to share it. He passed away before the project was completed. It almost seems as if the restoration isn't really done, just because he never saw it.

The Moline was featured in *Farm & Ranch Living* in 1994, and I was excited—but disappointed Grandpa wasn't able to share in my "fame". He had encouraged me to submit the photographs and would've been surprised at the response I received. It seemed as though everyone knew about my tractor!

I especially enjoyed talking with people who like old tractors. It's nice to see a spark in someone's eye as the conversation triggers memories.

I've never farmed or made a living on a tractor, but I like helping others remember their days on this equipment. Every farmer has a story. Sometimes it's nice to just listen.

FEW AND FAR BETWEEN. At first, Thomas Bickel just wanted to use his great-grandfather's old MM Z for parts and buy another Z to restore. He soon realized how few and far between Z's were, but he finally found one. That's it "before" at left and "after" below, with Tom.

NEW LEASE on life was given to 1950 Farmall C by Ray Horan, who enjoyed restoring the tractor used by his father and grandfather on the family farm. Ray exhibits the Farmall ("before" below and "after" left) at local tractor shows.

JUST LIKE GRAMPS USED TO DRIVE

By Ray Horan, Sycamore, Illinois

FOR MANY YEARS, my grandfather and father used a 1950 Farmall C on the family farm. In the late 1970's, they finally decided it was too much trouble to keep the old C running, so it was parked inside the barn and left there.

Its years of faithful service had seen most of the Farmall's paint weathered off or covered in old oil from gasket and seal leakage. Sitting idle in the barn for a decade and a half also left its engine frozen.

In 1992, I was asked if I wanted the Farmall. Since this was the tractor Gramps used to drive with me sitting on his knee, I said, "You bet!"

That summer, I disassembled the engine, unfroze the pistons and replaced the piston rings, rod bearings, oil seals, engine gaskets and much more. My goal was simply to get the old tractor running again

By the winter of '92, everything was back together and Gramps' tractor was running and sounding just like I remembered.

With the mechanical work finished, I now decided to complete the restoration by repainting the Farmall. I began in the spring of 1993, and by midsummer, the tractor was ready to "go out in public", so to speak.

I now exhibit it at our local Steam & Tractor Show. I'm mighty thankful I knew that everything on the tractor was completely original and that it was left resting inside a dry barn, just waiting to be brought back to life.

Tractor Talk

HENRY FORD EXPERIMENTS

The Ford Motor Co. was established in 1903. The company's first serious tractor experiments began in 1905 and were based on car designs. In fact, an early tractor experiment was dubbed the "automobile plow". In 1907, Ford had a lightweight machine that could pull a single-bottom plow.

Former Farm Boy Missed Music of 'Johnny Popper'

By Ronald Baertsch, Huber Heights, Ohio

I BARELY REMEMBER when Dad decided to give up farming with a team of aging horses and buy his first tractor. But I remember the tractor—a 1937 John Deere AR with the original steel wheels. As soon as I was big enough to climb onto the seat and shove the clutch lever ahead, I was driving the Deere for spring planting, fall harvesting and everything in between.

We used that tractor year-round, in every conceivable way. During our cold Wisconsin winters, when temperatures hovered around 30° below, the AR was often the only thing that would start. If you were strong enough to turn over the hand flywheel, it would start without fail. Then came the job of dragging the Ford pickup and car around the yard until they decided to start!

The last time I drove the Deere was at our farm auction in 1957. I didn't realize how much I missed the familiar sound of a "Johnny Popper" until many years later. I started attending threshing reunions and antique machinery shows and yearned for an old Deere to work on. It would be wonderful to hear the familiar sound of two cylinders at work whenever I wanted.

In July 1992, I bought a 1944 John Deere B, which reminded me of the one we borrowed from my uncle to cultivate corn. (The AR wasn't designed for that particular job.) After a lot of rebuilding, sanding, chipping and painting, it looked so good that I drove it in our local Fourth of July parade. Working on that tractor was the best stress reliever I'd found in years.

But what I really wanted was an AR. After a long search, I found a 1937 model near Duluth, Minnesota. I bought it sight unseen, except for a snapshot. The owner had it delivered to a small town in Indiana, where my son and I picked it up and hauled it home.

As I write this, there are tractor parts all over my garage. Some need repair, some are covered with rust and some are already a beautiful shade of John Deere green. I've had the AR running several times and hope to have it ready for the next Fourth of July parade. When that day comes, I'll have the "real Deere" I've wanted all these years.

FORMER GLORY. Ronald Baertsch is restoring this 1937 John Deere AR. A 1937 AR was the first tractor his family owned.

GATHERING RUST. Stan Davis of Live Oak, Florida restored this John Deere during the winter of 1994-95. "It was completely disassembled, then reassembled part by part from the ground up," Stan recalls. **"There's nothing special about it. I just enjoy working on Old Iron...and the satisfaction of getting one to run after years of gathering rust."**

PURRS LIKE A KITTEN. "I drove this 1925 McCormick-Deering 10/20 many times on my uncle's farm," says Curvin Study of Littlestown, Pennsylvania. Since having it restored, Curvin has driven it in two parades in his hometown. "It purrs like a kitten," he says. "I appreciate this old but reliable machine as an example of the high-quality equipment the United States produced in the early 20th century."

NOT MUCH MONEY. "This is what my husband's Allis-Chalmers WC-947 looked like before and after restoration," relates Cleona Van Camp of Jerome, Michigan. Reo Van Camp also has re-

stored three John Deeres. "Both of us were raised on farms," Cleona comments. "There was lots of hard work and not much money, but we didn't think anything of it," Cleona says. "Those were happy days."

Dad Was Proud to See His Favorite Tractor Live on

By Richard Vogt, Enid, Oklahoma

SMILING ALL the way, my father drove his brand-new Oliver 99 from the dealer in Hennessey, Oklahoma 30 miles to our farm. That was in November 1947. Dad was proud of that tractor for the rest of his life, even after he stopped using it. He often talked about how it had outpulled LA Cases and an International W-9 at a plowing party for a sick neighbor.

"Ollie" served Dad well right up until he retired from farming in 1979. But by then, the 99 was worth only scrap price. Dad couldn't bear the thought of it being scrapped, so he gave it to me to restore.

The 99 had been converted to propane around 1958, so I reconverted it to gasoline. The whole tractor was stripped down and sandblasted, the sheet metal repaired and the drawbar and battery box rebuilt. A valve job, new tires and steering wheel and a fresh coat of paint completed the restoration in 1986.

Dad was so proud of his old 99 that he told everyone it looked even better than when it was new. He seemed comforted by the fact that his favorite tractor would live on. When Dad passed away in 1993, I had a drawing of an Oliver 99 put on the memorial folder we handed out at his funeral. 🔧

BETTER THAN BEFORE. J.S. "Hap" Vogt bought this Oliver 99 in 1947 for $3,620, then happily drove it the 30 miles to his farm outside Enid, Oklahoma. Nearly 40 years later, when son Richard restored it, Hap boasted that it looked even better than when it was brand-new.

Prize-Winning Tractor Brought Dream Full Circle

HIS OWN TRACTOR. Peter Bucci drives his 1942 Ford Ferguson at the fair where he won a prize for the best restored tractor. He'd dreamed of having his own tractor since his youth, when he participated in 4-H tractor competitions.

By Peter Bucci, Amston, Connecticut

OUR FAMILY of nine converted from horses to tractors in the early 1950's, buying a 1942 Ford Ferguson 2N that had been repainted red and gray. My dream was to live with that tractor, make it my 4-H project and win the tractor award.

Our 4-H team did hours of garden and farm chores together and went on to compete in town, state and regional tractor-driving contests. We won every contest but the last one. In that event, we were required to belt up and operate a piece of equipment—something we'd never had to do in any other competition. We hurriedly lined up, threw on the belt, backed up and raised our hands as a sign that we'd finished.

Then the official said, "Throw it in gear." Uh-oh. We did—and the belts flew off. It took us several attempts to do it properly, and that cost us the contest. We lost by 5 points. The winner got a brand-new 1955 Ford tractor.

When I came home, I had a new goal—to someday own a tractor myself. I spent 37 years working for a jet engine manufacturer, but I never forgot about my dream.

After retiring in 1993, I bought a tired 1942 Ford Ferguson for $1,200. My friend Butch Tubbs and many tractor people helped me completely rebuild this baby, also painted Ford red and gray. We entered her in a fair and won the trophy and prizes for the best restored tractor.

CRUSHING CORN. This John Deere D has been in Buck Mays Jr.'s family since it was bought new, for $900, in 1928. Buck, of Marshall, Arkansas, recalls using the "poppin' John" to pull a large hammer mill all over the county to crush ear corn for other farmers. The two-cylinder tractor was restored after being damaged in a fire.

MIGHTY FOND OF FORDS!

By Donald Artman, Monee, Illinois

IN THE LATE 1940's, my dad farmed with a Ford 8N. It was a very handy tractor to have around, and we used it for everything. The 8N was the first tractor my three brothers and I ever drove.

I guess that's why I've always been partial to Ford and Fordson tractors, and I now have 15 of them. Although as a young man I left farming to go into construction, I started collecting tractors in 1973, when my wife, Myrna, and I purchased a small acreage.

The first tractor I bought was—you guessed it—a Ford 8N. Since then, I've acquired two more 8N's, both of which I've restored and will one day give to my 4-year-old twin grandsons. I also have a 1953 NAA Ford Golden Jubilee that I restored for their 8-year-old brother.

One of the 8N's was recently displayed at the Old-New Agricultural Equipment Show held at a shopping mall near our home. Myrna and I are members of the Ford-Fordson Club, and we've exhibited our tractors at various shows throughout the Midwest, including the Old Thresher's Show in Mt. Pleasant, Iowa.

CHRISTMAS GIFT. Ramona Lehar and her family restored this 1937 Farmall F-12 for her dad, Loren Gorman, as a Christmas gift in 1994. "We found the tractor in a fencerow in October," says Ramona, of Granby, Missouri. "With some help from our tractor club, we had it done by Christmas. We put in some long nights, but it sure was worth it to see the joy on Dad's face." Ramona restored her own 1935 F-12 in 1992; now she and her dad compete with each other in pulling contests. Pictured with Loren is grandson Ty Austin.

LABOR OF LOVE. Donald Artman and wife Myrna recently displayed one of his restored 8N's at an agricultural equipment show held at a shopping mall near their Illinois home.

HIS FAVORITES. Thomas Page has been collecting and restoring tractors since 1971, but these 1937 Eagles remain his favorites. "I bought the 6B at a farm sale in 1978," says Thomas, of Galva, Illinois. "It was in sad shape, but I worked on it for a year. Now it looks and runs real nice. I bought the 6A in 1985." Thomas also owns the first tractor he ever drove, a 1936 Case CC on steel.

Tractor Talk

HENRY AND HARRY SHAKE HANDS

Late in 1938, Henry Ford and Harry Ferguson made their famous "handshake agreement" whereby Ford was permitted to incorporate Ferguson's hydraulic hitch system on the Ford 9N, introduced in 1939. The patented system forced other manufacturers to develop their own versions, such as Fast Hitch, Eagle Hitch, Snap Coupler and others.

Teen's F-12 Restored in Time for Town's Bicentennial

By Susan Yaddow, Guilford, New York

THE FARMALL F-12 was introduced in 1932, finally making it possible for small farmers to consider replacing their horses and mules. The inexpensive four-cylinder tractor had low operating costs, and it used only 1 gallon of gas per hour, enabling a farmer to plow 4 to 6 acres a day.

A dull and dingy F-12 entered our lives when my husband, Larry, bought it from a neighbor and rebuilt the engine. Our son, Michael, has always

GIFT FROM DAD. Michael Yaddow, 16, restored his 1937 Farmall F-12 with help from his father and a family friend. Michael received the F-12 as a gift from his father when he was about 6. That's Michael on the restored tractor…and working with Dad to remove lugs.

been fascinated by tractors and machinery, so Larry gave the F-12 to him. Michael was about 6 at the time.

In 1995, as our town made plans for its bicentennial, Michael and Larry decided to restore the tractor and display it during the celebration.

A friend offered the use of his sandblasting and painting equipment. Michael, now 16, removed the steel lugs from the iron wheels so he could drive the tractor on the road, then started the slow trip from our rural home to our friend's shop in town. The bicentennial was only 2 weeks away.

The manifold, seat and gas tank were removed, and the sandblasting began. When that was completed, the painting started. What a change!

The tractor that emerged was what the original owner must have seen when he bought it in 1937. The first F-12's were gray, but the factory started painting them red in 1937—and what a gorgeous, shiny red it was!

The night before the bicentennial, Larry and Michael added the finishing touches, applied decals and made last-minute tune-ups.

The day of the celebration, heads turned when this proud young man drove his tractor around town. And no one could've been prouder than his dad and me.

Now Michael and Larry plan to work on one of the other tractors we've acquired over the years. Maybe it'll be a Fordson or a Farmall Regular. Whatever they decide, I'm sure that seeing another piece of our agricultural history restored will be just as exciting as the day that beautiful F-12 was driven down the streets of Guilford.

A GREAT GIFT. John Ridenhour of Gold Hill, North Carolina says this 1940 Farmall A is "the greatest gift I've ever received". His grandparents bought it for him in 1992, and his grandfather helped him restore it. He's competed in several tractor pulls and takes it to shows around his home state.

MOSTLY STOCK. "My tractor may be little, but it is an antique," writes Charles George of Orlando, Florida. "It's a 1968 Wheel Horse, and it's basically all stock except for the exhaust and rear tires." Charles competes in antique-tractor pulls in Ashton, Florida in the 1,000- and 1,500-pound classes.

Farmall Becomes Part of the Family

By Carol Dauner, Sawyer, Kansas

OUR OLD John Deere had served us well, but when wheat sold for $1.49 a bushel in 1945, Dad decided he could afford a new tractor. He found a sleek new Farmall H and had it fitted with wheel weights for better traction.

Dad used the Deere, and my younger brother, Casey, drove the new tractor. The Farmall was much faster, and when they worked the same field, Dad would scold Casey for turning the corners too short. "Johnny Pop" took a wide turn, and Dad just couldn't get used to the H's superior mobility.

When Dad was in a good mood, he'd let Casey take the H to the pasture to round up the milk cows. Of course, Casey had a good time driving around the pasture before he settled down to the task at hand.

Dad's turn came that fall, when Casey was in school. Drilling wheat was faster and easier with the H, and Dad took full advantage of his opportunity.

When my parents retired in 1973, the H was moved to our place. As we acquired larger, more powerful International tractors, the Case H was reduced to pulling the drag to grade the driveway and other small jobs. Eventually it sat forlornly next to the shed, its paint dimming and its engine deteriorating.

Our son Darin tried to repair it in 1982, but it was more than he could manage. We all wanted to fix it up but didn't know where to go. When a mechanic friend offered to restore it, we gladly agreed.

My husband, Jim, is part owner of the Ranchers Cafe in Sawyer, where the farmers gather every morning before daybreak. One morning in December 1988, they watched Jim proudly drive up on the Farmall, which had a big Christmas bow on its radiator.

Our Farmall will never again be abandoned to the mercies of time and the weather. It's a valued member of the family, just as it was when it first came home in 1945. 🚜

ALWAYS HELPS OTHERS. Robert Diffin restored this 1941 John Deere D in 1991. Sandy Walker of Durand, Michigan says her dad is so selfless that this project is one of the few things he's done just for himself. "When we had a big snowstorm in 1967, Dad tried to drive a tractor down a gravel road to get insulin for a neighbor who couldn't get to his house," she says proudly. "That's the kind of person he is. He'll always go out of his way to help someone else."

POPULAR PLACE. Carol and Jim Dauner pose with family members outside the Ranchers Cafe, where Jim first displayed their newly restored Farmall H. Jim is part owner of the cafe, a popular gathering spot for area farmers.

His Fiancee Knows 'Allis' Will Always Be Her Rival

NUMEROUS PIECES. When John Molette convinced a farmer to sell him this 1942 Allis-Chalmers B, the tractor was in numerous pieces. John spent an entire summer restoring it.

By John Molette
Byron Center, Michigan

WHEN I WAS 8 years old, we moved from the city to the country. It seemed like heaven, with all that room and fresh air.

Dad soon realized he needed a tractor for mowing and plowing—and probably to satisfy the boy in him. When his brand-new Ford was delivered, my brother and I thought it was the greatest thing we'd ever seen.

A few years ago, I decided I wanted my own tractor and started looking for the right one. After months, I found her—a 1942 Allis-Chalmers with a PTO output shaft and a belt pulley. It was as if she'd been waiting for me.

The owner told me he'd bought the tractor brand-new, used it for years and then retired it to the barn. He had just pulled it out of the barn, debating whether to sell it, when I came along. I finally convinced him to sell it to me.

"Allis" was in many parts and pieces when I got her, and I spent the whole summer restoring her. I knew it would be worth it. By the end of the summer, she was beautiful.

My fiancee and I are building a house and will be getting married soon. She's accepted the fact that "Allis" will always be her rival, but we believe the three of us can live happily ever after.

CHERISHED EVERY HOUR. Ray D. Robertson and son Ray R. marked this 1941 Farmall M's 50th birthday by restoring it in their farm shop in Madison, Nebraska. The elder Ray bought the Farmall the year before his son was born, and young Ray grew up learning to drive it. "It was hard to tell who was most proud—the father driving his restored tractor, or his son, who cherished every hour spent with his dad," says Ray R.'s wife.

Tractor Talk

"STOVE TOP" NOT ONLY IN THE KITCHEN

In the early days, tractors had to be started on gasoline and, once operating temperature was reached, switched over to kerosene, sometimes known as "stove top". In 1935, kerosene sold for about 6¢ a gallon, making the cost of operating a tractor very economical.

Proud to Help Dad with Restoration Work

By Stephen Tencza
New Milford, Connecticut

MY FATHER restored a John Deere B a few years ago. It was his grandfather's and he says it will always be in the family. When we bring it to shows, it attracts a lot of people.

When my father was restoring the B, a friend gave him a John Deere pedal tractor that was in bad shape, and my dad restored that. We show it next to the B, and the kids love it.

We also have a 1935 Farmall F-12 on iron wheels and a McCormick-Deering Standard W-6.

Both were rusted and in bad shape, but Dad restored them both. The F-12 had no hood and had sat outside for years. It looked like junk. Now they both look like brand-new tractors.

I was small when Dad restored the B, but now I'm 10 years old and am looking forward to helping restore the other tractors we have.

MORE HELPFUL. Stephen Tencza sits on the John Deere pedal tractor his father displayed alongside his Model B at a show in 1992. "I was small when Dad restored the B, but now I can help him restore the other tractors," Stephen proudly reports.

LOOKS WONDERFUL. "My father-in-law owned this B.F. Avery in the 1940's, and my husband decided to take it all apart and restore it," writes Jane Bujanowski of Baltimore, Maryland. Alarmed by all the parts littering the shed, she asked if he'd be able to put the tractor back together. It took 2 years, but he did. "It looks wonderful," Jane enthuses. "His dad would be so proud if he could see it now."

Tractor and Plow Display Reminds Him of Old Days

By Aubrey Dodson, Amelia, Virginia

WHEN GRANDFATHER deeded 80 acres to my parents in 1931, they cleared land for a home with axes, mules and dynamite. Dad bought an old Fordson tractor and an Oliver double-disk plow to work the land.

After I retired, my wife and I built a house of our own on the old home place. I started thinking about getting another Fordson and restoring the Oliver plow as a reminder of the old days.

In February 1994, a cousin found an old Fordson in the woods. A tree had grown near one of the wheels and had to be cut down before the tractor could be moved. As another cousin helped me haul it home, I imagined Dad saying, "Boy, what are you doing with that piece of junk?"

I took off all the parts I could, used quart after quart of rust treatment, found a picture in a tractor book and started to work.

The fuel tank had a piece of wood stuck where the cap should have been. I thought we might have an old cap in the toolshed, but I couldn't find one. I went back to scraping and painting.

But a voice seemed to be saying, "Go back again." I went back to the shed, pulled out an old bucket of nuts and bolts, and there on top was a cap with "Fordson" on it. It fit perfectly. Dad was helping me now.

The wooden steering wheel was gone, replaced by a rubber-coated one from a car. Dry rot had ruined the rubber. I took the base to a welding shop, had a steel rod made to fit and welded it to the steering spokes.

My brother-in-law found a toolbox from Dad's original Fordson. We also found a magneto that was used to fire the engine when the crank was turned. The tractor would be used only for display, so I didn't restore the engine.

When the Fordson was finished, I took the plow apart and cleaned, scraped and painted it. Now both pieces of equipment sit in front of our house, overlooking the fields my father once worked with another Fordson and that same Oliver plow. 🖝

FOUND ABANDONED. Aubrey Dodson restored this vintage Fordson after a cousin found it abandoned in the woods. Behind the tractor is an Oliver plow once used by Aubrey's father.

His Friends Had to Finish Restoring Bill's Super 'A'

By Jovita Swyers, St. James, Missouri

WHEN MY husband, Bill, was about 12, his family bought its first tractor. From then on, Bill was hooked on tractors. He not only loved driving the family tractor…he also wanted to know how it worked. When it wasn't being used around the farm, Bill tinkered with it. If something was broken, he'd fix it…if it wasn't, he'd take the tractor apart anyway.

He also liked hearing tractors run. Eventually he got so he often could tell what was wrong with a tractor just by listening to it.

When he graduated from school, Bill got a job as a lineman for the city of St. James and also repaired the utility's vehicles. At night or on weekends, he worked on farmers' tractors. For years, Bill had a dream—he wanted to own and restore a Farmall Super A. He not only liked Internationals…he figured a Super A was small enough to keep here at the house.

The problem was finding one. He asked all his friends—other linemen, electricians, farmers, the folks he had coffee with at the St. James Bakery—if they knew where he could get a Super A.

Finally he heard from a man in Salem, Missouri who had one for sale. Bill went to look at it…and came home with his tractor. It was pretty banged up and leaking oil.

Bill decided to start his restoration by replacing the brakes on the rear wheels. When he pulled one wheel off, he found a

JOB WELL DONE. Bill Swyers never saw his white Farmall completely restored—but his friends made sure the job was finished.

big surprise—the tractor had originally been painted white, not the typical red.

When he asked his friends whether they'd ever heard of a white Farmall, one—John Williams—gave Bill a copy of *Red Power* magazine. In it was an article explaining that IH had produced a limited number of white Farmalls as demonstrators that farmers could use in their fields while deciding whether to buy one. That really excited Bill—it meant he had an unusual tractor!

Then a terrible tragedy occurred. While he was at work, Bill was involved in an accident and was killed.

He had finished overhauling the engine on his little white tractor and was beginning to put the A back together again when he died. Bill's friends knew all about the tractor—he had kept them posted on his progress.

His friends created a memorial fund to complete the tractor. John and Doug Williams got the Super A running so smoothly that Bill would have loved the sound of it. Then Doug applied several coats of white paint to make the tractor a true demonstrator.

I keep the tractor at the house, just as Bill would have, and from time to time, I take it to shows.

The Super A is a demonstrator all right—it not only demonstrates one man's love for tractors, but the dedication of his friends who completed a project he wasn't able to. ☛

MANY MEMORIES. It took Harold Jensen of Penn Yan, New York about 6 months to restore this 1920 Samson, daughter Nancy Morse says. When he bought it in 1976, it had no fenders, so he borrowed some from another collector and used them as a pattern to make his own. "Dad has many memories of his father using a Samson around the farm in the '20's," Nancy says. "Today Samsons are a rarity at the gas engine shows Dad trucks it to."

Taking Different Route Led Him To Dad's Tractor

By Clifford Harrison, Salem, Oregon

FOR 10 YEARS, I looked for my dad's old tractor every time I went back home to Magrath, Alberta. Dad had bought the Massey-Harris 22 in 1950, when I was 14, and sold it in the early 1960's. I'd left home by then and didn't know where the tractor went. No one else in the family knew, either.

On a trip to Magrath in July 1994, my wife and I decided to take a different route. As we drove along, I saw some old tractors in a farmer's field. One of them looked like Dad's.

I stopped and checked further. It *was* Dad's. I talked the farmer into selling it, and we made another trip to Magrath to bring it home. I spent a year restoring it.

Since then, I've bought three Massey-Harris Pony tractors, one more 22 and an old Oliver tractor. I plan to restore all of them, but none will be as special as that first one that belonged to Dad.

IN A FARMER'S FIELD. The black-and-white photo shows Cliff Harrison, his dad, two brothers and the family's Massey-Harris 22 when it was 3 years old in 1953. The two color photos show the 22 as Cliff found it in a farmer's field in 1994, and after Cliff restored it.

Oliver 66 Does Double Duty

By Robert White, Columbus, Ohio

A FEW YEARS AGO, I bought a 1949 Oliver 66 Row Crop that my wife and I restored. We learned that this tractor was one of the first made after the strike in 1949.

Over the past year, I exhibited the 66 at 13 antique steam engine and tractor shows in Ohio. At the Dover show, I belted a saw to the tractor pulley to cut wood for the steam engines.

The saw has a 30-inch blade on a mandril that I redesigned. The original design required wood to be lifted up to the blade.

My design uses ball bearings to move the table into the

OLIVER 66 ROW CROP restored by Robert White and his wife is used to plow and to saw wood.

saw and stainless steel pulleys attached to the rear of the table with cast-iron window weights to return the table to the starting position. This design eliminates the labor required to lift and push the table into the saw.

I also use the tractor/mandril assembly to cut wood for our two wood-burning stoves. I just set the tractor on low and it powers that saw through any wood!

The "Oliver Gang" held its 1995 Farm Days at the Roger, Althea and Keith Blue Farm, where 25 of us used our Oliver tractors to plow 80 acres.

In addition to the Oliver 66, I have a 1936 Farmall F-20, a 1937 Allis Chalmers WC, a 1954 AC WD and a 1954 Farmall Cub with mower. I'm planning to restore and exhibit all of these at shows across Ohio!

AN EXCITING MOMENT. "I learned to drive a tractor when I was 6, and I restored one when I was 12," relates Jeremy Johnson, Portland, Oregon. "The tractor I restored is a 1949 Case SC that I bought in August 1989. I wanted this tractor because I've always liked Case equipment. I've been on the farm since I was born. My great-grandfather had two tractors that are still in the family...that kindled my interest in tractors. An exciting moment occurred on my SC in 1990 at the Great Oregon Steamup in Brooks, just after I finished restoring the tractor. I got my picture taken sitting on the SC with Helen Case Brigham, great-granddaughter of J.I. Case!"

Chapter Eight

Build Your Own

Exactly what is a tractor? Folks who designed and built their own may have stretched the definition.

Backyard-Built Tractor a Godsend in Time of Need

By Robert Graham
West Davenport, New York

MY COUSIN, Cy Davis, was an engineer at General Electric in Schenectady, New York. In 1943, he "manufactured" a doodlebug in his backyard as a gift for my father.

The engine and chassis came from a wrecked 1931 Nash with 11,000 miles on it. Its transmission was left intact. The front axle came from a Studebaker and was reshaped and installed upside down.

The drive line was cut, leaving only room for a universal joint and another 2- or 3-inch section of drive line, which was attached to a Brockway truck rear end. The complete rear axle was used, including the 10.00 x 20 tires. When both the Nash and truck transmissions were engaged in reverse, the doodlebug would move forward at full throttle—about 1 mph.

Two milk cans filled with concrete were mounted at the rear for traction. With tire chains, the doodlebug would pull almost anything. It easily pulled a two-bottom plow, a corn harvester and a two-section spring-toothed harrow.

To make it even more useful, we modified several implements to use with it. Those included a dump rake, a mowing machine, a side-delivery rake and several wagons.

We used our "tractor" extensively for 5 years with no major repairs. I have no idea what it cost Cy to make, but for a family receiving it in a time of dire need, it was worth millions.

Tractor Talk

LONGEST PRODUCTION RUN

The 1923 John Deere D was the longest production run of a tractor. The D was made for 3 decades and 162,000 of them were sold.

Its two-cylinder engine was adapted from the Waterloo Boy rated at 22/30 hp and would pull a three-bottom plow. The decision to use the two-cylinder engine was one of pure economics, even though the competition was producing tractors with four cylinders.

The two-cylinder engine offered less maintenance and better fuel economy, plus they already had it. It proved to be a good decision. Thirty years is a long run—even for a Deere!

TEST DRIVE. Robert Graham, eager to take the family's doodlebug for a test drive, hopped into the driver's seat the day it was delivered in 1943. A cousin manufactured the tractor as a gift for Robert's father.

GRANDPA WAS BORN TO TINKER

By Scott Woethrich, Francesville, Indiana

MY GRANDFATHER, Earl Rockwell, always loved to tinker, and because he was born and raised a farmer, many of his inventions were aimed at making things easier for farmers.

One of his most successful creations was a tractor he named "The Beatall", as in the slang expression "Well, if that don't beat all!" He built this tractor in his machine shop back in 1957 by combining two tractor rear ends with a 471 GM diesel engine, capable of 105 horsepower.

The result was a four-wheel-drive tractor that was steered hydraulically and hinged in the middle for turning. Grandpa used this tractor in his own farming operation for quite a few years, then sold it to another farmer, John Simousek of North Judson, in 1971.

Grandpa still has the letter John sent him 2 years later in which he stated that The Beatall was the best tractor he'd ever owned, and that he'd yet to have a single breakdown with it. "That's more than you can say about most of the new tractors nowadays!" John added.

Bought "Beatall" Back

In 1991—20 years after he sold The Beatall to John—Grandpa and I bought it back. I'm now its proud owner, and Grandpa and I spent quite a bit of time restoring it to like-new condition. It still runs great!

Besides The Beatall, Grandpa also created another tractor he named "The Hybrid". This one was a two-wheel-drive rig with a 371 GM engine and a wide front end taken from a truck. It's still in our area also, and we've been trying to buy it back for another restoration project.

Yet another of Grandpa's homemade articulated tractors was "The Worm", which is still being used by its owners. Grandpa also modified an old Rambler station wagon into a camping trailer, and he helped a couple of other area farmers, Elmer Swing and Elwin Gunnerson, develop a portable conveyor, mounted on a truck chassis, to facilitate loading and unloading grain bins.

Grandpa is now 89 years old, and he still loves to tinker. And as you can probably guess, I enjoy giving him a hand with his projects!

CREATIVE GENIUS. Earl Rockwell has come up with a number of inventions to make life a little easier for farmers around Francesville, Indiana, including the "homemade" tractors shown here. The Beatall, the blue tractor featuring a red beetle logo (seen clearly at left—that's Earl at the controls), was created from two tractor rear ends and a 471 GM diesel engine. The Worm, an articulated tractor sporting a cab, still sees daily use by its Indiana owners. The Hybrid (black-and-white photo) utilizes a front end taken from a truck.

Unusual Tractors Deserve Their Place in History

By Beth Applegate, Sutherlin, Oregon

WHEN MY BROTHER, Dick Harwood, moved to his farm near Devon, Montana in the late 1960's, he found he had a problem. He either needed more machines and hired hands than he could afford, or more hours of daylight to do all the work himself.

The solution to his problem, he reasoned, was bigger, faster, more fuel-efficient equipment that would allow him to cover more ground in a day and use less fuel. Dick says the tractors then on the market did not fill these needs.

What was he to do? Well, Dick is quite a mechanic...he decided that if he couldn't buy such tractors, he would make 'em himself.

After thinking it through and doing some research, he hooked two John Deere 80's together end-to-end, with the nose of one on the drawbar of the other. He then removed both sets of front wheels and axles, and hooked the tractors together with a heavy tubular-iron hitch that could swivel and pivot.

Unneeded Parts Removed

Using the rear tractor's power-steering hydraulics, Dick rigged up a cylinder to ram-steer or "jackknife" the two units. All unneeded parts were removed from both tractors, and the throttle, gauges, gear shift and clutch were modified so they could be used from the rear, or "pusher", tractor.

Dick also made a weatherproof cab for the rear tractor. He then greatly strengthened the hitch on the rear unit so it could pull the weight of much larger equipment.

The elongated monster Dick had created now had 140 horsepower and could pull 36 feet of chisel plow, with twisted chisels for stubble mulching. It could also pull 36 feet of seeding drills and plows together as one unit.

Covered Lots of Ground

Now Dick had what he needed—power to pull big equipment fast across lots of ground. In a day, he could cover 150 acres on 40 gallons of diesel fuel. He figured that eliminated the need for two additional tractors, the hired men to run them and the fuel they would consume!

The savings helped Dick, his wife, Jenny, and their three kids through some mighty lean years.

Other farmers heard about Dick's strange tractor and asked him to build one for them. Over the next few years, he built 48 of them and sold them to farmers as far away as North Dakota and parts of Canada.

On his own elongated tractor, Dick removed some of the water from the tires and a few of the wheel weights to reduce soil compaction. He explained that the tractor was now more maneuverable and had more leverage because of the weight in front.

TANDEM TRACTOR. This is one of Dick Harwood's homemade tractors. Beth Applegate thinks her brother's tractors deserve a place in farming history.

Dick made elongated tractors for only a few years, working on them in his spare time during the winter. Then the major tractor companies began selling four-wheel-drive articulated tractors that more or less did what Dick's tractors did.

Dick is now 75. His unique tractors helped a number of farmers get the job done when nothing else could. For that, I think Dick and his elongated tractors deserve a place in farming history.

Tractor Talk

DIESEL EXPERIMENTS

In 1893, Rudolph Diesel of Germany published a paper that described his high-compression engine. He produced the first engine in 1895, and 2 years later, the famous brewer, Adolphus Busch from St. Louis, went to Munich to see Diesel.

After thoroughly examining the engine with scholars and engineers, Busch paid Diesel a $1 million licensing fee to produce the engine in the U.S. beginning in 1898.

Family's Home-Built Tractor Seldom Let Them Down

By John Millsapps, Boulder, Colorado

VERY SLOWLY. Clarence and Keith Millsapps' father built this "mostly Model T" tractor in the 1940's to use on their Colorado farm. Their brother John often drove this rig very, very slowly pulling a walk-behind plow. "Note the hard rubber tires and chains for traction," John points out.

IN THE 1940's, we used a home-built tractor to work our acreage near Denver, Colorado. Dad built it from different parts he had around the place, including a Model T truck frame, worm-drive differential and a touring car cowl.

The one "non-T" component was a three-speed Chevrolet transmission mounted behind the three-pedal planetary transmission. This combination gave the tractor six forward speeds, or seven if we put both transmissions in reverse. Then the tractor went forward at an even slower pace than with the low-low combination.

I learned to drive this rig in the late 1940's. For the most part, my "driving" consisted of holding down the clutch pedal in low gear and keeping the wheels in the furrow while one of my brothers handled the walk-behind plow.

It was a tough way to plow a field, but it was the best way we had at the time. Although conventional tractors were available, money wasn't, so we made do. Our tractor seldom let us down. 🔧

Old Photos Spark Memories

By Winifred Chesborough
Truth or Consequences, New Mexico

MY HUSBAND, Lawrence, farmed 160 acres of land in Otter Tail County, Minnesota when he was 16 years old. (His father had died when Lawrence was still quite young.) The first time a tractor was used in his fields was in 1937, and it was a rather unique machine.

A neighbor had converted an Oakland car into a tractor and welded two walking plows to its rear end. Lawrence paid the man a dollar an acre to plow the fields, and he could plow about an acre per hour, compared to about a half acre per hour with horses.

The first tractor Lawrence bought was a used 1937 McCormick-Deering F-12 with lugs, and it cost $699. He built a board-and-canvas cab on the tractor to help protect him from the elements.

I snapped a picture of him and our small son, David, just before Lawrence left for the field one morning (above left). In the photo, he's wearing boots, gloves, a heavy cap and a sheepskin overcoat—early spring in Minnesota can be bitterly cold! 🔧

LOOKING BACK. Winifred Chesborough shared these photos of early tractors. The steel-lugged 1937 McCormick-Deering features a homemade board-and-canvas cab made by her husband, Lawrence, shown with their son, David. A neighbor converted an Oakland car into the tractor shown at left; he equipped it for fieldwork by welding two walking plows to its rear end.

50 Years After Selling Do-All, Onetime Farmer Bought It Back

By James Keenan, Omaha, Nebraska

I STARTED farming in eastern South Dakota in 1933, during the drought and Depression. That first year, I used horses borrowed from my father and brother-in-law. I bought a few pieces of horse-driven machinery and borrowed the rest from neighbors and friends.

Like most young farmers, I thought I should have a tractor and started looking for a cheap used one. I found a 1928 Rumely Do-All convertible with a mounted cultivator in Sioux Falls. The asking price seemed in order, and the dealer was willing to sell it to me on credit, with a small down payment and a promise to pay it off from my 1934 harvest.

The dealer had a good reason to make the financial arrangements I needed, but I didn't know it at the time. I later found out my tractor was manufactured only from 1928 to 1931, then discontinued when Rumely became part of Allis-Chalmers.

I had bought an orphan, with no local service dealer and no chance there would ever be one. But the Rumely was in good condition and served me well for the next 2 years.

I truly loved driving the Rumely. As a "convertible", it could be used in either three-wheel or four-wheel form. The four-wheel form was for jobs like plowing, disking, harrowing and mowing.

The three-wheel form was for using a rear-mounted cultivator. The front wheels were removed, and the Do-All used one single caster wheel in the rear. I could cultivate about 20 acres in a 10-hour day.

It was a pleasure to drive the Do-All in three-wheel form when cultivating. When I came to a row end, I could un-lock the rear tail wheel, step on the brake for the wheel in the direction I wanted to turn and get right back on the next two rows. I still enjoy demonstrating the tractor's quick turning ability at antique tractor shows and parades.

After 3 years of farming, I decided to quit and do something else. I sold the Do-All to a neighbor for $400 in July 1936, moved out of state and forgot about it for years.

Many years later, when visiting relatives back home, I met a younger relative of the man who'd bought the Do-All. When I asked about it, he told me it had been abandoned in a grove of trees on their farm. I wanted to buy it back, but it wasn't for sale. The present owner intended to restore it himself when he retired.

I offered to buy it many times after that. Each time, I was told it still wasn't for sale. But it hadn't been restored, either.

I finally suggested to the owner that neither of us were getting any younger. If one of us didn't restore it, it might be lost forever. He finally agreed to sell it back to me for $800.

Fifty years to the month after I'd sold the Rumely, I had it back home again. It hadn't turned a wheel for 44 years and was in pretty bad shape. After a year of hard labor and making parts, I had it restored and ready to display and demonstrate at antique tractor shows.

Rumely made about 3,194 Do-Alls. There were two models, with four distinct styles—convertible in three-wheel form with rear cultivator; convertible in four-wheel form; tricycle with front-mounted cultivator; and the standard, non-cultivator type.

Since 1986, I've acquired and restored all four types, and I displayed them together at various shows in 1995. These tractors are quite rare. Few, if any, Midwest collectors have or show all four of the different Do-Alls.

I enjoyed driving and farming with that 1928 Do-All when I was 24 years old, and I enjoy driving it as much today at age 84.

SAME POSE. Jim Keenan is shown sitting on his 1928 Rumely Do-All—except that more than 50 years elapsed between photos. The black-and-white was taken on a farm near Flandreau, South Dakota in 1934...the color at Jim's home in Nebraska in 1987.

One-of-a-Kind MM Tractor Was 'Lost' For Decades

By Mrs. Dale Casteel
Cambridge, Illinois

OUR Minneapolis-Moline IT Experimental isn't just unusual—it's the only one in existence.

MM collectors knew of this tractor through pictures from the company's archives in Minnesota but feared it had been scrapped long ago. A family near Prophetstown, Illinois had used the tractor on their farm in the early 1940's while testing MM plows. After they finished with it, the little tractor was lost for a long time.

A couple of years ago, the *Henry County Advertiser* ran an ad for an MM tractor for sale—nothing more. My husband and our son went to check it out. Lo and behold, sitting there in a pasture was the long-lost IT Experimental. The hood had been painted black, which probably saved it from the elements.

Dale bought the tractor then and there. He brought it home, took it apart and began the extensive process of restoration. Now we have a very rare and beautiful little tractor. We've taken it to quite a few shows.

One former MM block man believes he saw this tractor in 1935 at the company's main plant in Hopkins, Minnesota. The unusual hood styling would make it unforgettable.

COMPLETELY UNEXPECTED. When Dale Casteel responded to an advertisement for an MM tractor, he never dreamed he'd find the long-lost IT Experimental. MM collectors had feared for years that the tractor had been reduced to scrap.

CIRCUS CAT. The Ringling Brothers, Barnum & Bailey Circus once used this 1955 Caterpillar D4 to pull equipment at Madison Square Garden in New York City. In the early 1970's, a farmer in Pitcher, New York bought it and added a Dakotah blade attachment. Current owner Mark Tanis bought the "circus Cat" from his neighbor in 1992 and restored it. Another neighbor, Walt Grewe, is at the wheel. "The circus Cat has just over 3,000 hours on its meter and runs great," Mark reports.

'Gertie' Came to Life Not Once, But Twice

By Paul Workman, Chillicothe, Ohio

IT ALL STARTED in 1940 in Ora Workman's machine shop in Pricetown, Ohio. His son Russell walked into the shop one day and saw his dad working over two large channel iron beams lying parallel on the floor.

"What are you doing now?" Russell asked. "Well, son, I've decided to build one more tractor," Ora replied. "Ol' Gertie" had begun to take form.

Ora was my grandfather...Russell my dad. Together they had designed and built several tractors for farmers in the area, each a little different. Several were built with parts from Model A Fords, one had front-wheel-drive, one had a chain drive and so on. But Ol' Gertie would be the granddaddy (or grandmama) of them all.

To form the chassis, they salvaged components from an assortment of junked vehicles and adapted them to the channel beam frame. A 1928 REO Speedwagon truck provided a heavy-duty differential, rear axles, brake assembly, radiator and steering gear. The front axle and wheels came from a 1930 Pontiac automobile. Rear wheels were formed by welding together two large spoked steel wheels with the center cut out.

Handcrafted Hood

The drive train featured a 1930 Pontiac flat-head V-8 engine and two transmissions (one three-speed, one four-speed), for a total of 12 forward speeds. Fenders from an old Reliable tractor covered the rear wheels. The hood was handcrafted from sheet metal. A seat was formed from wood planks, iron and a spring cushion from a Model A Ford.

One feature truly set Ol' Gertie apart from other tractors of the time—a hydraulic lift on the front. Made from a hydraulic pump and cylinder from an old dump truck, it was used primarily to operate a buck rake.

The project took about 3 months from conception to completion. Grandpa and Dad found many of the parts at a salvage yard in nearby Hillsboro, and they named the tractor in honor of the lady who'd handled many of their transactions.

After a few test drives, it became clear the Pontiac engine and the two transmissions weren't a good combination. Grandpa and Dad replaced them with a six-cylinder engine and four-speed transmission from a 1930 Dodge Imperial 80 truck.

Gertie's steel wheels were replaced with large rubber-rimmed tires around 1943. For the next 10 years, she did most of the fieldwork, but eventually more modern tractors took over. For 40 years, Gertie sat idle, slowly deteriorating and sinking into the earth.

Put Doubts Aside

In April 1994, Dad decided Ol' Gertie would live again. Several family members and neighbors gathered to carefully raise her and tow her home. About all that was still usable was the main frame, differential and front axle.

I'm sure some of us had doubts about the project, but we were all willing to help. We removed the dirt and loose rust, then reinforced the frame with an additional length of channel iron on each side. New rear wheels and tires came from an Allis-Chalmers Gleaner combine. A 1971 Ford 1-ton truck supplied a motor, four-speed transmission and radiator.

Other parts were gathered—a gas tank from a 1986 Dodge Colt automobile, rear fenders from an old Oliver tractor and steering gear from a 1955 International 2-ton truck. A new hood and dashboard were made from sheet metal, much as they had been 50 years before.

By October 1994, when Dad celebrated his 80th birthday, Ol' Gertie was ready for another test drive. The 360 V-8 engine fired, then roared, the transmission engaged and Gertie was backed out of the garage. She has great power and speed, and although many of the components are different, the "new" Gertie very much resembles the old one.

Four generations of the Workman family have now driven Ol' Gertie—a tribute to the mechanical talent and ability that has been passed down from father to son.

GUSSIED UP. "Before" photo at left shows Ol' Gertie at the start of her restoration. "After" photo below shows Ol' Gertie gussied up and ready to again take to the field. Her fancy grille (above) was taken from a truck. At right, Paul Workman's dad, Russell, is about to cut into a "Gertie birthday cake" on his 80th birthday, just after the restoration was finished.

He Ran into Trouble Driving Dad's 'Mongrel'

By Franklin Paddock
Rutland, Massachusetts

MY FATHER bought his first tractor from an inventive local mechanic around 1936.

The parts came from several different automobiles and small trucks. It had a six-cylinder Chevrolet engine, a Dodge rear end, an REO radiator and two transmissions hooked up in tandem. The steel seat came from an old horse-drawn hayrake.

My father was quick in teaching me how to drive this contraption—or, rather, how to steer it. At 8 years old, I wasn't tall enough to push the clutch in far enough to get it out of "drive".

Dad often let me drive the tractor from the field to the barn. He'd walk ahead of me and wait at the open barn door so he could throw in the clutch and take it out of gear. Then I'd jump down from the seat, and Dad would get on and drive the tractor into the barn.

One day on my approach to the barn,

ASSORTED PARTS. The first tractor Franklin Paddock's father owned was this "mongrel" pieced together by a Massachusetts mechanic. The parts came from several different cars and trucks, and the seat was taken from a horse-drawn hayrake. Franklin and his wife still live on part of the same property his dad bought in 1929.

I grabbed the hand throttle on the steering column and the tractor rapidly picked up speed. Dad lunged for the clutch, but the risk of getting pinned between the tractor and the door forced him to back off.

I managed to make it into the barn—and then drove straight through the closed double doors in the back! The tractor stopped when the rear wheels got caught on the 8-foot beam that supported much of the barn.

The tractor came to rest with one of the 12-foot doors sitting on the radiator and steering wheel. Fortunately, I'd tried to push in the clutch when I hit the door and had slid forward off the seat. When the door crashed down, my head was safely below the steering wheel.

Dad came running over to me, but before he could say anything, I quickly reassured him that I wasn't hurt. That was probably one of the scariest moments either of us ever had.

Our mongrel tractor wasn't damaged, but it took four men to lift the door back on its hinges.

STEAMED UP. "This 'tractor' made from a 1929 Model A was used on my grandparents' farm for about 10 years," writes Robert Lussier of Clifton Park, New York. The family used it to drag, disk, plow, pull a corn harvester and power a buzz saw. It also doubled as a doodlebug for trips to school. "As you can see from the steam in this 1948 photo, it was being worked," Robert observes.

Tractor Talk

A BIG SUCCESS

One of the first highly successful small tractors was the Bull produced by the Bull Tractor Co. of Minneapolis in 1913. The Bull was rated 5 horsepower at the drawbar and 12 horsepower at the belt. In just 7 months, the company sold 3,800 tractors for $335 each—all for cash.

MAKING THE GRADE. "Before the advent of tractors, my great-uncles came from Norway with their parents to live on a 200-acre farm near Butterfield, Minnesota," reports Mrs. G.M. Hardesty, Pasco, Washington. "One of them built a little tractor that was the first in the area. His name was Ole Kjobstad…that's him standing near the rear of his tractor, resting his hand on the roof (at right). In the second photo (below), Ole (on the right) and Great-Uncle Herman (left) stand next to Samson tractors for which they built the cabs. The third photo (bottom) also shows Ole—he's next to the grader. His brother Oliver stands beside the Rumely OilPull they used to grade roads and also run their threshing ring."

CHANGED HIS MIND. Don Brown had always been an Oliver man—until he spotted this Silver King at a sale in 1961. The tractor was manufactured for 20 years by the Fate Root Health Company, which also made locomotives.

Handsome Silver King Is One of the Family

By Betty Brown, Durand, Illinois

OUR SILVER KING is part of the family. All nine of our children have driven it, and now our grandchildren are learning on it, too. It gets lots of attention.

My husband, Don, has farmed all his life. For years, he and his father never used anything but Oliver equipment.

Then in 1961, Don went to a farm sale near Rockford, Illinois. He had no intention of buying a tractor—until he saw the King. A neighbor had owned a fast, sleek King when Don was a boy, but that was the only one he'd ever seen. I was quite surprised when he drove the King into our farmyard, honking the horn.

The Fate Root Health Company manufactured the Silver King in Plymouth, Ohio from 1934 to 1954. Ours has a road gear of 25 mph, a Continental engine and a PTO.

The tractor is very versatile, and we've used it for many jobs. Our son overhauled the engine in 1969, and in 1984, we decided to rejuvenate its looks, too.

We contacted the factory for information on the original paint color and were lucky enough to find authentic decals. Through the company, we also learned that the tractor had been manufactured in 1946.

We started taking the King to parades in 1994. It's won first place many times in the antique tractor division. We also attended a convention in Plymouth featuring over 100 Silver Kings from all over North America.

Old Gibson Due for Some Applause

By Pete Pedigo, Ringgold, Georgia

IN THE EARLY 1950's, Daddy bought an unusual tractor—a Gibson. I was 8 or 9 years old, and even though I could barely reach the brake or clutch pedals, I learned to drive on that tractor.

One of the most unusual things about the tractor was the way you steered it. It had a tall, straight lever sticking up higher than the gear shift that you pulled backward to turn right or pushed forward to turn left.

There was no cowling or sheet metal on the tractor, so you could see the engine, frame and most of the moving parts. The rear wheels had conventional tractor rubber with V treads, and the engine was a 6-horsepower air-cooled Wisconsin.

The tractor was started by winding a rope around a pulley in front of the engine. You stood just outside the right front wheel and gave the rope a big tug.

When I first started driving the tractor, Daddy always had to start it for me—I just wasn't big enough to give the rope the pull it needed. Once, Daddy forgot to take the three-speed transmission out of gear, and when he pulled the rope, the tractor took off across country, with him chasing it!

My wife and I still have that old Gibson. It's parked out in the barn, where it doesn't get the attention it deserves. I love anything mechanical and keep promising myself that one day soon, I'll give the Gibson some spit and polish and run it in a parade where it'll get some overdue applause!

THE THIRTIES PUT SOME COLOR IN THE FIELDS

During the 1930's, manufacturers were giving their tractors a make-over in order to make them more visible in the fields and more salable at the dealers.

International-Harvester changed their drab gray to bright red. Allis-Chalmers went from dark green to Persian orange. Case changed from bluish gray to Flambeau Red. Massey-Harris droped its steel gray for bright red and Minneapolis-Moline changed from gray to Prairie Gold.

Tractor Cultivator May Have Been First of Its Kind

By Robert Hawthorn, Castana, Iowa

IN 1916, I graduated from college as an agricultural engineer with big ideas. My father had passed away, leaving my older brother and me to operate our 250-acre farm. I wanted a tractor in the worst way, but I saw no point in owning one and still keeping all our horses for cultivating.

That fall, we saw a Bates Steel Mule tractor being demonstrated. The Bates was said to have cultivating capability, although no cultivator was available. This was 6 years before the appearance of the first general-purpose Farmall.

The Bates had a single-crawler tread centered under the rear, with two wheels in front for steering. The front wheels were wide enough to straddle two rows of corn, with 30 inches of clearance under the frame.

Less Soil Compaction

The tractor also had three control wheels on a concentric shaft, like the hour, minute and second hands on a clock. The big wheel was for steering, the middle one was the clutch and the smallest was the gear shift. It had three gears—two forward, one reverse—and no brakes.

The salesman said the crawler tread not only provided tremendous traction, but distributed the tractor's weight over a wide area, causing less soil compaction than a man walking. "I don't care what he says," one farmer said. "I'd lots rather have a man standing on my foot than that monster."

We were impressed, though, and bought the tractor for $895, convinced we could improvise a cultivator on our own.

That winter, we hitched a pivotal-axle, two-row horse cultivator to the drawbar. Two single-row cultivators were connected on each side, with a sliding track operated by a hand crank. This allowed the outside cultivators to be steered in and out to conform to irregular row widths. Four operators were required—one to drive the tractor, and one for each cultivator.

The neighbors thought we were off our rockers. Tractors just weren't used for cultivating. But when they inspected behind the rig, they admitted it did a better job than they could do with horses.

Set Shovels Deep

Any farmer with a heart was inclined to lift up shovels to lighten the load on his sweating team. We didn't feel sorry for a tractor, so we set the shovels deep. The steady speed kept dirt moving uniformly around the corn. The steering crank on the outside units and the steerable inside cultivator enabled the operators to stay centered for a precision job.

Today, it would seem preposterous to have four men on a four-row cultivator. But at 4 mph, with no stopping to rest the horses, we covered 40 acres per day—twice the output of four men with horses. Farm equipment historians tell us this is the earliest record of a four-row tractor cultivator.

In addition to tending 100 acres of corn, we used the Bates to pull a three-bottom plow, two 8-foot disks, a six-section pegtooth harrow, a grain binder, a 10-foot grain drill and a road grader.

After 3 years, the Bates was a wreck. Crawler pins broke frequently. The transmission, with plain bearings and no seals, was worn beyond repair. The engine was in fair condition, though.

We sold the tractor to a neighbor, who powered his sawmill with it for many years. It was finally sold for scrap during World War II. 🔧

"MY FOLKS drove this 1926 Dodge as a car for 8 years, then converted it to a tractor," recalls A.M. Hansen of Bismarck, North Dakota. "We used a Buick transmission behind the Dodge transmission, a Model T truck worm drive and Greyhound bus tires. In the picture, taken in 1936, that's me and my dog, 'Bruno', spreading grasshopper bait—a mixture of arsenic and bran. We also used the tractor for pulling the manure spreader, fixing fence, grading roads and running errands. It was very versatile and would travel at 1/2 mph, with both transmissions in low gear, to about 18 mph in high gear."

Tractor Talk

JOHN DEERE STYLED AND UNSTYLED

"Unstyled" to a John Deere enthusiast refers to most models manufactured prior to 1939.

"Styled" was the look that followed, which was inspired by the automobile industry. The "bolted-together look" was left behind, and hoods and grilles were given a more streamlined look.

Invention Kept Farmers Warm, Saved Factory Jobs

By Evelyn Habenicht, Bettendorf, Iowa

WHEN WORLD WAR II ended, the Fort Dodge Tent & Awning Company in Fort Dodge, Iowa faced many layoffs. They'd run three shifts a day making tents for the war effort, but now they'd have to return to a prewar schedule, making awnings, canvas tarps and far fewer tents. Dad had been a supervisor during the war, and Mom and many of her friends worked for him.

Meanwhile, Dad wanted to make something to keep my Uncle "Happy" warm when he drove his tractor on bitterly cold days. Uncle Happy's solution had been to place large pieces of cardboard alongside the motor so the heat would bounce back.

Dad figured canvas stretched on a tubular metal framework would do the job more efficiently. It also would cost much less than a cab, which most farmers couldn't afford.

After a lot of experimenting, reworking and adjustments, the prototype was ready. Dad's invention was named the "Heat-Houser". The Tent & Awning Co. had a new product to manufacture, people had jobs, the farmers were keeping warm and Dad had a patent pending. We were going to be rich!

The gravy train derailed when it was discovered that another man in the Midwest had come up with the same idea and was busily manufacturing the "Comfort-Heater". He, too, had a

A LITTLE PROTECTION. Art Halligan sits on a Farmall equipped with the Heat-Houser he invented to keep tractor operators warm on cold days. His daughter, Evelyn Habenicht, says the product's name was later stenciled on the side of the canvas.

patent pending. No one knew who had applied for the patent first, so both manufacturers agreed they would not reveal the application dates and would simply go on with business pretty much as before.

Unfortunately, that meant Dad's royalties stopped. But it was great while it lasted!

He Drove from New York to Nebraska to Buy a Rare 98

By Joseph Detrick, East Concord, New York

THERE WERE only 500 Massey-Ferguson 98's built, and I was searching for one. After placing want ads in several magazines, I got a response from a man in Holdredge, Nebraska. He had two 98's and sent photos of both.

As soon as I saw one of the photos, I knew I had to have that tractor. But it was 1,300 miles away. Oh, well. I had to have that tractor!

We made a deal over the phone, but I wasn't able to pick up the tractor until a year later. I rented a flatbed, and two friends and I drove to Nebraska to bring it home.

I restored the tractor in 1993 and now take it to local shows and parades. I also do some plowing with it, using a four-bottom trailer plow. The tractor is powered by a three-cylinder Detroit Diesel engine with about 89 horsepower.

This rare tractor was actually built by the Oliver Corporation, which sold them to Massey-Ferguson. That company then added its own grille and hood and painted the tractors in the Massey color scheme.

LONG HAUL. Joseph Detrick really "went the distance" to bring home this Massey-Ferguson 98. He and two friends drove 2,600 miles round-trip to pick up the tractor in Nebraska and haul it back to Joseph's home in New York.

Youngster Builds His Family a Tractor

By Donnie Morris, Simpson, Illinois

IN 1948, when I was 14 years old, I designed and built the first tractor my family had on our farm. Up till then, we'd used Grandfather's team of mules for all of our work.

My tractor had seven speeds forward and three in reverse. To accomplish this, I used two transmissions from Chevrolet cars. I also used the rear axle of a Plymouth so that the tractor would have hydraulic brakes.

The engine was a Briggs & Stratton that I ordered from Sears and that arrived by rail. The tractor had a front wheel from a wheelbarrow and could go from 1 to 30 mph.

We didn't have electricity on the farm when I built the tractor, so I had to do the cutting and drilling with hand tools. A local shop did a small amount of welding.

From the time I learned to read, I especially enjoyed *Popular Science* and *Popular Mechanics*…it was those magazines that really inspired my tractor project.

In 1951, I bought a 1936 Farmall F-12 that took over some of the work from my homemade tractor. I still have the F-12 and hope to one day restore it to its original condition.

WITHOUT ELECTRICITY on the farm, Donnie Morris, shown sitting on the tractor he built, had to do all the drilling and cutting by hand. But the homemade tractor became his family's first.

Papa's 'Thirty' Put a Twinkle in His Eye

By May Voris, Gustine, California

MY FATHER, James Salmina, came to California from Switzerland before the turn of the century to work as a butter maker for his Zio (Uncle) Piazzoni in the Carmel Valley.

After saving enough money, he started his own dairy, and in 1917, he and my mother packed up and moved to San Luis Obispo.

Papa purchased the first tractor in Los Osos Valley in the early 1920's. It was a rich gray color with the word "THIRTY" on each side of the radiator. Across the top of the radiator was the name "CATERPILLAR" in bright red letters.

The name Caterpillar came about in 1904, when the Holt Tractor Company of Stockton, California tested a steam-driven machine that moved on wooden tracks. A photographer was there to take numerous photos of the experiment, and he remarked that the machine moved just like a caterpillar.

Mr. Holt liked the name and began using it for his tractors. The Caterpillar Tractor Company was formed in 1925, when Holt merged with Best Tractor Company. Six years later, the now-familiar yellow paint was adopted.

Papa's Caterpillar Thirty had a galvanized, corrugated top with canvas curtains on each side. The curtains were to protect the engine from dust, as grit was especially hard on the engines in those days. Papa eventually got rid of the curtains, as the adobe soil turned out to be too heavy to stir up very much dusty grit.

He used the Thirty to run a stationary baler in the fields. The tractor was kept a distance from the baler to prevent the possibility of sparks near the hay. A long belt from the tractor ran the baler.

Papa used his old Thirty until the 1940's, when a larger tractor became necessary. The beloved Thirty went to a neighbor with a small farm at Baywood Park, where it received the same loving care that Papa had always given it.

I remember our family taking a Sunday drive while I was still a little girl to see if the old Thirty was okay. When we saw the tractor, the twinkle in Papa's eye and his little smile was proof to me that our Thirty had a good home.

Chapter Nine

Monster Collections

When it comes to collecting
old tractors, sometimes
the goal is to have both
quality and quantity.

'G Fever' Left Precious Legacy for Children

By Alice Doughty, Prescott, Wisconsin

THE Allis-Chalmers G isn't like every other tractor out there. My husband Bruce's love of G's started in Arkansaw, Wisconsin in 1949 or '50, when his father bought one.

One way the G is different is that its engine's in back, giving the operator a clear view of what's ahead of him. It also makes the tractor look like a big orange grasshopper.

Bruce was just 8 or 9 when he first became acquainted with the G. His dad used it for about 10 years, then sold it to a cousin. About that time, Bruce left home to join the Army. We were married in 1962, and 2 years later, we settled in the small town of Prescott, Wisconsin.

One day while visiting Arkansaw, Bruce found his dad's old G for sale and decided we needed it to plow our driveway. Besides, Bruce really wanted that tractor back in the family.

The G became Bruce's toy. He worked on it, took the kids for rides on it and—when necessary—plowed snow with it.

Could Spot One a Mile Off

We later moved to a place in the country, and I discovered Bruce had "G fever". Whenever he'd spot one in a field or yard—and he could spot them a mile off—he had to check to see if it was for sale.

If he saw an auction bill listing a G, he just had to go. Every time he left, I told him, "You'd better not come home with another tractor." That didn't deter him much.

First he had just one. Then there were two, and then four. He'd bring the tractors home, clean them up, tinker with the engines, restore them and polish them until they looked like new. Most times he'd pick up a few implements, too.

I had to pretend to be really upset (well, sometimes I really was) when he "accidentally" slipped and told me he'd acquired another Allis. With a twinkle in his eye, he'd tease me back to good humor and proceed to buy more orange spray paint.

Bruce would hang the parts on my clothesline for spray-painting. The neighbors never knew what was going to be on my lines. The kids bought Bruce what they called "corporate orange" paint for Christmas and his birthdays. He used a lot of it!

When he had five G's, he told me he had one for each of the kids and one for me. But, of course, we needed six, and he soon found it. For years, I thought that was it. Then one day, I was in the shed with him and counted seven. That didn't even include the original Allis, which was always kept in the garage. So we had a total of eight. Surprise, surprise!

You may wonder how a man could buy so many tractors without his wife knowing about it. Bruce would probably tell you it wasn't easy, sneaking those Allises past the house when I wasn't looking. He had a lot of help from our neighbor and his brother-in-law.

I once told our neighbor Bruce's greatest joy in life was his tractors. He laughed and said, "No, it was sneaking them past you!"

The original became a showpiece. Bruce and our oldest son, David, equipped it with hydraulics and attached a steel blade in the center that can be removed simply by pulling two pins. It also has the original wood blade in front, and dual wheels.

The other tractors are all equipped with different attachments—a hay mower, a corn planter, a cultivator, a disk plow, a moldboard plow. All these implements are the original equipment made for use with the G.

Displayed Along Highway

Twice a year, on Memorial Day and Labor Day weekends, Bruce polished his "toys" and displayed them in a row at the edge of our yard, right along U.S. Highway 10. He so enjoyed having people stop and ask, "What are they?" or "Are they for sale?" or "How come you have all the same kind?"

On May 6, 1994, Bruce was diagnosed with terminal cancer. He died 21 days later. As a tribute to him, we decided to display his tractors. The boys got them out of the shed, washed them and lined them up at the edge of the yard. In the background, the flag was flying at half-staff. It was Memorial Day weekend.

Each of Bruce's children now has one of his tractors. David has the original G his grandfather bought almost 50 years ago. Perhaps when David has children, he'll take them for rides on the G, just as his father did.

Our G's flood us with memories of a sweet, wonderful man who loved his family, his friends, his tractors and life. Bruce was as unique as the G's he collected. ☗

FINAL TRIBUTE. Bruce Doughty's family got his Allis-Chalmers G's out of the shed on the day of his funeral. Note the first one in his collection with its two blades and dual wheels.

121

'Total Wreck' Collection Began with Memorable Trip

By Mildred Long, Vernal, Utah

MY late husband, Denver, began collecting and restoring antique tractors in 1967, when friends told us about a Mc-Cormick-Deering 22/36 in Lava Hot Springs, Idaho.

We drove out there, found the owner and paid him $30 for the tractor. Then we came home and made preparations to come back and pick it up with our 1949 International logging truck. Denver's sister Sylvia and her family made the trip in their car, and our two younger children came along, too.

Along the freeway north of Salt Lake, the minimum speed was 45 mph, and our old truck could hardly go that fast. But we finally made it to Lava Hot Springs, got the tractor loaded and started back home.

Outside Montpelier, Idaho, the truck blew a head gasket. All we could do was set up camp off the road for the night. In the morning, we loaded everything we could into the car and drove home to get parts for the truck. It was a good thing Sylvia and her husband were along to provide transportation.

The next morning, we got up early and drove back to the truck. Fixing it was quite a chore for the guys, but they got it done and we returned home without further problems.

When we got the McCormick-Deering home, it didn't even run. Denver overhauled it completely, buying new parts, grinding valves and doing other work. His hobby had begun.

His next "find" was in Eddyville, Iowa, where we were visiting his Uncle Happy, who had a McCormick-Deering 10/20. Denver asked if he could buy it.

Uncle Happy replied, "By golly, if you'll come and get it, you can just have it." Little did he know he'd just given it away, for Denver would do exactly that.

One day in late October 1968, Denver and I set out in the old International with our camping gear. We spent the first night with Denver's sister Elise in Glenwood Springs, Colorado.

The second night, we camped at an abandoned farmhouse somewhere in Nebraska. We slept in the back of the truck with a tarp overhead, but we still got a little wet in the rain overnight.

The next day, in an Iowa town not far from Uncle Happy's, the head gaskets blew again. Denver found a friendly household, asked to use their phone and called Uncle Happy. He was lucky enough to find the part we needed and brought it to us.

With the truck fixed, we went on to Uncle Happy's, had a nice visit and got the 10/20 loaded. On the way home, another problem popped up—an oil leak. It was Sunday, and few garages were open. We finally found a mechanic who charged us $150 for the job, which delayed us for a long time and didn't do a nickel's worth of good.

We bought a can of Wynn's Stop Leak as a last resort and poured it in. With very little oil pressure, we worried at every turn in the road.

That night, we camped in a snowstorm outside Omaha, Nebraska. With the tractor loaded, there was hardly enough room for us in back, but the tarp kept some of the snow off us, and the sleeping bags kept us warm.

Our biggest worry was getting over two passes outside Denver, Colorado, but to our surprise, the leak stopped. We didn't have to keep pouring in oil. But we never did get the oil pressure to register properly again.

The night of November 2, 1968,

PARKING PORCH. Bill Lucabaugh has more than 100 tractors in his collection, including these two Allis-Chalmers, says Amy Benham, who lives nearby in Hampstead, Maryland. Amy reports, "When one of his grandsons asked why the tractors were on the porch, Grandma replied, 'Because he can't get them in the front door.'" Bill's collection includes 35 AC's, 26 Fordsons and assorted Farmalls, Massey-Harrises, Cases and John Deeres.

when Richard Nixon won his first term as President, we rolled into our driveway, once again victorious in our endeavor to collect an antique tractor.

Needless to say, we didn't take any more real long trips in that old International. Denver built a trailer and pulled it with a pickup to haul his treasures home. Each trip was a lot of fun, despite the trials and hardships.

Denver eventually acquired more than 50 antique tractors and other pieces of equipment—Cases, Fordsons, Allis-Chalmers, an Oliver, a 1913 Avery and a Power Horse among them. We got a Farmall F-30 from a junkyard and traded an antique icebox for a John Deere.

Our collection also includes a 1925 Model T Ford school bus, a McCormick-Deering binder, a homemade tractor, a horse-drawn grader, and a 1926 dump truck that was once used at Yellowstone Park.

For 6 years, we displayed everything at an event we called the "Total Wreck Antique Machinery Show". We didn't restore everything—some things were used for parts, and others we just got running. To us, that was restoring. We couldn't afford to get everything "like new" again.

Our Model T bus and an antique one-horse baler are now on loan to a museum, but we still have everything else on the farm. I just wish I had a building big enough to store it all! 🗝

Tractor Talk

PARTS MISSING?

In 1937, Minneapolis-Moline introduced its Model R with 154 fewer engine parts than conventional engines. This innovative design not only made the engine easier to maintain but also caused better combustion, resulting in greater fuel efficiency and more horsepower. No one ever complained about the "missing parts".

Family's First Deere Got Farm Boy Hooked

By Wayne Smithback
Stoughton, Wisconsin

MY PARENTS farmed with horses near Utica, Wisconsin until 1939, when Dad bought a John Deere H, a two-bottom 12-inch plow and a two-row cultivator for $675.

I was 10 years old and drove the Deere for the first time while coming home from haying in our marsh. It was so much fun that I drove the whole way in low gear—and that was very slow!

After that, I started cultivating corn from daylight to dusk. I was enjoying myself so much I didn't even stop for dinner—I just kept on driving. I also did custom cultivating for $1.25 an acre.

Now that I'm retired, I still enjoy the thrill of driving the two-cylinder John Deeres. I have a collection of 22 of them, all restored. 🗝

A BIG FAN. Wayne Smithback has been a fan of two-cylinder John Deeres ever since his father bought one in 1939. Wayne now owns 22 restored Deeres, including this H shown "before" and "after".

Dad's Old KT Was The Start of His Collection

By Pete O'Brien, New Effington, South Dakota

IT WAS the fall of 1949, and Dad was 63 years old. "This was my last year of threshing," he announced as he drove his 1930 KT tractor into the far corner of the pasture and parked it beside the old Case threshing machine, thinking this would be the KT's final resting place.

From time to time, Dad's friends would come by needing a part from the old KT, and Dad would always help them out. Fenders, head, block, gas tank and radiator were all eventually taken. All that remained were the wheels, rear end and bottom block.

After I retired from farming in 1990, I occasionally talked

A CHALLENGE. This is all that was left of his dad's old KT tractor when Pete O'Brien decided to restore it. With a lot of hard work and parts salvaged from another tractor, Pete completed the job.

about restoring one of my tractors. A friend suggested I restore the old KT, so one day, I pulled it into my shop.

Upon closer examination, the same friend said, "You'll never get that old wreck running!" I took that as a challenge, and I started watching the magazines and checking out posters for upcoming tractor auctions.

Finally, in August 1992, I located an auction at Napoleon, North Dakota with a 1934 KTA listed for sale. I was sure most of the parts would fit my KT, so I attended the auction, bought the KTA and hauled it home.

The engine was stuck on the KTA, and the head and the gas tank were missing. The morning after I got the tractor home, I wanted to find out how tight the engine was stuck, so I took a chance and jumped on the crank.

To my surprise, the engine came loose. I got a gallon can of gas and hooked it up to the carburetor, turned the engine over about 20 times and got it started. I decided it ran too well to "junk out".

The KTA's previous owner had told me he had another one sitting out in a pasture near Braddock, North Dakota. He said it was complete but only good for parts. The next week, I went back and picked up this second KTA, and it provided me with enough parts to completely restore the first KTA and Dad's old KT.

These two tractors now appear each year at the threshing bees at Rosholt, South Dakota and Dalton, Minnesota. In addition, the KT now runs my 28-inch Minneapolis-Moline threshing machine.

Besides these, I have also restored 13 Minneapolis-Molines and several Cases, Internationals and Massey-Harrises. When Dad parked his KT out in our pasture, neither he nor I could have dreamed where it would eventually wind up, or that it would be the start of a wonderful pastime for me!

Collecting Couple Is Always Looking for 'Just One More'

By Evelyn Alpers, Stover, Missouri

WHEN WE bought our first Massey-Harris Pony back in 1958, my husband, Robert, and I never dreamed it would be the start of a collection of small tractors. Today we own 25!

Robert does all the restoration, and he straightens the metal hoods and fenders to get the tractors ready for painting. (He doesn't paint them himself, because he's too particular.) Over the years, he's figured out ways to make some parts and has found places to buy those he can't make himself.

A few years ago, old tractors were more plentiful, and we sometimes spotted them behind barns or in fields as we traveled. Now there are many more collectors, and old small tractors are difficult to find.

We usually check out ads or auctions, looking for "just one more tractor". Of course, we were looking for "just one more" with the last 15 to 20 we purchased! As Robert says, "If you quit wishing, you might as well not be living." So we keep looking.

We've acquired tractors in Missouri, Kansas, Ohio and Iowa. Our current collection consists of nine Massey-Harris Pony tractors (model years 1947-50), four John Deere LA's (1941-44), three Avery V's (1946-47), three Allis-Chalmers G's (1948-50), a 1939 John Deere H, a 1950 John Deere M, a 1943 Case VAI, a 1950's Allis-Chalmers B, a 1950's Allis-Chalmers C and a 1947 Farmall Cub.

One benefit of collecting tractors is that Robert and I spend more time together. When people ask how we like retirement, our answer is, "If we'd known it would be this enjoyable, we would've tried it a long time ago."

We especially enjoy displaying our tractors at farm shows and parades throughout the Midwest. Sometimes people ask if the tractors are new. They can hardly believe the tractors look so good and run so smoothly after 40 to 50 years.

Collecting tractors—and meeting so many nice people in the process—renews our confidence in people, helps us realize what a great country the United States is and allows us to reminisce about the past.

If you're ever in central Missouri, look us up. We're always glad to hear about other collections, and we'd be glad to share ours with you.

FAVORITE TRACTOR. This gleaming lineup shows seven of Robert and Evelyn Alpers' nine Massey-Harris Pony tractors. The Pony is their favorite model, but their collection also includes 16 other small tractors.

He Never Lost His Enthusiasm for John Deeres

By Tom Coppess, Elwood, Indiana

MY SONS and I have a collection of 36 antique John Deeres, six of which were once used by relatives to farm. One of those—a 1938 A that I bought from my oldest brother, Clem—has been in the family for about half a century.

My experience with John Deeres began in 1938, when I was 5. That year, Dad traded a Fordson with a front axle that allowed you to move the wheels in or out, for a brand-new John Deere B. When the dealer delivered the tractor in a stock truck, I thought, "Boy, what a beautiful machine!"

One day that spring, we used the new B to make furrows so we could plant potatoes. It got dark before we covered the potatoes up, and Dad—who had a job in town—said that I'd have to do the job the next morning, using the B to pull the drag.

The only problem was, I wasn't big enough to start the tractor. I got Mom to help me and showed her what to do. She pointed the gas lever down, then turned the flywheel. Once the engine started, I had her point the fuel lever backward so the engine could switch over to kerosene.

I felt like I was king of the world—not only did I get to drive the tractor; I had to show Mom how to start it. After that, I never lost my enthusiasm for John Deeres.

I did have one incident that you might think would cool my enthusiasm a little, but it didn't. Recently I was backing my 1926 D out of the old semi trailer that I'd taken the wheels off to use as a garage.

When the rear wheels hit the ground about 8 inches below the bed of the trailer, the seat on the tractor broke off and I went tumbling. I wasn't hurt…and the tractor didn't run over me!

What may have saved my life was the fact that I was using the clutch lever as a brake. When I fell off, I pulled harder on the lever and it turned down past center. When the top end of the lever touched the platform, the pulley-brake locked on, stopping the tractor.

The seat was a pan on a leaf-spring. When I looked at it later, the metal did not seem to have been rusted or previously damaged. Even today, I cringe when I think what might have happened

126

'Dad Said It Was a Tractor, But It Sure Didn't Look Like One to Me'

By Charlotte Garrett Springer
Snyder, Texas

BECAUSE my parents, Bill and Geneva Garrett, had been busy farming all their lives, they'd never had time for a hobby. Then one day in 1985, my father suddenly decided to take us all to a tractor show.

I was 18, and the only tractor I knew anything about was the one I plowed with—a fancy John Deere with a cab and air-conditioning. Going to a show to look at old tractors that didn't even have cabs seemed kind of pointless…and a little boring.

The next thing I knew, my father was dragging home old piles of junk. He explained that each pile was a vintage tractor. The first one was a John Deere A…but it didn't look much like a tractor to me!

What it did look like was one of those heaps of rust you sometimes see in the corner of a field as you whiz by on the highway. After many long hours that turned into weeks and months, Dad restored that A…and opened my eyes!

His A was a beauty—it looked brand-new and ran really well, and I'd never seen him so excited. Today I am very proud of him…he not only introduced our family to new hobbies and interests—he's helping preserve some of this country's farming history!

It's been more than 10 years since we went to that first tractor show. Now the whole family enjoys going to shows…and we each have our own hobbies.

Dad is, of course, still collecting and restoring tractors. At last count, he had 17 in mint condition, including a 1917 Holt Caterpillar. He also has old engines, an oat press and many other antique farm implements.

Not to be outdone, Mother has a collection of old wooden washing machines that she fixes up and displays. My younger sister, Cynthia, has restored two old wagons and now has an all-original covered wagon.

With some help from Dad, I have restored a Fairbanks-Morse Z engine.

Most of all, I've come to realize how important it is to hold on to our past …and collecting and restoring old farm equipment is one of the best ways to do that!

MANY DEERES. Above are seven of the 36 tractors in the collection belonging to Tom Coppess and his sons. From left to right, they are a 1936 BR, 1938 B, 1936 A, 1938 A, 1938 G, 1937 D and a 1926 D. That's Tom at far left driving a 1951 John Deere A that belonged to his dad, and at left with his 1926 John Deere D after the pan seat broke off.

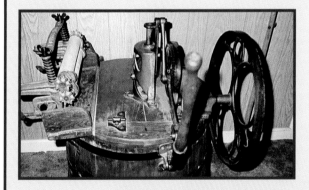

if the seat had broken while I was backing down a ramp out of a trailer at a show!

We keep all the tractors in our collection as original as possible, but I've since put a seat from a later model D on my 1926 D.

The B that Dad bought new back in 1938 was used for about 10 years, then sold. Despite its small size, the B pulled a PTO-operated combine with a 42-inch cut…a hay baler for custom baling…a plow, a disk and other implements.

Now I have a B just like it in our collection. I also have a 1941 B and a 1951 A that Dad owned…a 1938 G and a 1950 G that my brother Gene farmed with…and a 1951 G that my wife's uncle, Tom Fagan, used.

I think Dad would really be proud of the condition his old tractors are in…and he'd enjoy our whole collection as much as my sons and I do.

CAUGHT THE BUG. This John Deere resting under a tree was one of the first "old piles of junk" brought home by Charlotte Springer's dad, Bill…but it hooked him on collecting Old Iron. It also got Charlotte's mom, Geneva, interested in collecting and restoring old wooden washing machines like the one above.

Love Those MM's!

By Phillip Myers, Marion, Indiana

GOTTA HAVE 'EM! That's the way Phillip Myers, at right with his 1957 MM 335, feels about Minneapolis-Moline tractors. His collection includes everything from a huge G900 to a child's pedal tractor.

THE FIRST TRACTOR I remember driving was a Massey-Harris four-wheel-drive. It was 1936, and I was 10 years old. My father let me drive the Massey to rake hay, and I've been a "tractor nut" ever since.

Our next tractor was a Farmall A, which we kept until after I returned home from the service in 1945. My folks were farming 80 acres and decided we needed a bigger tractor, so they purchased a Minneapolis-Moline R.

That was the beginning of my love affair with Minneapolis-Moline tractors. Coincidentally, during the same year we acquired the R, I met and fell in love with my wife-to-be, Marilyn.

I farmed my folks' place for 7 years with the R, then traded it for two MM ZA's. We also acquired additional equipment, including a combine, corn picker and baler. If it was made by Minneapolis-Moline, I thought we had to have it!

We continued farming until 1965, and during this time, Marilyn and I raised three sons and a daughter. Then I went to work as a heavy equipment operator for a local company. I cash-rented our farm and traded off most of my MM equipment.

I did keep one of my precious MM's, however—a 1962 Jet Star. And by 1986, I missed those Minneapolis-Moline tractors so much that I started a new collection. My first purchase was a 1968 G900.

In 1988, I retired, and Marilyn and I decided that I should keep myself busy collecting and restoring more MM's. My collection now includes an R, ZA and U from 1950; a 335 and 445 from 1957; a 1954 UB; a 108 Garden Tractor from 1963; and a 1950 pedal tractor.

Marilyn and I have been married for 47 years, and we're proud members of the Prairie Gold Rush Club. I like to point out to folks that my two great loves have the initials "MM"—my wife, Marilyn Myers, and Minneapolis-Moline tractors!

SEEDS PLANTED. "Over a period of several years, some of my friends would drop by to suggest that I fix up an old tractor and enter it in a pull," reports Earl Reynolds of Bayside, California. "I resisted—why fix up a tractor, then risk damaging it in a pull? Then I heard about a 1952 Case LA that wasn't much more than a pile of junk. I guess the seeds my friends had planted had taken hold. I went and got the LA, restored it, entered pulls...and won! Now I really had the bug...I decided to collect and restore every model Case made between 1940 and 1954. So far, I have seven. I can see this project is going to keep me busy for a long time!"

DRIVING MULES LED TO COLLECTING TRACTORS

By Gordon Grice, Guymon, Oklahoma

PAPA raised mules and kept a mammoth jack named "Jumbo". I grew up farming with mules, which I regarded as punishment because all of our neighbors had tractors.

Finally, in the early 1930's, Papa bought a worn-out 1929 John Deere D. I was overjoyed, but there was something wrong with the tractor that caused it to frequently die. Since neither Papa nor I had any previous experience with tractors, we couldn't figure out the problem.

Whenever the tractor died, I would crank it and crank it to get it restarted—sometimes it seemed like I cranked it more miles than I actually drove it!

A mechanic friend of ours, Amos Enslinger, eventually figured out that the screws holding the spark lever to the magneto were loose, and this was what caused the D to die so frequently.

Once we tightened up the screws, the situation improved considerably...except that this was during the Dirty Thirties, and I frequently got the tractor stuck in piles of "blow sand". The D's steel-lugged wheels were absolutely helpless in blow sand.

When rubber tires came out about 1934, a neighbor told me that they would take a tractor right over blow sand. I remember telling him that I would have to see it to believe it!

Ironically, about 4 years ago, I found an old John Deere D half-buried in a blow sand pile near home, and I bought it to restore. I now have about 40 tractors, the oldest of which is a 1923 McCormick-Deering 10/20.

My collection also includes the 1926 John Deere D, an International Harvester Farmall 560, an Oliver 90 and several Twin City FT's and FTA's—I have a lot of Minneapolis-Molines, in fact.

Our antique tractor club here in the Oklahoma panhandle is called the No Man's Land Antique Power Club. When we sponsor tractor pulls, we frequently attract entries from Texas and Kansas, as well as quite a few locals.

I often trail nine of my Twin City tractors together and pull them in parades. Three days before Christmas one year, I pulled them from my home to Elkhart, Kansas for the town's John Deere Day celebration.

The distance is about 45 miles, and it only took me 6 hours to cover it one way!

QUITE A CARAVAN! Gordon Grice frequently trails nine of his Twin City tractors, several of which can be seen here, in tandem for parades. His collection also includes a 1926 John Deere D he found buried in sand.

Chapter Ten

Feats and Bragging Rights

There are many ways to get into
the pantheon of tractors—
win a pull…plow through
snowdrifts…save a life.

What Started with Disappointment Ended with Pulling Tractors Out

By LeRoy Lambert
Sharon Springs, New York

MY DAD started farming with International Harvester and McCormick-Deering equipment in the 1930's. He also had a milk truck route from the mid-'20's till 1950.

If it wasn't for his two hired hands and the McCormick-Deering 10/20, he never could have kept both the milk route and the farm going. Then in 1941, Dad decided to get a Farmall M.

The war was under way and tractors were scarce, but he made a deal with a dealer to buy the M. When he went in to pick it up, he discovered that the dealer had sold it to another farmer for $500 more.

Because he was so angry, Dad went over to an Allis-Chalmers dealer. That dealer said he wasn't going to get any new tractors in for the foreseeable future, but he had an Allis WC that he could "power up" and add new tires to so it would meet Dad's needs.

Well, Dad took the deal...and thus began a long love affair between our family and Allis-Chalmers. Dad used the WC until 1948, when the dealer replaced it with a new WD. The WD and the McCormick-Deering were the only tractors on the place till 1953.

That's when Dad got a Farmall C, the tractor I learned to drive on. We kept the 10/20 but retired it, using the C in its place. For several years, I didn't drive the WD, and when I finally did, I didn't like it.

They say familiarity breeds contempt. That wasn't true with me and the WD ...the more I drove it, the more I liked it. Eventually I became as big a fan as Dad.

In 1961, Dad bought a second WD at an auction. It wasn't in very good shape, but with a little work, it ended up being another great tractor. About four years later, my older brother was driving it and threw a rod after tripping the governor.

The dealer said he couldn't repair the WD, but he did have a WD-45 he could put a bigger engine in. So Dad bought our fourth Allis-Chalmers, with 56 horsepower instead of the 42 it was supposed to have.

In 1970, shortly after I got married, I decided that with even more horsepower, I could spend less time in the field and more time with my family. So Dad went back to the Allis-Chalmers dealer and looked at a 190 XT.

He couldn't make up his mind whether to buy it, and a few days later, the dealer brought the tractor out to the farm for us to try. It was right in the middle of a huge snowstorm, so Dad immediately put the XT in his garage.

Neighbor Needed Help

A couple hours later, a neighbor called—he'd gotten his tractor and manure spreader stuck in a deep snowdrift and needed help. I took our WD-45 down to pull him out...and immediately got stuck myself. I then borrowed my brother-in-law's Oliver 770...and got that stuck, too!

Next, I got the old McCormick-Deering 10/20 out of retirement. We'd kept it in running order, and I figured that with steel wheels and lugs, it might have enough traction to pull us out of the snowdrift.

You guessed it—I also got the 10/20 stuck! If it hadn't been so miserable out, it would have been funny seeing four tractors and a spreader all stuck in the snow.

Sooo...this time, I went to Dad's garage and got the 190 XT. You know what's coming next—the XT pulled each of the tractors and the spreader out of the snow, one by one...and that sold me on it! We called the dealer the next day, and the XT was ours.

Today I'm semi-retired because of an injury. But we still have all three Allis-Chalmers—the WD we got in '48 ...the WD 45 from the mid-'60's...and the 190 XT that couldn't be defeated by a little snow. They are not just old friends...they're part of the family. After all, they've experienced pretty much what we have.

What began with Dad having a temper tantrum way back at the beginning of World War II turned into a lifelong affection for Allis-Chalmers tractors.

NEVER BEATEN. When Dave Langworthy bought this 1936 Oliver Hart-Parr 18/28 at a farm auction, it had been sitting under a lean-to for over 30 years. "The only repairs needed were to the carburetor, magneto, exhaust valve (it was stuck) and one spark plug," Dave relates. "We had it running in 3 hours. Now we enter it in pulls at threshing bees in Toledo, Washington, and it hasn't been beaten yet!" Pictured with Dave is his son Troy.

BOUGHT IT BACK. "This 1956 Allis-Chalmers WD-45 was Dad's favorite tractor," remembers Jeff Rott of Naperville, Illinois. "After he passed away, I bought it back from the estate for more than Dad paid for it in 1957." Bernard Rott never wanted the tractor restored, fearing the job wouldn't be done well. "I put a lot of love and money into restoring the tractor," Jeff says. "I think if Dad were here, he would approve."

Her Dad Was First to Farm With a Tractor In Montana

By Gloria Casinelli, Rogers, Arkansas

IN 1912, my father became the first person in Montana to use a tractor for farming. At age 21, he was hired to plow a section of land on a dry-wheat ranch in the Missouri River Valley. It was wide-open country, with dirt wagon roads and no fences.

A Rumely factory representative taught Dad how to run the tractor. Dad said the complete rig consisted of the tractor, two 26-inch Emerson disk plows (a gang of eight), two double-disk harrows, a wide-tooth harrow and a heavy plank drag. The rig was 75 feet long and made 15-foot furrows.

Dad plowed, disked, harrowed and dragged all in one operation. "When we were done, you'd think we were going to plant lawn seed," he said.

Later in 1912, a four-cylinder Hart-Parr was brought in, but Dad said it gave the farmers so much trouble that it was discarded.

BIG SURPRISE. "It was my birthday and there was a special present awaiting me in the barn," writes 12-year-old Alex Terwilliger of Eagle, Michigan. "When I saw it, I was really surprised! It was a 1948 Farmall Cub that my dad had seen sitting out under a tree. He bought the tractor, and my grandparents, Bill and Mary Lehman, restored it. It was all done in secret so I wouldn't find out. The man Dad bought the Cub from, Ed Shaw, was the original and only owner...till now! Boy, what a present...the Cub is the best restored tractor I've ever seen!"

'Johnny' Rescued Busful of Children

By Tom Pomeroy, Salem, Oregon

THE PART of Oregon where we live doesn't often get big snows, but we did one Tuesday night in 1932—and our family had the school bus contract. Dad had no trouble on his route, but Uncle Grover got stuck in a drift and had to call for help.

We ran the local John Deere agency, which I watched while Dad and Uncle Grover were driving the buses. There was a rubber-mounted tractor on the floor, so I fueled up old "Johnny", wrapped myself up, and set out to get the bus and kids through the drift.

It was a cold 3-mile ride, but Johnny kept right on plowing through the drifts and breaking a path. When I finally got to the bus, the kids were nearly frozen. We hitched up and I pulled them down the road to the point where I'd broken a trail, then pulled over so Uncle Grover could drive them on to school.

The kids got to school about an hour late. I made it back in time for my 11 o'clock class, freezing but glad we were all safe. I don't think I'll ever forget how cold that ride was.

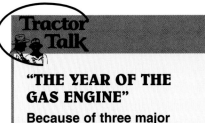

Tractor Talk

"THE YEAR OF THE GAS ENGINE"

Because of three major accomplishments occurring in 1903, it can be called "the year of the gas engine". First, the Wright brothers sustained the first heavier-than-air controlled flight... second, there were three gas-powered crossings of the United States...and third, 16 agricultural gasoline traction engines were sold by the Hart-Parr Co.

WHEN DOCTOR NEEDED TO GET TO HOSPITAL, MM DELIVERED

By Glenn Wiltse, Wahpeton, North Dakota

DURING THE early 1960's, I was in the second decade of my family medical practice. We lived about 2 miles from the local hospital, on acreage our son and I farmed with a Minneapolis-Moline.

One Sunday afternoon, I received a call from the hospital's maternity floor. My services were needed in the delivery room. But our community had suffered a spring flood, and one look out the window convinced me the water was too deep for an automobile. My thoughts immediately turned to the tractor.

I drove the MM at full speed (about 18 mph) to the hospital, arriving just in time to assist the baby into the world. When I told the nurses how I'd gotten there, they wouldn't believe me—until they looked out the nursery window and saw my faithful MM parked on the street.

That was the only time a tractor was used for transportation by a member of the medical staff at St. Francis Hospital in Breckenridge, Minnesota.

PAYMENT FOR A BILL. Bill Jensen of Independence, Kansas acquired this 1937 John Deere as payment for a fertilizer bill. "One of our landlords couldn't pay his share of the bill and asked if I'd take the tractor as payment," Bill recalls. "We really couldn't afford not to get the money, but we jumped at the opportunity anyway." Since Bill finished restoring it, the Deere has won several trophies in antique tractor pulls and has appeared in exhibits and parades.

Chapter Eleven

Fun and Games

Tractor teeter-tottering…
entering pulls…makin' believe
in an old OilPull—they're all
ways to enjoy Old Iron.

Driving Tractors to Shows Can Be More Fun Than Hauling Them

By Mary Priesgen
Rubicon, Wisconsin

MY FAMILY and some of our friends don't just restore old tractors—they often drive them long distances to parades and shows. Each trip turns into a unique and enjoyable outing.

It all began several years ago when my husband, Eugene, and his brother, Gerald "Butch" Priesgen, restored a couple of tractors. Butch has a 1936 Allis-Chalmers that has been in the family for more than 50 years…Eugene fixed up a 1950 John Deere B.

They then joined a group of other guys with restored Old Iron and all of them decided to attend shows and parades that they could drive their tractors

READY TO ROLL. Six members of the RATs line up their tractors for a group photo just before setting off on a 6-1/2-hour trip to a show in Baraboo, Wisconsin.

to. Each year between early June and mid-September, they head off down the road to at least five or six such events.

Their longest trip to date took them 6-1/2 hours of driving one way and required crossing a river on a ferry. This trip took the group 70 miles to the Badger Steam & Gas Engine Club show in Baraboo, Wisconsin.

Months of planning were required for this trip, and the guys chose roads with shoulders so that the tractors could get out of the way of traffic. For part of the trip, they took a carferry across the Wisconsin River near Lodi (it's one of the few free carferries in the nation).

They pulled a trailer loaded with water, gas, tools, blankets, rain gear and food. They also had a trailer with a homemade John Deere 5-hp "hit and miss" engine built by club member Donny Thomas.

Donny drove his 1945 Allis-Chal-

mers WD. The others on that trip to Baraboo were Donny Multhauf on his 1952 Massey-Harris 44, Fred Albrecht on his 1950 Massey-Harris 44 and Gary Becker on a 1952 Massey-Harris 44 that is owned by Fred.

Everyone but Eugene and Butch is from Hartford, Wisconsin. The men call themselves "RATs"—members of the Rubicon Antique Tractors Club.

One interesting aspect of the trip: In 1950, Butch and Eugene's grandfather bought a John Deere tractor in Baraboo and drove it home to Rubicon. Because of that, this trip was like repeating a little slice of history.

Many owners don't like putting miles on their restored tractors. The RATs, however, feel that driving is one of the best parts of having a restored tractor. On an old tractor, you stay in the "slow lane" enjoying the scenery, the relaxed pace and the old equipment all at the same time.

In a single summer, the RATs may put as many as 650 miles on their tractors. Usually the wives meet their husbands at the tractor show or parade, and everyone enjoys a great weekend away from home!

'Don't Feel Bad...There's Always Next Year!'

By Shelley Keeler Canupp, Sebastian, Florida

I WIPED the perspiration off my hands and onto my jeans, then looked at my watch. The tractor pull would begin in just 5 short minutes. All around me, tractors were roaring so loudly I could barely hear the crowd.

"Class B over here!" a man in a John Deere hat shouted. I climbed on board my little red 1967 Massey-Ferguson and started the engine, then wheeled the tractor around to where the man was pointing. I left the engine running so it would be warmed up by the time my turn came.

My dad came over to tell me not to worry. He was completely confident...or at least that's what he wanted me to think. It didn't help—I was still shaking like a leaf.

I spotted my tiny two-person cheering section amidst the blur of faces and hair that was the crowd of spectators. Mother and Grandmother stood side by side, waving at me.

This was my third pull. Three years earlier, when I was only 16, I'd won my first pull, the only girl in the field. Last year, I placed second, a few agonizing inches behind the winner.

This year I was determined to win.

"Welcome to the Ashtabula County Fair's annual tractor pull," the announcer said over the public-address system... and all the tractors not already running started up with a deafening roar.

I watched nervously as the tractors ahead of me took their turns trying to pull the heavy sled. One tractor that I thought looked like a lemon turned out to be...it conked out before it had even budged the sled.

Then I heard the announcer call my name. After I was hitched to the sled, an official hopped onto my drawbar. I shifted into third gear and gently let off the clutch.

The engine strained at first, but then it thundered. The tires gripped the earth and we began to roll faster and faster. Even above the roar of the engine, I could hear the crowd applauding.

I felt like a star performing on a stage...then my tires began to slow and I knew my "show" was about over. "Stop!" instructed the official on the drawbar, tapping my shoulder.

Good Enough to Win?

I hit the brake and heard the PA announcer exclaim, "162 feet, 8 inches! How about that, folks?"

As I left the field, my stomach finally unknotted. It had been a good pull...maybe even good enough to win. "You've got it!" my dad assured as I climbed up on the fence to watch the other competitors.

One after another, the other tractors competed and failed to equal my distance. Then along came a mean-looking Oliver driven by a boy who looked very confident. Just before pulling the throttle down, he glanced over at me with a superior-looking grin.

The Oliver's engine ground as its wheels clenched the dirt. Farther and farther along the course it went till at last the engine slowed and died—"171 feet!" hollered the announcer. "Here's our winner, ladies and gentlemen!"

My tiny cheering section moaned. I moaned. I even thought I heard my Massey-Ferguson moan. Second place wasn't bad...but it sure wasn't first.

I glanced over and saw Dad just standing there, head down, looking discouraged. Now it was my turn to encourage him. I got down off the fence and put my arm around him.

"Don't feel bad," I told him softly. "There's always next year!"

OVERNIGHT CAMPOUT. "In 1960, this 1954 Farmall Super H hauled my dad and his friends to an overnight campout on Big Pocono Mountain in Monroe County," writes Ann Lichtenwalner of Stroudsburg, Pennsylvania. They traveled along an old railroad bed, hauling a wagon filled with food, a picnic table, two Coleman stoves, and hay bales for seating. A canvas-covered frame fitted over the wagon to provide shelter for the night. "The tractor is still as beautiful as it was then," Ann says.

Boys 'Drove' Old OilPull as It Sat Abandoned in a Gravel Pit

By John Damisch, Northfield, Illinois

ONE COLD DAY in March 1931, I watched from the doorway of the corn-crib as Dad pulled his brand-new Farmall F-20 nose to nose with our 1920 Rumely OilPull. Because it was so blustery out, the OilPull had refused to start.

Dad put a belt between the pulleys of the two tractors. He revved up the F-20, the belt spun, the pulleys turned—but the OilPull refused to start. In fact, it never started again.

The OilPull was towed to the gravel pit in the back pasture, where it sat until World War II, rusting away. But it wasn't abandoned. My brothers and I "drove" it for years.

When Dad plowed with the F-20, we "plowed" with our OilPull, and later in the season, we used it to thresh and fill silos. The OilPull was a steam engine on the Milwaukee Railroad, pulling 100 freight cars. It was a semi hauling cattle to the stockyards…the bridge of the *Titanic*…the cockpit of Lindbergh's *Spirit of St. Louis.*

My older brother usually was the engineer of the train, captain of the ship or pilot of the plane. The rest of us were his crew. From the ancient OilPull's high wheels, we jumped into lifeboats, parachuted out of an airplane and leaped from the cab just before the locomotive hit an oncoming freight train.

In 1939, our world began to change. We graduated from our one-room country school and went off to high school in town. In 1943, the junk man hauled the OilPull out of the gravel pit, and it was melted down for the war effort.

Today, my wife and I farm 425 acres of corn and beans. At harvesttime, our custom harvester arrives with two John Deere 9600 combines, two 900-bushel grain carts pulled by Deere 8000's, and several semis and grain trailers.

The combined horsepower makes our old OilPull, huge as it was, seem like a 10-ton weakling. But the fun of driving it in the gravel pit will never be forgotten. ☞

Tractor Talk

ALLIS-CHALMERS SOLD

In 1985, Allis-Chalmers was purchased by a subsidiary of Klockner-Humboldt-Deutz AG of Germany and became the Deutz-Allis Company. Deutz-Allis tractors were painted sping green. When it was again sold in 1990 to a group of executives and U.S. investors, the company became AGCO. The Persian orange color returned to all domestically produced machines.

Tractor Teeter-Totter Foils Most Who Try It

By Robert Steele, Morris, New York

BALANCING ACT. Bob Peck, who designed and helped build "The Frustrater", uses his 1950 John Deere A to try to balance on the teeter-totter.

ONE YEAR, the members of the Mohawk Valley Power of the Past Association decided we wanted to have a tractor teeter-totter for our annual show. Using a tractor to balance a teeter-totter so that neither end touches the ground can be quite a challenge…and lots of fun!

We talked one of our members, Bob Peck, into designing and building the teeter-totter. He'd never seen one before and had to figure out what it should look like and how it should work.

Bob decided our teeter-totter should be very simple, have a variable pivot and be made of steel for low maintenance. He also realized we would have to be able to transport it easily to different tractor shows.

After getting the club approval of his design, Bob held a "build it" night in his shop, and members pitched in to put on the deck and complete the teeter-totter. What a big kick everyone got out of seeing it in action at its first show!

After the show, someone asked Bob whether he thought the teeter-totter should have a name. "You bet!" Bob responded. "After seeing the expression on folks' faces when they thought they'd mastered it, only to discover in the next instant it had mastered them, I think we should call it 'The Frustrater'."

So Bob put a name on the teeter-totter…and ever since, The Frustrater has been living up to that name! ☞

Getting Wed with Tractors Had Dad's Blessing

By Carol Schimnich, Sauk Rapids, Minnesota

MY HUSBAND, John, and I first met on December 16, 1993. I was raised on a farm, and I quickly discovered that he also farmed and liked restoring old tractors.

Less than 2 weeks later, on the afternoon of Christmas Eve, my dad died very suddenly of a massive heart attack. John and I had only dated once prior to this, so he never got to meet Dad in person. He came to Dad's wake, however, where he met the rest of my family.

We continued to date, and I soon got to see his farm and his collection of antique tractors. His favorite, he told me, was a steel-wheeled 1928 McCormick-Deering 15/30 on which he'd given rides to visitors from as far away as the Ukraine.

We became engaged on November 4, 1994. As we began making our wedding plans, we both came up with the idea of traveling from the church to the reception hall on a tractor-drawn wagon.

Dad had always enjoyed giving his grandchildren wagon rides when they came to visit the farm, so we agreed that any of my nieces and nephews who wanted to ride on the wagon could do so. I asked Mom if we could use Dad's favorite tractor, an Allis Chalmers WD-45, and she said that we could, although I suspect she thought the idea was a bit silly.

Once I had Mom's okay, I began praying and asking Dad to indicate his happiness for us by providing good weather for our tractor ride from the church to the reception.

We were married on May 19, 1995. John's best man was a good friend named Jonathan Jude who, as a teenager back in 1988, had helped him restore the 15/30.

I will never forget walking out of the church after the wedding ceremony and seeing the sun shining on a perfect spring day. I knew then that Dad was giving John and I our wedding present—and his blessing. I also suspected he was having a good chuckle at the way we had chosen to get from the church to the reception! ⛏

GOING AWAY IN STYLE! Carol and John Schimnich chose her dad's favorite tractor to convey them from the church to the reception following their wedding. John's best man, Jonathan Jude, helped him restore the 1928 McCormick-Deering 15/30, driven by Carol's brother-in-law, David Esinger.

Driving a Tractor Was Fun, Not Work

By Elsa Kerschner
Kunkletown, Pennsylvania

DRIVING A TRACTOR was something I considered fun, not work.

Pulling a disk around a field had many advantages, like the birds that came to look for worms in the freshly turned soil, and the rich scent of that soil.

When streams of sunlight broke through a cloud, they were like stairways to heaven, turning the world into an outdoor cathedral. ⛏

Drag-Racing Fantasy Left Teen Feeling Guilty

By Jerry Oster, Slidell, Louisiana

WHEN I WAS growing up on our farm near Greeley, Colorado, Dad owned an Oliver Row Crop 70 made in the early 1940's. I spent many hours on this sturdy old tractor. It was like a friend to me.

The six-cylinder engine ran smoothly compared to Dad's bone-rattling four-cylinder Farmall F-12. The throttle was inconveniently located way down on the floor, between the clutch and brake pedals, and it had a unique "double H" gear-shift pattern. I can still hear the distinct sound of each of its six gears. And I well remember the fearful sound of third gear. That was my secret.

As a young teenager in the era of fast cars, I liked to pretend the old Oliver was a dragster. As it groaned back and forth across freshly plowed ground, I'd daydream that I was speed-shifting down a drag strip, wheels squealing, blue smoke billowing, front wheels high off the ground.

One day after working a field with the 70, I stopped to unhook the harrow for the drive home. I was looking for a little excitement. Could this tractor really perform like a dragster and "pop a wheelie"?

My better judgment told me that I could damage the tractor. But then I reasoned, this tractor is tough. I put my better judgment aside.

Dad Wasn't Watching

I looked around to make sure Dad wasn't watching, then put the tractor in third gear. I reached down, pulled the throttle all the way out and let the engine rev up to full rpm. After checking again for Dad, I popped the clutch.

There was no squealing of tires, no blue smoke, but the front wheels did pop a few inches off the ground for just a moment. I speed-shifted into road gear and flew down the road toward home.

I could hardly wait to tell my friends that I'd popped a wheelie with the tractor. I knew better than to share my excitement with Dad or my older brother.

The next day, my brother was getting the 70 ready for the day's work when I heard him call to Dad. "Come here and listen to this knocking sound when you drive the 70 in third gear," he said.

Dad listened, and so did I. There was, indeed, a distinct knocking. Dad shook his head with a troubled expression.

My heart began to pound. Did I damage third gear when I popped the wheelie? No, I told myself, the tractor was getting old and wearing out. Besides, third gear was the one we used most.

But I still felt guilty. I dared not say a word. I feared the worst—a ruined transmission and a big repair bill.

Knock Never Stopped

Fortunately, the tractor kept going, but always with that distinctive knock. Whenever I heard it, words of Scripture sounded in my ears: "Be sure your sin will find you out."

A few years went by, and the knocking continued to haunt me. When newer implements required a tractor with a three-point hitch and a hydraulic system, Dad reluctantly traded in the 70 for a new Oliver 660.

After the new tractor was delivered and unloaded, I helped load the old one onto the truck. I felt some sadness at saying good-bye to my old friend— and relief at watching the truck drive away with my "secret".

I no longer live on the farm, although my heart is still there. Now I'm a pastor, and the story of my secret has provided me with material for more than one sermon. 🚜

SUNTAN MADE DISKING WORTH THE BUMPY RIDE

By Ruby Walton, Tucson, Arizona

BEFORE TRACTORS had enclosed cabs with padded seats, spring disking in Wisconsin was a challenge. Winter snows turned the soft plowed dirt into something resembling lumpy concrete. Riding an open tractor over that ground was like riding a bucking bronco—except that with a bronco, you could hope to be thrown off after a few minutes. Not so with a bouncing tractor. You stayed on...and on...and on.

Yet I liked driving the tractor. The monotony of going back and forth across the field was broken by the various birds that disputed my right to be there. The tractor's roar prevented me from hearing their songs, but it also prevented them from hearing mine. I could warble to my heart's content, and not even I had to listen. I like to sing, but my voice sounds much better when drowned out by a tractor.

My main purpose in driving the tractor, however, was getting a suntan. This came as a surprise to my husband. He'd thought I did it to see how much machinery I could break, how many fence posts I could knock down with the disk and how often I could run out of gas a mile from the house.

Our field sat back from the road, so on warm days, I could wear a swimsuit on the tractor and tan just as nicely as if I were lolling at the beach. I hung a hat, shirt and jeans on a convenient fence post so I could don them before a sunburn started.

Every time I turned around at the end of the field, I had to check to be sure my legs weren't being shaded by the tractor, then move accordingly to ensure an even tan. Then I could check to see whether I was steering down the right furrow.

I thought maybe the pilots liked seeing a pattern on the fields below that was a little different. That was fine, as long as they didn't swoop lower to see why our neighbor kept stopping his tractor at our end of the field to clean the dirt off his plow!

At the end of the day, I could face the bushel of ironing stuffed behind the pantry door with a clear conscience. Driving the tractor gave me a beautiful tan—and a perfect excuse to leave my housework behind. 🚜

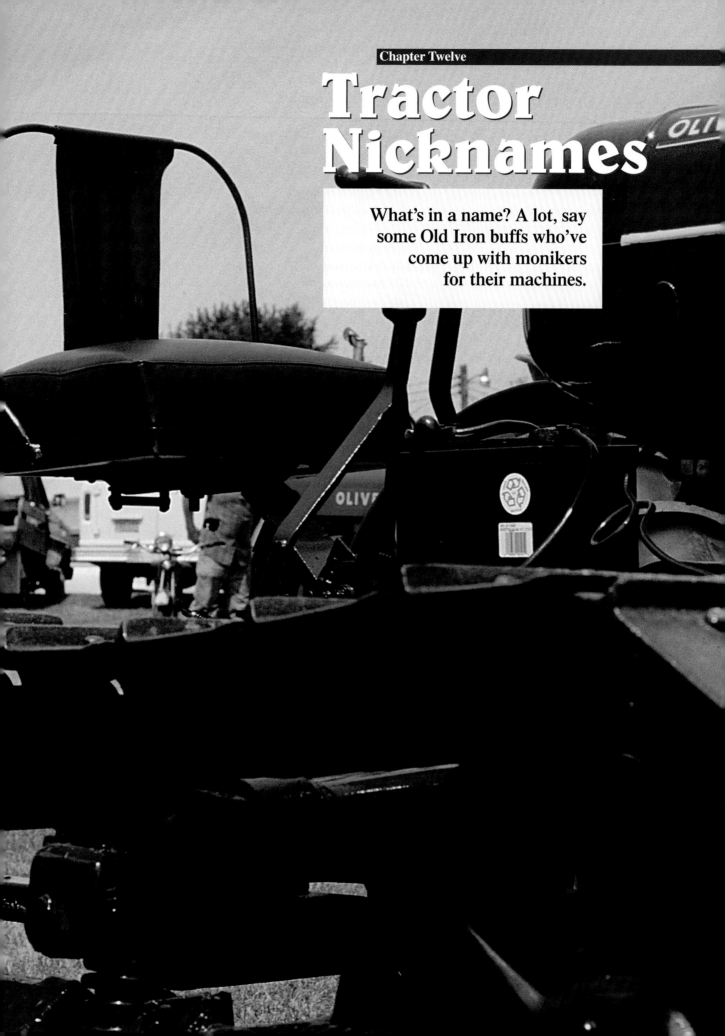

Chapter Twelve

Tractor Nicknames

What's in a name? A lot, say some Old Iron buffs who've come up with monikers for their machines.

'Lulu Belle' Finds a Home

By Nancy Winters
Moorpark, California

LITTLE did we imagine, back in 1962, that the tractor we purchased for $125 would become such an important member of our family. We named her "Lulu Belle".

Although we had only 1-1/2 acres of walnut trees, the little 1934 Cletrac made us feel like real farmers. Besides helping us perform the necessary farm tasks, she was also a source of entertainment when friends came to visit. Her orchard seat gave an exciting ride over bumpy terrain, kind of like riding a bucking bronco.

As the years passed, the walnut trees gave way to 4-H animal pens. Fewer trees were producing, so we finally decided Lulu Belle should be sold. We advertised her but got very little response.

As our sons grew older, they would disk around the remaining trees just to drive Lulu Belle. In 1978, we sold 1/2 acre and built a new home on the remaining acre. By this time, most of the walnut trees had died, and so had Lulu Belle's head gasket.

Larry, my husband, parked her under a tree on the lower corner of our property. The boys and their friends still played on her and even "decorated" her with camouflage paint. Dirt washed down the hill, and over the next 17 years, her tracks became buried.

Because she'd been with us so long, no one in the family could bear the thought of Lulu Belle being cut up for scrap. One of our sons, Matt, said he'd take her, but where does one put a 3-ton toy that doesn't run and can't be moved?

Our predicament was further complicated when Larry got a new job in Arizona and our house had to be put on the market.

Determined to find a home for Lulu Belle, I called a longtime rancher friend for the names of tractor clubs and anyone else who might be interested in the old Cletrac.

To our surprise, one of those names was a representative of the historical society from our county, Ventura. Larry, Matt and I waited apprehensively for Mr. Pfeiler to arrive.

He took one look at Lulu Belle and said he'd like to have her, as well as her disk, for the newly planned Tractor and Farm Machinery Museum. We were thrilled!

Now it was time to dig her out, jack her up and tow her free. With a lot of manual labor and a little help from a neighbor's Caterpillar, we finally managed to extricate her.

A few weeks later, Mr. Pfeiler came to pick her up. With more work and maneuvering, Lulu Belle was finally loaded and on her way.

A PLACE IN HISTORY. This 1934 Cletrac, purchased by Nancy and Larry Winters and named "Lulu Belle", has been restored for display at the Ventura County (California) Tractor and Farm Machinery Museum.

As of today, Lulu Belle is sitting in a barn in Oxnard, almost as good as new, waiting for the museum to open. She has the honor of representing one of the first practical small track-laying tractors in Ventura County, replacing horse-drawn vehicles.

We're proud of Lulu Belle's part in history and especially pleased that she's found such an appreciative home. In years to come, our grandchildren can visit the museum and tell their kids, "That was Grandpa Larry's tractor."

'Rudolph' Rises from Ashes to Lead Parade

By Lynda Bulla
San Joaquin, California

EVERY CHRISTMAS since 1951, an International Farmall A utility tractor had served as "Rudolph" in our Christmas parade, pulling Santa's sleigh. "Rudolph" was lettered on the tractor's side, and a red light and antlers were wired to the front.

Early each December, city employee Jim Fish would dust off the tractor and pray that it would start. There was only one time it didn't—that year, Rudolph was towed by a truck, much to Jim's dismay. After each parade, Rudolph returned to his regular duty of disking city lots.

When Jim retired, Rudolph was given to him as a retirement present. In turn, he gave Rudolph back to the city, with the stipulation that it be used only to pull Santa's sleigh.

Then tragedy struck. On June 25, 1995, a fire swept through the city utility yard where Rudolph was stored. The tractor, sleigh and all the town's Christmas decorations were destroyed.

'Kerosene Annie' Meant Good Food for This 14-Year-Old

By Myron Elliott, Yuma, Arizona

WHEN I was a lad of 14, my father had a 25/45 Rumely OilPull teamed with a 32/56 Aultman-Taylor thresher, and we served three threshing rings in our area. The Rumely weighed about 24,000 pounds—that's a lot of "Old Iron"!

While Dad oversaw the thresher, I was in charge of controlling the speed of the Rumely's engine. I would slow the engine when the bundle wagons came up or stop and start the thresher as needed.

I liked being the "engine man" on the crew, but one chore I didn't relish was filling the water tank before each day's run—the Rumely held about 90 gallons! Because it burned a mixture of about half water and half kerosene (due to its rather unusual cooling system), it was nicknamed "Kerosene Annie".

One of the perks of being engine man was that I got to eat at the first table. Some of the Welsh farm ladies in our area could really cook, and as a growing boy, I could really eat. In fact, it's a wonder that some of the other kids on the crew, who had to eat at the last table, didn't "polish my plow" out of resentment!

All of this took place in 1928, just before I started high school. I'm now 82, and if I were a bit younger, I'd be tempted to try restoring an old Kerosene Annie like that one we had back in northwest Ohio!

After reading the story in the *Fresno Bee*, Don and Ron Weber volunteered to restore the tractor. They spent more than 200 hours lovingly bringing Rudolph back to life. Then they called Jim on the phone.

"Here, listen to this," they said and held the receiver next to the tractor. When Jim heard the engine start, tears came to his eyes.

"I feel like a damn fool," he said, "but I can't help it. This has a heart and soul in it. I love that old tractor."

At Christmas, our community again gathered for a day of fun and fellowship, with Rudolph leading the way. Other volunteers rebuilt and restored the sleigh, and individuals and organizations donated funds for new decorations.

The old tractor taught us all a lesson: With caring people, lots of hard work and plenty of prayer, anything is possible. The spirit of Christmas is alive and well in San Joaquin.

RED-NOSED TRACTOR. This International Farmall A has served as "Rudolph" in the San Joaquin, California Christmas parade for more than 40 years. Six months after this photo was taken, fire reduced the tractor and sleigh to a pile of rubble. Volunteers restored the tractor and sleigh in time for the annual parade the next year.

Winning Tractor Pulls Is 'Pipe Dream'

By Elmous Smoke, Newark, Ohio

FOUR GENERATIONS of our family have enjoyed farming and competing in tug pulls with Cockshutt tractors.

Although I'm nearly 80 years old, retired and living in town, I was born and raised on a farm near Etna, Ohio. My dad also lived there most of his life, and we did all of our farming with horses while I was still at home.

My wife and I started farming in 1951, and while working for the Farm Bureau in the '50's, I sold Cockshutt tractors. After seeing all the advantages of farming with a Cockshutt, I finally decided I had to have one.

That feeling carried over into the next generation. Both of my sons, Larry and Tom, have acreage and own tractors, and Larry has restored several older Cockshutts.

The first one he restored was a 1954 Cockshutt 50 that he named "Pipe Dream". This tractor compiled a pretty impressive record; Larry won 20 straight tug pulls with Pipe Dream.

He also restored a 1947 Cockshutt 30 he named "Utopia", and he just recently restored a 1947 40. He gave the 40 to his son, Todd, another Cockshutt fan.

Besides Larry, Tom and Todd, my daughter Marlene's son, Chad, and Todd's son, Tory, also either drive or cheer at the tug pulls. Like I said, enjoying and competing with our Cockshutts is definitely a Smoke family tradition!

PRAIRIE GOLD TURNS WHITE

In 1969, after 40 years of successful farm machinery production, Minneapolis-Moline merged with Oliver and Cockshutt of Canada to become White Farm Equipment Co., a division of White Motor Co.

RARIN' TO GO! Larry Smoke and "Pipe Dream" give it their all at a tug pull. Four generations of Smokes have enjoyed farming and competing with Cockshutt tractors.

BEST FRIEND. "This 1946 Allis-Chalmers B belonged to my best friend, who used it for many years to plow gardens and truck patches," says DeWayne Jackson of Brooksville, Florida. "We worked on it a lot to keep it going. When he died, he left it to me. I restored it and named it 'Jack' in his honor." Now DeWayne uses the tractor to plow his and his friends' gardens.

'Johnny' and 'Red' Make Good Workers And Great Friends

By Jeb Lloyd, Fayetteville, North Carolina

I AM 15-1/2 years old. Whenever I can, I visit my grandfather, who has a big 5-acre garden behind his house in Jacksonville, North Carolina.

He owns two tractors, a 1960 Farmall 140 named "Red"

"RED" AND "JOHNNY" are the tractors' names…Jeb Lloyd and his granddad are the people. When Jeb was 2, his grandfather would let him steer Johnny.

and a 1947 Ford named "Johnny". When I was only 2 years old, Grandfather would carry me on his lap while he plowed his garden with Johnny.

I noticed even back then that when Johnny was in second gear, the transmission made a strange noise that sounded like grumbling. Grandfather has had Johnny overhauled, but the transmission still makes the same sound.

Once Grandfather drove Johnny 5 miles up the freeway to a garage for some repairs. On the way back, it started to rain like there was no tomorrow…then Johnny ran out of gas in the middle of a bridge.

My uncle had to go fetch gasoline in two milk jugs. In the meantime, traffic was slowed down for several miles. When Grandpa got home, he didn't stop at the house to dry off …instead, he drove Johnny to the shed and dried him off!

Another time, Grandfather was working in the garden with his 500-pound plow hooked on Johnny's back. When the plow snagged a big root, it caused Johnny's front end to rear up. Because the plow was set at an angle, the tractor turned in midair so the front wheels landed in a 5-foot-deep irrigation ditch.

Grandfather stepped off Johnny without getting hurt…but the tractor ended up on its side in the ditch. One rear wheel was spinning in the air, and about 4 quarts of oil spilled out.

It took a tow truck to get Johnny out of the ditch. But the hardy tractor was soon back in operation as if nothing had happened.

Whenever I go to see Grandpa, I always also go to see Johnny and Red. Grandpa and I are very close, partly because we both enjoy working with Johnny and Red.

MANY NEW FRIENDS. Dave Takacs of Demotte, Indiana has been interested in Farmalls since his childhood, when he drove the tractors for his uncles. In addition to this 1946 H, he also owns a 1953 Super M, a 1946 A and a 1938 F-20. "Restoring the H was fun and educational for our family, and we made lots of new friends," Dave enthuses. "So many people are willing to help you locate parts, and the vendors at the shows are more than helpful."

Dad Names Tractors After Previous Owners

By Janet Gum
St. Charles, Missouri

MY DAD, Ray Gum, grew up on a farm and began driving a tractor before he was big enough to see over the steering wheel. After he and Mom were married, he left the farm for a career driving an 18-wheeler, but he never lost his love for tractors.

When my sisters and I finished school and were out on our own, Dad began collecting antique tractors. He purchased most of these at auctions in Missouri and Illinois.

To honor the tractors' previous owners, Dad has always named his new additions after the folks from whom he bought them. In the past 15 years, he's had a "Clarence", a "Doyle", a "Milton", a "Frenchie" and a "Ralph", just to name a few.

Two years ago, Dad held an auction of his own and sold Clarence and Frenchie. It was a very emotional day for him, because he felt like he was losing a couple of old friends. Since that day, however, he's added several new friends to his collection…which will probably continue to grow until my sisters and I inherit it!

SURE TO BE NAMED after their previous owners are these two recent additions to the collection of Ray Gum, shown here with his wife. Daughter Janet says her dad feels his tractors are all good friends and he dislikes parting with any of them.

AND THEN HE SAID...

"After restoring my 1954 Farmall Super C, I felt I had accomplished a nearly impossible task. But what really made me feel good was when I was driving it in our Fourth of July parade and a retired farmer stepped out and said, 'I used to have a Super C just like that. You sure did a good job on it!' "
—*Victor Mathis*
Indian River, Michigan

Their Little Family Grew and Grew, Then Got Small Again

By Gaynel Drumm
Yorktown, Indiana

FOR A few years after World War II, we had only "Little Allis" in our family. She was a 1945 Allis-Chalmers AC that we inherited when we bought our farm.

The farm consisted of 32 acres, a house, a barn, one cow and Little Allis. She became our best friend, plowing our garden and helping to disk and plant the fields.

Later, she also pulled our kids on sleds along snowy roads in winter. One time, Little Allis even rescued some friends—a husband and wife and their two children who got stuck in a snowdrift. That day, Allis carried five people home without complaining at all.

As time went on and our farm got bigger and more complicated, we needed more power than Little Allis could provide. So my husband, Eldon, went out and bought "Grandma Allis", a 1937 Allis-Chalmers WC.

Because she was larger and older than Little Allis, Grandma Allis took over many of the harder chores like most of the fieldwork. Later still, we decided we needed even more power, this time enough to run a big combine.

One day, Eldon brought home the third member of our tractor family, an Allis-Chalmers WD 45. After that, "Grandpa Allis" did the really big work on the farm.

Eventually, however, it came time for Eldon and me to slow down. Like even the best tractor, our parts were beginning to wear out.

We decided we needed to part with two of our tractors. Eldon put an ad in the paper, and one day a nice man dropped by the farm. He'd seen the ad and said he loved Allis-Chalmers tractors as much as we did.

He bought Grandma and Grandpa Allis and took them away. We said "farewell" knowing they were in the hands of someone who would take good care of them and treat them with respect.

So Eldon and I are back to where we started. We have a little farm with a house, a barn and a cow… and, of course, Little Allis. Now she spends a lot of time sleeping in the barn.

But when we need her to plow our garden or help a neighbor, she's eager to go to work. She also pulls our camper out of the barn whenever Eldon and I decide to take a trip.

After all these years, Little Allis, Eldon and I are a close-knit family. Long live Little Allis!

Chapter Thirteen

Good for a Laugh

You've read every other kind of tractor story...now it's time for some that'll tickle your funny bone.

After Hours of Work, Boys Fired up Engine on The Sly

By Raymond Graham
Ulman, Missouri

WHEN I WAS a kid, my grandfather had two Nichols and Shepard steam engines and we kids played around them a lot. The little 10-horsepower model once was used at a sawmill on a neighbor's farm. At some point, it was brought home and parked next to a small pond, where it sat for several years.

One summer day, my little brother and I decided it would be fun to fire up this little engine. Everyone was gone except our great-grandmother, who was at the house and didn't know what we were doing, so we got started. I was 9 or 10 at the time, and George was about 4.

First we had to put the manhole cover in the boiler at the bottom. We didn't have a wrench, and Granddad kept his shop locked, so we tightened it as best we could by hand. Then George and I got buckets and started carrying water from the pond. We carried water for hours and dumped it into the boiler, tadpoles and all.

Around noon, we could see water in the glass, but we were getting pretty tired. We decided to go see if Great-Grandmother had lunch fixed for us, rather than have her come looking for us. Sure enough, she had corn bread and butter, and fried potatoes with onions. Believe me, we cleaned our plates that day! She never asked us what we'd been doing, so we beat it back to finish the job.

Cornstalks Burned Quickly

We started carrying water and tadpoles again. I don't know how we knew how much water to put in the boiler, but when we had half the glass filled, we decided there was enough to build a fire.

For fuel, we used cornstalks left over from the cattle's winter feed. We built a fire in the firebox and soon saw a little smoke coming out of the stack. The cornstalks burned faster than we could carry them, but we didn't give up. We just kept carrying cornstalks. Then we heard the water beginning to boil. We were in business!

The manhole was leaking badly, but we couldn't do anything about that. We found an old lard can and put it underneath to catch the water—as if that would help. George and I just kept carrying cornstalks and putting them in the firebox. After a little while, we had enough steam to blow the whistle, but we didn't dare make a sound.

In Memory of Grandpa

RAYMOND GRAHAM was my grandpa. He died in 1987. He actually wrote this story about 15 years before that.

He not only loved old tractors…he loved swapping stories about them. This 1912 Leader was his pride and joy. When he found it, it had been sitting in the woods for about 50 years and had a tree growing through the frame!

He spent 2 years restoring it. After he died, the tractor remained in our family. In this photo (above), my husband, Ed, is driving the tractor and my uncle, Gary Graham, is operating the clutch and throttle.
—*Lysha Keeth*
Ulman, Missouri

When we got a reading of 50 on the gauge, we thought that was plenty and opened the throttle. Sure enough, the old engine began to turn, but you could've heard it screech for a mile. It hadn't had a drop of oil in years. We let it run awhile, then got more cornstalks and fired up again.

Now it was time to see if the engine would move itself. It had just a forward gear, because Granddad had taken one of the rods off while using it on the sawmill to make it quieter. We found a piece of shafting and stuck it through a hole in the flywheel and on into the clutch.

The engine had been sitting in the same place so long that its wheels had sunk into the ground, and we never did get it to pull itself out. And it was a darned good thing, too, because the tree right in front of us had limbs hanging well below the smokestack and governors.

We finally decided to leave well enough alone and quit before we got hurt. Then, too, we were thinking about the razor strap that would land on our pants—my pants for sure—when Dad got home.

For the rest of the afternoon, George and I just took it easy, waiting for our parents to come back. Believe it or not, we didn't get the razor strap. I still think we should have.

20 Years of Pulling Their 'Green Mule' Taught Them to Be Patient

By Linda Templin, Steele, Alabama

FOR 20 years, our family has tolerated a 1952 John Deere tractor. This stubborn mule has pushed us into a life of patience. Sometimes it's pushed us to the limit.

When my husband and I first found this green machine, it was parked behind the tractor dealer's building, like a horse tied to a hitching post. While I sat and waited, dreaming of the nice tractors on display, my husband strolled out back and bought that old tractor. All my dreams of the pretty ones out front faded in the wind.

The Deere was pushed onto a trailer, since it wouldn't crank, for delivery to our place. When it arrived, it had to be pushed off again.

From that day on, we've pushed and pulled that old green tractor to start it every single time we've used it. It's been a hard worker, and it always got the farming done—except when it ran hot and stalled in the middle of the field.

Each year, we became more patient and tolerant. Soon the tractor was part of the family. Every spring, people would slow down to watch this housewife dragging the tractor behind a pickup to encourage it to start plowing the garden. Seeing us drag the tractor around was a sure sign of spring.

The children grew up with this stubborn machine, and the sight of Ma pulling Pa every time it was used. But now the sons pull Pa around. Ma sits in the swing under the sweet gum tree, wondering why Pa bought that tractor anyway. Then she hears a yell from yonder field, and knows that Pa needs help with that green mule.

We've promised ourselves that someday we'll just park this old tractor, plant daisies around it and buy a new one. But pushing and pulling it has become such a habit that we can't seem to break it.

Right now it's sitting at the end of the garden with a flat tire. But there's a whisper of fall in the air. We know that when autumn arrives, we'll pull it again, hook the rotary mower on the back, and mow down the weeds and the memories of the hot summer. And next year, when spring arrives, we'll probably do it all over again. ☙

Tractor Talk

ALLIS-CHALMERS' FIRST TRACTOR

The 1914 Allis-Chalmers 10/18 was the company's first tractor. It was powered by a two-cylinder engine that started on gasoline and then could be switched over to kerosene. It had one forward gear and one reverse and traveled at 2-1/2 mph in either. It stood on three wheels with the front wheel off-center, which made steering difficult.

Hay Seeds Were Culprit in Cub's Balky Start

By Warren Knicley, Parsons, West Virginia

I ONCE OWNED a service station and garage, repairing cars, farm machinery and about anything else that got broken. One day a friend brought in his Farmall Cub, which had sat in the barn all winter and wouldn't start.

The engine would turn part of the way, then stop. I tried taking off various parts that might be causing the problem, with no luck.

Then I took off the head and found there were so many hay seeds on top of one piston that it couldn't turn over—the hay seeds were hitting the head. I cleaned them out, and the Cub started right up and ran fine.

To this day, the owner doesn't believe this story, but it's the truth. I don't think I could make up a story like that! ☙

IN BOY'S EYES, FARMALL WAS 'BRIGHT AS THE BREAK OF DAWN'

By Thomas Holmes, Raleigh, North Carolina

THE DAY our Farmall A was delivered in 1940 was one of the happiest of my youth. For years, I'd admired the tractors shown at the Altamont Fair, longing for the day we'd have one of our own.

For $500, Dad got the tractor, a two-bottom plow, a disk harrow and a set of cultivators. It wasn't brand-new, but to me, that red tractor was as bright and shiny as the break of dawn.

We did more work with the tractor in 2 days than we could do with the horses in a week. I wasn't sad to see the animals go. I subscribed to Henry Ford's philosophy—it was a waste of a man's life to walk behind a slow-moving team of horses.

Little did I realize that I'd go on to spend 20 years in the tractor and implement business. A lot of interesting things occurred during those years, but one memory is especially vivid.

When I operated a Ford dealership, I got a call from a farmer named A.C. Meadows. He couldn't locate the serial number on his tractor and wondered if I could look it up for him.

"Sure," I said, "but why?"

"I'm making out my will and I want that tractor buried with me," he replied. "I haven't been in a hole yet that that tractor couldn't get me out of."

Couple Had Unique Way of Fighting Fierce Winds

By Kay White, Bartlesville, Oklahoma

I SPENT THE summer with my grandparents in Mountain View, Oklahoma when I was 13. Grandpa's brother owned a large farm just north of town, and Uncle Kinley and his wife invited me to spend a few days with them.

It was plowing season, the wind was blowing and dirt devils were spinning tumbleweeds several feet into the air. Before Uncle Kinley went out to plow, Aunt Anna Lee took an old sheet, tore it into long strips about a foot wide and tied the strips together.

Uncle Kinley climbed onto his John Deere, and Aunt Anna Lee climbed on behind him. She wrapped the sheet around them until they were tightly bound to the tractor, and off they went.

My uncle was a tall thin man in his 70's, and the wind sometimes blew so hard that it actually knocked him off the tractor. With Aunt Anna Lee behind him, and the two of them lashed to the tractor, he couldn't blow off.

I wish I had a picture of them plowing. Seeing them tied to the John Deere brought a whole new meaning to "family togetherness".

MEMORABLE POSES. Clif Erickson (at left) and brothers Rog, Dick and Curt posed atop their Allis-Chalmers WC in 1937. Then, 54 years later, they did their best to re-create those poses. "The 'old' WC was our pride and joy from 1937 to the early 1950's," recalls Clif, of Palm City, Florida. "After we all left the farm, Rog found the 'new' late-'30's WC so we'd have a tractor to play with."

$15 Pile of Fordson Scrap Forced Dad To Eat His Words

*By Jerald Wallace
Crawford, Nebraska*

IN THE 1940's, my dad had four Mc-Cormick-Deering 15/30's. I drove the 1927, my cousin and brother drove the 1926 models and Dad drove the 1925.

We also had a John Deere mower, which Dad put on "his" tractor. The power shaft didn't run in high gear, so we had to mow in second.

In 1946, my brother and I bought a Fordson tractor that had been scrapped for the war effort but was never picked up. We paid $15 for the pile.

Dad was so mad at us! "Those Fordson tractors aren't worth much, and you just wasted your money!" he said. I told Dad I was going to mow hay with it. He retorted, "I could eat all the hay it could mow!"

When Dad wasn't around, I worked on the Fordson, replacing the parts that were broken when it was scrapped. It ran well, but I wanted to put a governor and magneto in it, too. I worked off the farm to earn the money to buy those.

The Fordson didn't have a power shaft, so my brother and I built one from a Model T Ford and ran it off the belt pulley. Then we put the mower on the Fordson and hid it in our little shop over the hill.

One day, before I had a chance to try it out and see if the pulleys were the right size, Dad told me to put the mower on one of the 15/30's. Instead, I went to the shop and got the Fordson while Dad went out to milk the cow. He stopped in his tracks when he saw me getting the Fordson ready to mow.

By the time Dad was done milking, I had mowed the field by the house. It worked just great! Dad came down to me and asked when I'd done all this work on the Fordson. "When you were gone," I replied.

"That sure is a good outfit," he said.

"Yes," I said, "except it needs a gear shift pulley." He told me to order one, and he would pay for it.

I asked him if he still planned to eat the hay. He just smiled and walked away.

Grandma's 'BR' Is Still Everyone's Favorite

By Joan Dahl, Bow, Washington

MY HUSBAND, Loren, was born on a dairy farm and lived there his entire life. In 1975, he decided that we should make the switch to row crops, but we would also raise dairy replacement heifers.

Among our equipment was a cute little John Deere BR that I dearly loved. Although we now couldn't afford to keep any equipment that wasn't useful, the BR was in perfect condition and we used it to grind grain for the heifers.

One day, however, the BR rubbed Loren the wrong way …almost literally. He was backing it out of the barn—it moved faster backward than forward—and he accidentally hit our new Massey-Ferguson combine.

The BR was adorable (at least in my eyes), but that combine was his pride and joy. Loren said we should get rid of the troublesome BR, so we sold it for $300. I was heartsick and told him we'd be sorry.

As the years passed, we rented the farm and then eventually sold it, but Loren, still a farmer at heart, began collecting old engines. He now drove a feed truck and I worked as a paralegal, and we started attending antique tractor shows regularly. Every time I saw a John Deere BR, I coveted it.

A few years ago, we bought a 1941 Allis-Chalmers B that was very much like the one we had when we first started farming. Loren restored it perfectly, and it was nice to have

JOHN DEERE BR was in pretty bad shape when purchased in British Columbia to replace the one owned years earlier by Loren and Joan Dahl. By putting in hundreds of hours, Loren restored the BR to showroom condition, and now it's the family favorite.

a tractor again, but I still really wanted a BR!

In 1993, while watching the tractor pull at a show in Lynden, Washington, we noticed a gentleman with a sign on his back saying that he had a few tractors for sale. We introduced ourselves, and he told us that one of the tractors was a 1945 John Deere BR.

He said his name was Eric Joel and that he was from Kelowna, British Columbia. The BR was in the upper Okanogan area near Shoswop Lake, and he used it mostly to scrape snow in the winter.

That fall, we went to visit Eric Joel and see the BR. Although it was in pretty bad shape, we bought it on the spot—for six times more than we sold ours for in 1975! We didn't have a trailer with us to haul the BR home, so we went back up the Kokahala Highway (300 miles one way) in the spring of '94 to pick it up.

It was fun bringing the BR back across the U.S.-Canadian border because all of the inspectors were interested in what a great little tractor we had found and how we were planning to restore it to "showroom" condition.

After hundreds of hours—and lots of late nights—Loren completed the restoration in August of that year. We took the BR to the same show in Lynden where we'd first found out about it, and it was one of the best-looking tractors there.

Now the little BR is a proud member of our family, and our grandsons especially like it. Whenever they come over, it's always, "Hey, Grandma, can we drive your tractor?" Sure they can, anytime.

We still have the Allis-Chalmers B, but there's no question that Grandma's little BR is everyone's favorite. The joke's on us for getting rid of something we eventually went to a lot of work to get back!

Brushing Against PTO Threw Him for a Loop

By Lola Herron, Pasco, Washington

AN OLD PAIR of jeans belonging to my husband needed the belt loops sewn back in place. He kept asking me to do it, but I had a house and six children to care for, plus weeding sugar beets, irrigating and doing other chores. So the sewing didn't get done.

One day, he left wearing a shirt, an old sweater and those beat-up jeans. A little later, I heard the tractor returning, and my husband came into the house with the jeans in his hand, and his legs in the arms of the sweater.

He'd gotten too close to the PTO on the tractor, and it tore the jeans right off his body. When he told me what happened, I replied, "Aren't you glad I didn't sew those belt loops?"

He Changed 'Target' In Mid-Field

By Andrew Lowry
Harrodsburg, Indiana

I GREW UP on my grandparents' dairy farm in California's San Joaquin Valley in the 1960's and '70's. My grandfather and uncle milked 100 Holsteins and grew hay and corn for silage.

We always had a tractor or two on the place, and one of the first I remember was a '68 Ford 4000. As a youngster, I thought the odor of the burning diesel and the rap of the engine was mighty exciting.

When I was 12, Grandfather purchased a second 4000. He apparently thought the first 4000 would be more tolerant of my youthful shortcomings as an operator, so he set out to teach me how to plow straight furrows with the older machine.

He began by showing me how to "open" a field for plowing by making a couple of initial rounds. Then at the far end of the field, he got up from the driver's seat and told me to take the steering wheel.

He gave me specific instructions on how to plow a straight line, saying that I should line up the "north end" of the Ford with a fence post at the far end of the field and use that as a sight to guide the tractor.

"Just keep the north end on that post and you'll plow a nice straight line," he said. As I picked out a post, I noticed most of our cows were lying contentedly on the other side of the fence.

Grandfather climbed down and I started off down the field, black smoke bellowing from the Ford. Everything was going great and I was homing in on my post, but for some reason, I decided that one of the cows would make a better target—after all, it was quite a bit bigger.

All continued to go well until I was about halfway down the field. That's when my cow decided to get up and walk off. Of course, without the cow to line up the front end of the tractor, I was soon bobbing and weaving, and my previously arrow-straight furrow began to look like the track of a sidewinder rattlesnake.

After making the turn at the far end of the field and heading back, I could see my grandfather over the hood of the 4000. He was waiting for me, feet apart, hands on his hips and his hat on the ground. It wasn't a windy day, so I knew the reason his hat was resting on the freshly turned earth was because he'd thrown it there.

Better it than me, I thought! ☛

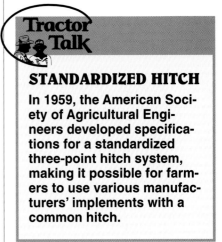

Tractor Talk

STANDARDIZED HITCH

In 1959, the American Society of Agricultural Engineers developed specifications for a standardized three-point hitch system, making it possible for farmers to use various manufacturers' implements with a common hitch.

Dad's Strong Words Brought Fordson to Life

By Forrest Cooper, Jackson, Tennessee

TIMES WERE HARD in the hill country of east-central Mississippi back in the mid-1930's—most people did whatever they could to eke out a living from the land. My dad, Dee Cooper, owned a small farm and operated a sawmill powered by a Fordson tractor.

A preacher named Brother Bill showed up in our community one summer and started preaching under a "brush arbor", a rough pole structure with brush piled across the top to make a roof. After he'd been there a few weeks, someone donated an acre of land to him on which to build a permanent church.

Brother Bill asked Dad to saw some logs into lumber for the church, and Dad agreed. They set up the mill on the site of the new church and met one morning to start making lumber.

The Fordson was an old iron-wheeled tractor that burned "tractor fuel", probably a low grade of kerosene, or coal oil as we called it. The Fordson had a hand crank mounted on the front end that engaged a socket on the crankshaft, and you had to crank the engine by hand.

These engines were fairly hard to turn over, and our Fordson had to be the king of the hard-starters. After about 10 minutes of spinning the engine, most men were weak in their knees.

Dad and Brother Bill took turns cranking the Fordson that morning, but to no avail. Eventually Dad lost his patience and said to Brother Bill, "I know what's wrong with this thing—it has the Devil in it!"

Brother Bill replied, "Dee, do you really think a piece of steel machinery can have the Devil in it?"

"Yes, I do," Dad said. "If you walk off beyond earshot, I'll talk to this thing."

Brother Bill said, "If you think it will do any good, go ahead," and he walked off a good 50 yards or more.

Dad told me later that he flew into that old Fordson and gave it several minutes' worth of first-rate cussin', then called Brother Bill back. "Give that crank a whirl," he told the preacher. Brother Bill spun the crank and on the first turn, the engine roared to life.

Dad said all the preacher could do for the next several minutes was shake his head in disbelief and repeat, "Well, I never!" ☛

PLAYING IT SAFE. Barge Massey vividly recalls the day he and his brother had to deal with a rather comical spinout on their family's Farmall. He's holding a model of the same tractor (far left) and one of a Ford 8N, similar to the Ferguson TO-20 they also owned.

Low Gear Didn't Keep His Brother Out of Trouble

By Barge Massey, Merlin, Oregon

WHEN I WAS a child back on my parents' ranch in Colorado, we grew several hundred acres of livestock feed, mainly corn and alfalfa.

For years, we managed to do this with two teams of horses and various pieces of horse-drawn equipment, but in 1949, my father finally bought our first tractor, a Ferguson TO-20, similar to a Ford 8N.

The tractor came with a side delivery rake and skyline hydraulic loader, buck rake and stacker combination, a two-way plow, disk plow and various other pieces of equipment—all for less than $3,000 new.

This equipment put our teams out to pasture, but my father kept the horses until they died of old age. He just could not imagine a world in which horses wouldn't continue to be used for farming.

In 1952, my parents acquired more property, which included an old Farmall F-20. We used both tractors for farming, and one day, I managed to end up with the two of them out in the field at the same time.

I decided to let my 6-year-old brother (who's 10 years younger than I am) drive the old Farmall back to the house while I drove the Ferguson. I put the Farmall in low gear for him and he started for the house with me following close behind.

My intention was to stop the Ferguson when we got to the house and then quickly climb on with my brother and stop the Farmall for him, as his legs were too short to reach the brake and the clutch.

This would have worked just fine, except that when we turned into the yard, he saw our mother outside hanging up laundry on the clothesline. He decided to show off a bit by showing her that he was now big enough to drive a tractor.

He turned the steering wheel too sharply, which locked the turning brake on one wheel and caused the tractor to go into an immediate spin right there in the yard. Mother started screaming for me to do something to stop him.

Well, I leaped off the Ferguson and tried to get close enough to the Farmall to jump on, but every time I thought I had it timed right, the Farmall's governor would open up, sending the front end flying around again and forcing me to jump back.

Mother kept screaming, and my brother was too scared to do anything but hang on to the steering wheel and keep spinning. I finally did manage to scramble on the tractor with him and stop the tractor.

Needless to say, this incident was pretty tough to explain to Mother, who by then was nearly hysterical. Luckily, however, she never mentioned any of this to our father—if she had, I'm sure I wouldn't be here to tell the story! ⊶

Radiator Became Target For Pitching Practice

By Betty Barnes, Lawton, Michigan

IN MAY 1972, my husband found a Cat 4-Pull tractor he'd been looking for ever since hearing about it 4 or 5 years earlier. It took months for Ray to convince the owner to sell. He finally brought the Cat home that fall and parked it in a spot where the neighbor kids played ball.

One day he caught the kids hurling baseballs at the Cat's radiator. When he asked why, they said they wanted to see how close they could come to hitting the same target each time. When he removed the radiator later, it was jammed in 11 different places!

Over the next 2 years, Ray spent more than 4,700 hours restoring the Cat. He once said the long hours nearly made him give up, but the joy of seeing it come together and the thrill of hearing it run gave him the spirit to keep going.

When Ray died in 1985, he willed the Cat to our grandson, Michael Betz. As a small child, one of the first words Mike ever said was "trac-toor". Wherever Grandpa was, Mike was there, too. Now he always has a part of Grandpa with him. ⊶

For 10-Year-Old, Starting John Deere Was a Miracle

By Tennyson Collins, Manhattan, Kansas

THREE OF our neighbors got John Deeres when I was about 10. George Hoerner and Dan Clark got B's, and Everett Abbott got the bigger D. I tried to talk Daddy into getting a tractor, but his two draft horses were in their prime, and he couldn't see the point.

Robert Hoerner and Alvin Abbott were about 4 years older than me, and I was always hanging around pestering them to let me ride along or help. The B didn't have fenders, so the only place to ride was on the drawbar, hanging on to the seat. Robert was smart enough to not let me ride there much.

The D had big wide fenders, and Alvin let me ride along while he did fieldwork. I was on the fender once when the radiator began hissing. When the big cast-iron cap blew off, I landed 50 feet away. It was a while before I got back on.

One humid summer morning, I went to the Hoerners' to see Robert. He was preparing to get the B out, which was fine by me. He set the gas and spark levers, opened the petcocks, switched to gasoline and pulled it over. But it wouldn't start.

Flywheel Needed Muscle

The flywheel took a lot of muscle to spin. To make it easier, each cylinder had a petcock to release some of the air. After the engine started, the petcocks were closed. A good man didn't always have to open the petcocks, but 14-year-old boys did.

Robert tried several times, checked the valves and levers and tried some more, but still it was no go. I tried, which was something of a joke. I had never been able to start a John Deere, hot or cold. I couldn't give it a fast enough twist. But I tried anyway.

We decided to ask Dan Clark to try pulling it, but the Clarks weren't home, so we went to the Abbotts'. Alvin said his dad was using their D, so the three of us decided to borrow the Clarks' tractor. But we couldn't get that started, either!

The Clarks' driveway had a good slope, and someone suggested we push their B there to get it started. It wasn't far, and we were full of vigor. Well, I was—Robert and Alvin were a little "pooped out" from pulling on flywheels.

We got it to the top of the slope, and one of the older boys climbed into the seat. After giving him lots of advice, we pushed him off. The tractor zipped down the hill. Everything would've been perfect, except he'd forgotten to put it in gear.

Up the Hill Again

There was nothing to do but push the tractor back up the hill and try again. It was a real chore, but we did it. After checking the shift lever several times, off he went. This time it started! It took only a few minutes to chain that tractor to the Hoerners' B and start pulling. Up and down the road we went, but it wouldn't start. By then, it was time for dinner. Alvin returned the Clarks' tractor on his way home, and we left the dead one smack-dab in the middle of the road.

I was the first one to get back to it, so I gave the flywheel a spin—and it started. It was a miracle! Robert came out when he heard it running. I was ecstatic. I never did let the older boys forget that I'd been able to start it when they couldn't. They got pretty tired of hearing about it.

I now know the humidity caused moisture to condense in the magneto, so the plugs weren't getting a proper spark. After the tractor sat for a while, it dried out, and all the boys' pulling warmed it up so it was ready to start for me. Of course, the magneto could've been taken off and dried out in a few minutes, but what do 10- and 14-year-old kids know?

He 'Gave Away' His Daughter But Can't Part with Tractor

By John Blanchard, Beaver, Oregon

AFTER GRADUATING from high school, I worked on my uncle's dairy farm. He used horses, and I became a pretty good teamster. But I knew that when I was on my own, I wanted to get my horsepower from a motor.

After returning from duty in World War II, I bought my own dairy farm. It was small and run-down, but it was mine.

In 1950, I took my wife to the hospital to deliver our baby. She was in labor for more than a day. On the second day, I was so nervous that I had to leave the waiting room and find something to do. What I did was visit the local implement dealer and buy a Farmall A.

Well, 19 years later, our baby girl got married…and I still owned the tractor. Now another 26 years have gone by—45 in all since we brought both our daughter and the A home to the farm—and I still own the tractor. It's running great!

I've had other tractors over the years, but when I sold my place, all of them had to go, except the Farmall. My daughter likes to remind me that when I walked down the aisle with her, I was willing to give her away, but never my Farmall A.

He Thought 'Tractor' Was Part of His Name!

By Florence Tolbert Readyville, Tennessee

ONE EVENING 23 years ago as I got our little boy ready for bed, he was telling me, as usual, about his day on the tractor with Daddy.

I said, "Darling, you talk about tractors all the time." He looked me squarely in the eye and declared, "My name is Charles David Tractor!"

Co-op's Legendary Speed Left Truck Driver Fuming

By Charles Beall
Ames, Iowa

THE ROAD SPEED of the Co-op tractor was a legend in its time. My cousin Allan and I put horns on ours to warn cars and trucks of our approach.

One day, Allan was driving the Co-op on a narrow country road and came up behind a neighbor in his Ford AA truck. Allan didn't want to stay behind the truck, so he honked his horn. The neighbor moved over, apparently thinking a car wanted to get past. When he realized he was being passed by Allan, he was so startled that he drove into the ditch.

The neighbor called Uncle Harold to complain, saying Indiana law prohibited tractors from passing cars and trucks. If there had been such a law, a lot of Co-op, Moline and Silver King drivers would've been in trouble.

I spent a lot of hours on our 1937 No. 2 Co-op, sometimes driving it 24 hours or more without a break. It was easy to drive standing up, and in the wee hours, I sometimes fell asleep doing just that. I never fell off or ran into a fence, which was probably pure luck.

The local vo-ag teacher told me he often dozed off driving his father's Farmall Regular. Few farmers in that area had fences then, and the only way to locate the edge of your own field was by noting the direction of the furrows. The teacher sometimes woke up and wasn't even sure he was still on his father's farm.

Fordson Barked up the Wrong 'Tree'

By R.C. Loyd
Statesville, North Carolina

THE TRACTORS of my youth were all memorable in one way or another. Among the most memorable was the Oliver "Tip Toe" owned by neighbor Bevin Holland. The rear wheels consisted of steel rims with rather wicked cleats welded on each side of the rim.

At the rear, the Tip Toe's only contact with the ground was those cleats, which gave the tractor its nickname. It also had no fenders, and further compounding the risk, it was a tricycle-type, with only a single wheel in front.

This meant it would overturn easily if you hit a rock or stump while driving it. If this ever happened, you tried your best to jump clear rather than fall under those dangerous rear wheels.

The Fordson tractor of that day had no fenders either, but it did have a wider "footprint". Besides the Tip Toe, Bevin also owned a Fordson, and he used this tractor for plowing. In fact, the Fordson was the best plowing machine invented up to that time, at least for our smaller fields.

The plow consisted of an extra-long front axle, extending about 2 feet past the right front wheel, with two disks mounted on the axle. As you plowed, the tractor's right front wheel ran in the old furrow and the right rear wheel ran in the new furrow.

One day when Bevin was plowing with the Fordson, he happened to catch a front wheel on a light pole, newly installed by the REA. The Fordson tried to climb the pole, so Bevin quickly pushed down the clutch pedal. But try as he would, he could not get the transmission out of gear.

He tried to kill the engine by backing off the throttle and retarding the spark, but to no avail. Every time he tried to kill it by releasing the clutch, the Fordson would start climbing the pole again. He couldn't allow that, figuring the tractor would flip back on top of him before he could jump clear.

There was only one alternative—hold the clutch down and hope someone would come along the nearby road and see his predicament. A neighbor did eventually happen by and cut off the fuel, and Bevin said later it was just in time—his leg had started quivering and he didn't believe he could have held in the clutch another second! ☛

Clever Crows Stayed One Step Ahead of Farmer

By John Arnold, Leesburg, Florida

WHILE PLOWING a wheat field early one October morning, I was visited by a half dozen crows. They hopped along just ahead of the Ford Ferguson in the newly formed furrow, looking for worms, totally oblivious to me and the tractor.

Around 10 o'clock, I went into the house for a drink of water, and picked up my .22-caliber rifle. I nestled the stock along one of the tractor's hydraulic arms, with the barrel next to the seat. When I returned to the field, the crows were perched in the treetops way off in the adjacent woods, sassing me.

When I went back home for lunch, I left the rifle at the house. When I returned to the field, the crows were back in the furrow, just ahead of the tractor! At 3 o'clock, I went back to the house and again fetched the rifle—and when I returned, the crows were back in the treetops!

I repeated this sequence for days and never once fooled the crows. Somehow they knew when I had the rifle with me and always stayed out of target range. ☛

Grandpa's First Ride on Tractor Was Also His Last

By John Baker
Aurora, Minnesota

SOME PEOPLE emerged from the horse-and-buggy era gracefully, even with enthusiasm. My grandfather was not among them.

But one day in the early 1920's, my father convinced him to try driving a tractor. Dad borrowed a Fordson, got it started and parked it at the edge of an open field, aimed toward the middle.

He showed Grandpa how to push down the clutch, shift into low gear and let the clutch out again to get moving. Grandpa climbed onto the tractor and followed these directions very well.

But Dad had forgotten one small point: He hadn't shown Grandpa how to stop the tractor, and the minute Grandpa realized this, he jumped off! Dad went running after the tractor as it zigzagged through the field, stopping it just before it ran into a rather large boulder.

To my knowledge, Grandpa never drove a tractor again.

Pile of Dirt Left Visible Evidence of Plowing Mishap

By John Vitt
Bartlesville, Oklahoma

MY MOST embarrassing moment on a tractor occurred one night when I was plowing wheat stubble in western Kansas. I was using a John Deere D, and once it was in the furrow, it stayed there until you got to the other end. Well, the field was a mile long—and I fell asleep.

I woke to the sound of a fence post cracking. It took a few seconds to figure out where I was, and by then, I had plowed down through a ditch next to the highway. I pulled the lift rope just before the plow hit the concrete.

But as I turned around on the highway, all the dirt fell off the plow in the middle of the road. Boy, did I take some kidding for that—the evidence was there for everyone to see.

TENDER YEARS. Three-year-old Crawford Ifland of Versailles, Kentucky just had to have his picture taken on this Massey-Ferguson while visiting his grandparents in Arkansas. Despite his tender years, Crawford displays a remarkable knowledge of tractors.

3-Year-Old's Already a Whiz with Tractor Lore

By Joan Ifland, Mountain Home, Arkansas

OUR GRANDSON Crawford is extremely interested in tractors. Shortly before his third birthday, he was sitting quietly in the car. His mother asked what he was doing.

"I'm thinking about a tractor," he replied.

"Oh, a John Deere?" Mom asked.

"No," said Crawford. "It's an Alice Charmer."

Crawford knows the names of most tractors, and his information about them is always correct. He not only recognizes different makes of tractor—you can describe a tractor for him, and he can name it!

Crawford recently asked my husband to mail him a picture of his Massey-Ferguson. When he visited us later, he had his picture taken on it. And he was pleasantly surprised to discover that Granddad also owned a Kubota.

At one point, Crawford casually mentioned to Granddad that the Massey-Ferguson and the Ford have the same hydraulic system. Grandma has just one question: What's a hydraulic system?

Dad Played Unexpected Comic Role in Deere Film

By John Tjoelker, Quincy, Washington

DAD WAITED 3 years for his new tractor, a John Deere B. He ordered it in 1943, but World War II was on, and farm machinery was mighty hard to come by.

When the tractor finally arrived in 1946, it cost a little over $1,300. That was $200 more than when Dad had ordered it, but it had lights and a self-starter. My brother Frank always found something to do on the tractor at night so he could use those lights—and show off for the neighbors.

The Deere dealer wanted to interview Dad about his new tractor, and the factory representative came along with his movie camera. The interview was filmed in front of Dad's large red and white barn, with Mount Baker in the background.

That fall, the whole town turned out for the local John Deere show at the school auditorium. The film shown during the presentation featured Dad and other Deere owners.

Suddenly the projector stopped and the film began to roll backward. There was Dad up on the screen, taking a Copenhagen tin out of his back pocket. He removed the lid, put his fingers in his mouth and retrieved his tobacco, put it back into the tin and returned it to his pocket.

The crowd roared, and Dad didn't even seem embarrassed—he was laughing too hard. 🚜

5-Year-Old Tried to Stake Claim to Tractor for Dad

By Beverly Gillette, Rochester, New York

WHEN our children were small, we were renting a farm in northern New York, trying to make ends meet. We didn't even have a tractor.

One day in 1963, our 5-year-old, Joey, was playing outside under a maple tree. His sisters were taking a nap, so I decided to make a cake for Grandpa's birthday. I checked on Joey, and he was still happily playing, so I started on the cake.

A little later, when the cake was in the oven, the phone rang. It was our neighbor down the road. "Do you have a little boy missing?" he asked. My heart went to my throat, but I said no. My little boy was playing under the tree.

The neighbor said, "You'd better look, because I think he's sitting on my Ford tractor." I looked. Sure enough, Joey wasn't under the tree.

I turned off the oven, grabbed the girls and raced to the neighbor's. There was Joey, sitting proudly behind the steering wheel on a huge tractor. His first words to me were, "Mommy, I found a tractor for Daddy and I'm bringing it home."

After a lot of explaining, I finally convinced him to get off the tractor and come home. The story soon was all over town about the 5-year-old boy who tried to take a tractor to his daddy because he didn't have one. 🚜

Stubborn Fordson Got Jump-Starts From Mule!

*By Ray Bledsaw
Hillsboro, Illinois*

I LEARNED HOW to drive our Fordson tractor in 1931, when I was 13. Dad said that I didn't handle the horses too well, and he didn't want to mess with the tractor, so if I could start it, I could drive it. For the next 4 years, the tractor was all mine.

The Fordson had iron cleats and ran on a magneto and kerosene. It was good and steady for plowing, disking and mowing—but it had a personality. I had to wear a rubber boot on my left foot so the grease spilling from the transmission didn't burn me. In cold weather, I warmed the oil by burning corncobs underneath the tractor.

The Fordson needed a lot of cranking to start. When that didn't work, our mule would drag the tractor until it started. The mule was so accustomed to this that he always stepped out of the way so the tractor didn't bump him when it began running! 🚜

Tractor Talk

FIRST RIDING PLOW

In 1874, Deere & Co. introduced the first plow a farmer could actually sit on—the Gilpin two-wheel sulky. It was a single-bottom plow pulled by three horses, and it could plow 3 acres in a 12-hour day.

Time to switch off the engine, tip up the metal seat so it won't get wet overnight and head on in for supper. As the sun dips down toward evening and the air is filled with the aroma of just-chopped fodder, you get a special feeling in your chest—together, you and this old tractor have finished yet another day's work. When you reach your pickup, you steal a glance back at the tractor sitting there in the dusk. "Sleep well, ol' gal," you whisper. "I'll be back again tomorrow."

Resources

OVER THE YEARS, many readers of *Farm & Ranch Living* magazine have asked for help in locating such things as manuals and parts for old tractors. Here is a list of resources that we hope will be helpful. Included in italic wherever possible is a brief description of what an organization or publisher does.

This list was compiled from a number of sources, especially from Old Iron buffs who kindly sent us information. The list is certainly not inclusive—there are many other resources out there. We just hope that the list will be of help to folks new to restoring Old Iron or owning a tractor just for fun.

We apologize to those organizations not on this list. Drop us a note, and if we ever run another list like this one, we'll try to include your name, too.

By the way—if you do write to any of the folks or businesses listed, *please include a self-addressed stamped envelope*. Many organizations on the list are small and can't reply without a stamped envelope.

Books • Videos

American Society of Agricultural Engineers
Preserving our agricultural past through books and videos
2950 Niles Rd.
St. Joseph MI 49085
1-800-695-2723

Antique Power Magazine
P.O. Box 562
Yellow Springs OH 45387
1-800/767-5828

Country Store
Books, videos and die-cast models, as well as country merchandise
P.O. Box 990
Greendale WI 53129
1-800/558-1013

Crestline Books
Historic tractor, car and engine books
2240 Oak Leaf St.
P.O. Box 2757
Joliet IL 60434
1-815/741-2240

Engineers & Engines
Tractor books, farm equipment, gas engines, catalog reprints
P.O. Box 2757
Joliet IL 60434
1-815/741-2240

Green Magazine
For JD Enthusiasts
Box 7
Bee NB 68314
1-402/643-6269

Stemgas Publishing Co.
Steam & Gas Show Directory, engine books, parts list, reprints
P.O. Box 328
Lancaster PA 17608
1-717/392-0733

Calendar

***Farm & Ranch Living* Old Iron Calendar**
c/o Country Store
P.O. Box 990
Greendale WI 53129
1-800/558-1013

Clothing

Connecticut Yankee Tractor Tees
Over 100 antique tractor T-shirt designs, including all brands. Send a self-addressed stamped envelope for full-line catalog.
85 Dayton Rd. Dept. FR
Waterford CT 06385
1-860/442-5182

Clubs • Organizations

BY TRACTOR MAKE

Antique Caterpillar Machinery Owners Club
10816 Monitor-McKee Rd. NE
Woodburn OR 79071
1-503/634-2496

B.F. Avery
R.R. 1, Box 68
1373E 100N
Paxton IL 60957

Ferguson Club
Sutton House
Sutton Tembury Well
Worcestershire WR15 8RJ
United Kingdom

Ford/Fordson Collectors Assn.
645 Loveland-Miamiville Rd.
Loveland OH 45140
1-513/683-4935

Gibson Tractor Club
4200 Winwood Ct.
Floyds Knobs IN 47119
1-812/923-5822

Hart-Parr Oliver Collectors Assn.
P.O. Box 685
Charles City IA 50616

Historical Construction Equipment Assn.
P.O. Box 328
Grand Rapids OH 43522

IH Collectors Assn.
R.R. 2, Box 286
Winamac IN 46996

International Cockshutt Club
2910 Essex Rd.
LaRue OH 43332
1-614/499-2961

International J.I. Case Heritage Foundation
P.O. Box 8429
Fort Wayne IN 46898

J.I. Case Collectors Assn.
Rt. 2, Box 242
Vinton OH 45686
1-614/388-8895

Maytag Collectors Club
960 Reynolds Ave.
Ripon CA 95366

M-M Collectors Club
22882 Lyndon Rd.
Morrison IL 61270

Shaw Du-All Club
22 Nesen Keag Dr.
Litchfield NH 03052

Silver Kings of Yesteryear
4520 Bullhead Rd.
Willard OH 44890
1-419/935-5482

Two-Cylinder Club
P.O. Box 219
Grundy Center IA 50638

LOCAL AND REGIONAL

Allis Connection
161 Hillcrest Ct.
Central City IA 53314
1-319/438-6234

American Thresherman Assn.
Box 58
Pickneyville IL 62274
1-618/336-5268

Antique Engine & Tractor Assn. Inc.
P.O. Box 267
Atkinson IL 61235

Antique Power Club of Alaska
P.O. Box 111905
Anchorage AK 99511

Badger Steam & Gas Engine Club
P.O. Box 255
Baraboo WI 53913
1-608/635-7772

Barry County Steam & Gas
P.O. Box 416
Hastings MI 49058

Butterfield Gas & Steam Engine Club
P.O. Box 194
Butterfield MN 56120

Camp Creek Threshers
Box 22
Waverly NE 68462

Connecticut Antique Machinery
P.O. Box 1467
New Milford CT 06776

Cooke Co. Antique Tractor & Farm Machinery Assn.
P.O. Box 895
Gainesville TX 76241
1-817/668-7861

Dakota Steam Threshers
P.O. Box 3
New Rockford ND 58356

Early American Steam Engine & Old Equipment Society
P.O. Box 652
Red Lion PA 17356

Eagle River Antique Steam & Gas Engine Club Inc.
4443 Chain O'Lakes Rd.
Eagle River WI 54121

Flat River Antique Engine
P.O. Box 641
Timberlake NC 27583

Fort Allen Antique Farm Equipment Assn.
P.O. Box 4064
Greensburg PA 15601

Granite State Steam & Gas
P.O. Box 200
Walpole NH 03608

Grease, Steam & Rust Assn. Inc.
P.O. Box 29
McConnellsburg PA 17233
1-717/485-9405

Historical Engine Society
Box 945
Burton OH 44021

Historical Steam & Gas Assn. of Centerville, Virginia
P.O. Box 375
Oilville VA 23129

LaGrange Engine Club Inc.
P.O. Box 91
LaGrange OH 44050

La Porte County Historical Steam Society
2946 Mt. Clair Way
Long Beach IN 46360
1-219/872-7405

Lawton Antique Tractor Club
P.O. Box 711
Lawton MI 49065

Long Island Antique Power Assn.
P.O. Box 1134
Riverhead NY 11901

Loyalsock Valley Antique Machinery Assn. Inc.
P.O. Box 174
Williamsport PA 17701

Makoti Threshers Inc.
P.O. Box 124
Makoti ND 58756

Mid-Michigan Old Gas Tractor Assn. Inc.
P.O. Box 104
Oakley MI 48649

Midwest Old Threshers
1887 Threshers Rd.
Mt. Pleasant IA 52641
1-319/385-8937

Minnesota Valley Antique Power
P.O. Box 226
Montevideo MN 56265

National Threshers Assn.
7873 Yankee Rd.
Ottawa Lake MI 49207
1-313/888-1345

Northern Arkansas Rusty Wheels
P.O. Box 36
Everton AR 72633

Northern Illinois Steam Power Club
P.O. Box 763
Pell Lake WI 53157

Northern Michigan Antique Flywheelers Club Inc.
P.O. Box 494
Walloon Lake MI 49796

Northwest Antique Power Assn.
P.O. Box 1670
Columbia Falls MT 59912

Oklahoma Steam Threshing & Gas Engine Assn. Inc.
P.O. Box 472
Pawnee OK 74058

Old-Fashioned Farmers Assn.
P.O. Box 164
Rockford OH 45882

Old-Timers Club
P.O. Box 8
Clifton OH 45316

Old-Time Historical Assn.
P.O. Box 220
Climax NC 27233

Old-Time Plow Boys Club
P.O. Box 215
Mertztown PA 19539

Pioneer Acres of Alberta, Canada
Box 58
Irricana AB Canada T0M 1B0

Rogers Pioneer Power Assn.
P.O. Box 43
Rogers MN 55374

Rosholt Area Threshermen Inc.
P.O. Box 85
Rosholt WI 54473
1-715/677-4734

Rough and Tumble Engineers Historical Assn.
Box 9
Kinzers PA 17535
1-717/442-4249

Steam & Antique Preservers Assn.
P.O. Box 133
Milton ON Canada L9T 2Y3
1-905/878-6576

Stephenson County Antique Engine Club
P.O. Box 255
Freeport IL 61032
1-815/232-2350

Solomon Antique Engine & Machinery Assn.
P.O. Box 75
Stockton KS 67669

Southwest Washington Two-Cylinder Club
P.O. Box 1202
Elma WA 98541

Teton Antique Steam & Gas
P.O. Box 278
Choteau MT 59422

Tri-State Antique Engine & Thresher Assn. Inc.
P.O. Box 9
Bird City KS 67731

Tuckahoe Steam & Gas Assn.
P.O. Box 636
Easton MD 21601

Magazines • Newsletters

Antique Power Magazine
P.O. Box 562
Yellow Springs OH 45387
1-800/767-5828

Antique Tractor Parts Finder Magazine
1-402/643-6269

Best Pulley Magazine
P.O. Box 83
Nokomis IL 62075

David Bradley Quarterly
206 Knob Creek Ln.
York PA 17402

Engineers and Engines Magazine
Steam, gas, tractor, locomotive and farm machinery
2240 Oak Leaf St.
P.O. Box 2757
Joliet IL 60436
1-815/741-2240

Farm & Ranch Living
With at least six pages about old tractors, it's the agricultural magazine for fun, not profit…and also the publisher of this book.
5925 Country Ln.
Greendale WI 53129

Gas Engine Magazine
For the tractor and stationary gas engine enthusiast
Stemgas Publishing Co.
P.O. Box 328
Lancaster PA 17608
1-717/392-0733
(fax 1-717/392-1341)

Golden Arrow Magazine
For Cockshutt Co-op, Black Hawk, Gawbles Farmcrest tractors
N. 7209 Hwy. 67
Mayville WI 53050

Heritage Eagle
International J.I. Case Heritage Foundation Inc.
P.O. Box 5128
Bella Vista AR 72714

I HC Journal
R.R. 1, Box 145
Reserve KS 66434
1-913/742-7425

Iron-Men Album
For the steam traction engine enthusiast
Stemgas Publishing Co.
P.O. Box 328
Lancaster PA 17608
1-717/392-0733
(fax 1-717/392-1341)

M / M Corresponder
3693 M Ave.
Vail IA 51465
1-712/677-2433

N-Newsletter
The N-cyclopedia for Ford collectors and enthusiasts
P.O. Box 235
Chelsea VT 05038

Old Abe's News and J.I. Case Magazine
J.I. Case Collectors Assn. Inc.
Rt. 2, Box 242
Vinton OH 45686

Old Allis News
Written for the Allis-Chalmers enthusiast
10925 Love Rd.
Bellevue MI 49021

Polk's "The Antique Tractor Magazine"
Classifieds, club listings, coming events
72435 S.R. 15
New Paris IN 46553
1-219/831-3555
(fax 1-219/831-5717)

Prairie Gold Rush Newsletter
Paul Lowry
R.R. 1, Box 119
Francesville IN 47946

Red Power Magazine
For IH and Farmall collectors
Daryl Miller
Box 277
Battle Creek IA 51006
1-712/365-4669

Rumely Collector News
12109 Mennonite Church Rd.
Tremont IL 61568
1-309/925-3932

Stationary Engine Magazine
Kelsey Publishing Ltd.
77 High St.
Beckenham Kent BR3 1AN
England

Swap Meet
Rt.1, Box 75 G
Bee NE 68314

The Hook
Magazine for antique tractor pullers
P.O. Box 16
Marshfield MO 65706
1-417/468-7000

Threshers' Review
Magazine for Midwest Old Threshers
1887 Threshers Rd.
Mt. Pleasant IA 52641
1-319/385-8937

Toy Farmer Magazine
For toy tractor collectors
7496-106 Ave. SE
La Moure ND 58458-9404

Wild Harvest and Massey Collectors News
For Wallis-Massey-Harris and Massey Ferguson collectors
1010 S. Powell
P.O. Box 529
Denver IA 50622
1-319/352-5524

Manuals • Technical Texts

Campbell Books
Originals and reproductions
R.R. 1, Box 348 Dept. FR
Newberry MI 49868
1-906/293-3744

Diamond Book Publishers
Sells new books on a large variety of tractors
P.O. Box 537
Alexandria Bay NY 13607
1-800/481-1353

Floyd County Museum
Oliver Hart-Parr literature
500 Gilbert St.
Charles City IA 50616
1-515/228-1099

Goodburn Books
Original and new books
101 W. Main St. Dept. FR
Madelia MN 56062
1-507/642-3281 or
1-507/642-8481

Iconografix
Tractor photo archive history books
P.O. Box 609
Osceola WI 54020
1-800/289-3504

Intertec Publishing Corp.
Tractor shop manuals
Box 12901 Dept. FR
Overland Park KS 66212
1-800/262-1954

Jensales Company
Tractor, stationary engine, magneto manuals
P.O. Box 1203
Alberta Lea MN 56007
1-800/443-0625
(fax 1-507/377-9727)

J.R. Hobbs & Son
Specialize in John Deere history and serial numbers
P.O. Box 317
Whiting IA 51063
1-712/458-2384

King's Books
Antique tractor, engine, manuals and literature
P.O. Box 86
Radnor OH 43066

Krause Publications Book Dept. IT
Tractor history books
700 E. State St.
Iola WI 54990-001
1-800/258-0929

Lloyd Wenger Books
Original literature for old tractors
831 Hill Top Rd.
Myerstown PA 17067
1-717/866-7147

McMillan's Oliver Collectibles
Shop, parts, operator manuals, Oliver models
9176 U.S. Rt. 36
Bradford OH 45308
1-513/448-2216

Museums

Carroll County Farm Museum
500 S. Center St.
Westminster MD 21157

Floyd County Museum
500 Gilbert St.
Charles City IA 50616
1-515/228-1099
(fax 1-515/228-1157)

The Hamilton Museum
900 Woodward Ave.
Hamilton ON Canada L8H 7N2
1-416/549-5225

Hesston Steam Museum
Steam train rides, weekends and holidays, noon-5 p.m.
La Porte County Rd. 1000N
La Porte IN 46360
1-219/778-2783

Midwest Old Threshers Heritage Museum
1887 Threshers Rd.
Mt. Pleasant IA 52641
1-319/385-8937

Minnesota's Machinery Museum
Agriculture and transportation
Rt. 2, Box 87
Hanley Falls MN 56245
1-507/768-3522

Old World Wisconsin
An outdoor museum of immigrant farm and village life
S103 W37890 Hwy. 67
Eagle WI 53119
1-414/594-6300

Ontarion Agriculture Museum
144 Town Line Rd.
Milton ON Canada L9T 2X3
1-905/878-8151

Sell Homestead Museum
Antique engines, tractors and cars (open by appointment)
1-1/2 miles north of
Booker TX 79005
1-806/658-4786 or
1-806/658-2253

South Lake County Agricultural Historical Society Inc.
P.O. Box 847
Crown Point IN 46307

Tired Iron Tractor Museum
Rt. 20 A
Leicester NY 14481
1-716/382-3110

Vintage Tracks Museums
Crawlers of yesterday
3170 Wheeler Station Rd.
Bloomfield NY 14469
1-716/657-6608

Tractor Parts

DECALS

Funfsinn, Kenneth
Rt. 2
Mendota IL 61342

Jorde's Decals
John Deere decals
935 Ninth Ave. NE
Rochester MN 55906

K&K Antique Tractors
Also reproduced parts
5995 N. 100
West Shelbyville IN 46176
1-317/398-9883

Maple, Jack
Rt. 1, Box 154
Rushville IN 46173
1-317/932-2027

R-M Distributors
3693 M Ave.
Vail IA 51465
1-712/677-2433

Shima, Dan
409 Sheridan Dr.
Eldridge IA 52748
1-319/285-9407

Wacker, Lyle
Rt. 2, Box 87
Osmond NE 68765
1-402/582-4874

PARTS AND ACCESSORIES

Fordson Parts
9113 Garney Ave.
Rosemead CA 91770

Fordson House of Tractor Parts Company
717 Stephenson Ave.
Escanaba MI 49829
1-906/786-5120

Snyder's Antique Parts
12923 Woodworth Rd.
New Springfield OH 44443

Specialized Auto Inc.
301 Adams
Houston TX 77011

GAUGES

Antique Gauges
Rt. 2, Box 225A
Laurel DE 19956
1-302/875-5255

Antique Gauges Inc.
12287 Old Skipton Rd.
Cordova MD 21625
1-410/822-4963

M&M
Reproduction gauges for Minneapolis-Moline and Oliver
6771 Everett Valley Rd. SE
Gnadenhutten OH 44629
1-614/922-3335

Zimmerman Oliver Cletrac
Cletrac gauges and all parts
1450 Diamond Station Rd.
Ephrata PA 17522
1-717/738-2573

IH AND CAT PARTS

Potts Repair Service
Repair and parts for International and Caterpillar
1027 N. U.S. Hwy. 231
Rensselaer IN 47978
1-219/866-8459

JOHN DEERE PARTS

Antique Tractor
Leaf River IL 61047
1-815/738-2251
(fax 1-815/738-2257)

Dennis Polk Equipment
72435 S.R. 15
New Paris IN 46553
1-219/831-3555 or
1-800/795-3501

Stephen Equipment
7460 E. Hwy. 86
Franktown CO 80116
1-303/688-3151

MUFFLERS

Oren Schmidt Mufflers
Rt. 1, Box 56
Homestead IA 52236
1-319/662-4388

Van De Wynckel Mufflers
R.R. 4
Merlin ON Canada N0P 1W0

PARTS—GENERAL

**Branson Enterprises Magneto
Service**
7722 Elm Ave.
Rockford IL 61115
1-815/633-4262

**Central Tractor Farm & Country
Warehouse**
*New, reconditioned tractor parts for
all brands*
P.O. Box 3330
Des Moines IA 50316-3330
1-515/266-3101

Denny's Carb Shop
Carburetor and ignition specialists
8620 N. Casstown-Fletcher Rd.
Fletcher OH 45326
1-513/368-2304

Gempler's
All types of tractor tires
P.O. Box 270
Mt. Horeb WI 53572
1-800/382-8473

Hercules Engine Parts
P.O. Box 142
10300 Fallsburg Rd.
Newark OH 43055
1-614/745-1475

J&D Productions Inc.
Tractor restoration videos
P.O. Box 38
Metamora MI 48455

John R. Brillman
Spark plugs and ignition parts
Box 333
Tatamy PA 18085
1-610/252-9828

K&K Antique Tractors
Reproduced parts
5995N 100W
Shelbyville IN 46176
1-317/398-9883

Lee W. Pedersen
Full line of restoration supplies
78 Taft Ave.
Lynbrook NY 11563

Lubbock Gasket Supply
Custom gaskets
402-19th St.
Lubbock TX 79408
1-800/527-2064
(fax 1-806/763-2801)

M.E. Miller Tire
Tires made from the old molds
17386 St. Hwy. 2
Wauseon OH 43567
1-419/335-7010

Minn-Kota Repair
Sterling wheel reproduction
R.R. 1, Box 99 FR
Milbank SD 57252

Molina gaskets
Antique gaskets
23126 Mari Posa Ave.
Torrance CA 90502
1-310/539-1883

Neilson Spoke Wheel Repair
New rims for old centers
3921-230th St.
Estherville IA 51334

Niagra Piston Ring Works Inc.
Custom piston ring service
4906 10A Park Dr.
Lockport NY 14094

Otto Gas Engine Works
Gasket and piston rings
2167 Blue Ball Rd.
Elkton MD 21921
1-410/398-7340

R.E.A.M. Corp.
Spark plug adaptors
P.O. Box 311
New Lothrop MI 48460

Restoration Supply Co.
*All kinds of parts for all kinds of
tractors*
18 Skyline Dr.
Medway MA 02053
1-800/809-9156

Schaffer's Shop
Third-arm kits and parts
1741 Franklin Rd.
Franklin Grove IL 60131
1-815/456-2114

Speer Cushion Company
*New and rebuilt replacement
cushions and assemblies*
431 S. Interocean
Holyoke CO 80734
1-800/525-8156

Steiner Tractor Parts
Replacement parts
G-10096 S. Saginaw
Holly MI 48442
1-810/695-1919
(fax 1-810/695-5032)

Starbolt Engine Supplies
Parts and supplies
3403 Buckeystown Pike
Adamstown MD 21710
1-301/874-2821 or
1-301/694-6840

Surplus Tractor Parts Corp.
*New, used and rebuilt tractor and
crawler parts since 1929. Call for
a free catalog.*
P.O. Box 2125
Fargo ND 58107
1-800/859-2045
(fax 1-701/280-2328)

The Shop
Restoration supplies
P.O. Box 279
Creston CA 93432
1-805/238-6997

Tip Equipment
Sand-blasting equipment
7075 Rt. 446
Box 649
Canfield OH 44406
1-800/321-9260

Tom Lein
Steering wheel reproduction
1400-121st St. W
Rosemont MN 55068
1-612/455-1802

Treadwell Carburetor Co.
*Tractor, industrial and antique
carburetors*
H.C. 87, Box 24
Treadwell NY 13846
1-607/829-8321

Welter Farm Supply
Rt. 3, Box 40
Verona MO 65769
1-417/498-6496

Wengers Farm Machinery
Full line of tractor parts
814 S. College St.
Myerstown PA 17067
1-800/451-5240